Teaching Statistical Concepts

371.3: 519 HAW

THE EFFECTIVE TEACHER SERIES

General editor: Elizabeth Perrott

THE EFFECTIVE TEACHER SERIES

Teaching Statistical Concepts

Anne Hawkins
Flavia Jolliffe
Leslie Glickman

LONGMAN
London and New York

Longman Group UK Limited,
Longman House, Burnt Mill,
Harlow, Essex CM20 2JE, England
and Associated Companies throughout the world.

Published in the United States of America
by Longman Publishing, New York

© Longman Group UK Limited 1992

First published 1992

ISBN 0–582–06820–7

British Library Cataloguing-in-Publication Data
A catalogue record for this book is available from
the British Library

Library of Congress Cataloging-in-Publication Data
Hawkins, Anne, 1948–
    Teaching statistical concepts/Anne Hawkins, Flavia Jolliffe,
Leslie Glickman.
        p. cm. — (The effective teacher series)
    Includes bibliographical references and index.
    ISBN 0-582-06820-7
    1. Statistics—Study and teaching (Higher)   I. Jolliffe, F. R.
(Flavia R.), 1942–.   II. Glickman, Leslie, 1945–1991.
III. Title.   IV. Series.
HA35.H39   1992
001.4′22′071173—dc20   92–7924
CIP

Set by 8E in 10/11 Times Roman
Printed in Malaysia by TCP

CONTENT S

EDITOR'S PREFACE

This new series was inspired by my book on the practice of teaching (*Effective Teaching: a practical guide to improving your teaching*, Longman, 1982), written for trainee teachers wishing to improve their teaching skills as well as for in-service teachers, especially those engaged in the supervision of trainees. The books in this series have been written with the same readership in mind. However, busy classroom teachers will find that these books also serve their needs as changes in the nature and pattern of education make the inservice training of experienced teachers more essential than in the past.

The rationale behind the series is that professional courses for teachers require the coverage of a wide variety of subjects in a relatively short time. So the aim of the series is the production of 'easy to read', practical guides to provide the necessary subject background, supported by references to guide and encourage further reading, together with questions and/or exercises devised to assist application and evaluation.

As specialists in their selected fields, the authors have been chosen for their ability to relate their subjects to the needs of teachers and to stimulate discussion of contemporary issues in education.

The series aims to cover subjects ranging from the theory of education to the teaching of mathematics and from primary school teaching and educational psychology to effective teaching with information technology. It will look at aspects of education as diverse as education and cultural diversity and pupil welfare and counselling. Although some subjects such as the legal context of teaching and the teaching of history are specific to England and Wales, the majority of subjects such as assessment in education, the effective teaching of statistics and comparative education are international in scope.

Elizabeth Perrott

A U T H O R S'   P R E F A C E

For a long time, we have shared a common interest in statistical education. Between the three of us we have wide experience of teaching statistics and statistical computing, and also an extensive knowledge of the related literature and research. Realising that such material was not readily accessible, and certainly was not available within a single source, we decided to write this handbook for teachers.

Computational formulae, and the like, which used to provide substantial textbook content, have become things of the past. This book is intended to lay a foundation for exploring how best to teach those applied skills which are now seen to be more relevant. It includes consideration of:

- changes taking place in statistics, for example in the areas of Exploratory Data Analysis, statistical computing and graphics;
- the conceptual difficulties which face teachers and students of statistics and probability;
- research into statistical education;
- management of statistical project work;
- developments in teaching methods and materials;
- the use and evaluation of teaching resources, including computer hardware and software, audio-visual aids and textbooks;
- assessment of statistical skills and understanding.

There is much to interest teachers of advanced statistics courses, although our focus will tend to be on how to provide for the needs of the majority of students, i.e. those students who (although studying it as a subject in its own right, or combined with mathematics or a 'user'-discipline) do not intend to become specialist statisticians.

To some extent, there exists a marginalisation of those statisticians committed to improving the quality of statistical education. Statisticians are trained to do statistics. Of these, a few are willing to train others to do statistics, while still working as statisticians themselves. Very few indeed, however, are willing to remove themselves so far from doing statistics as to spend most of their time training others to teach statistics. Although a

great deal of progress has been made in developing statistical
education during the past ten to fifteen years, much of the
impetus for this has come about through the efforts of relatively
isolated specialists and enthusiasts, although world-wide the
number of such persons is not negligible.

With the increasing recognition that statistics should be a part
of the core curriculum for the compulsory years of schooling for
all children, there is now an urgent need for teacher training in
both content and pedagogy, and the problem is not confined to
the UK. It is our intention that this book will go some way
towards improving the situation. We realise, however, that what
is really needed is the establishment of sufficient centres of
excellence, with adequate staffing levels and resources to
facilitate research. Statistical education must be recognised to be
as worthy a research area as is mathematical statistics. The
present situation where, despite its all-pervasive nature, statistics
education is not afforded the level of pedagogic research and
training considered to be necessary for other areas of the school
curriculum cannot be allowed to continue.

On a somewhat lighter note, we would like to make it clear
that no significance is to be attached to the ordering of our
names. In fact, readers may be amused to visualise us deciding
the issue on the floor of a cramped London office, in true
statisticians' style, by the throw of a random device!

Anne Hawkins, Flavia Jolliffe, Leslie Glickman

Leslie V Glickman – a tribute

It is with great sadness that we recall that our co-author Leslie Glickman died suddenly just two days after the manuscript for this book was completed. We first came to know Leslie in 1984 through the UK working group on probabilistic concepts and intuitions. We will remember him as a gentle and unassuming man, meticulous in his work, generous in his appreciation of others' efforts, and sensitive and economical in his criticisms. He was more than willing to consider and try out, as well as to originate, new ideas. He was good-natured and fun to work with, and our meetings with him were always congenial affairs.

We shall miss Leslie both as a colleague and as a friend, and it is undoubtedly the case that the area of statistical education will also feel the loss. He still had so much of value to contribute. With the manuscript completed, he was full of plans for future projects; researching and developing a new idea in statistical graphics, and further work on statistical concepts and intuitions with us.

Leslie's enthusiasm for probabilistic understanding and the work of the early probabilists is demonstrated in the articles which he wrote for 'Teaching Statistics'. His desire to make statistics accessible to a wider audience was obvious from the quality of his writing and the concern that he had for his students – both at the City of London Polytechnic, where he lectured for sixteen years, and at Brighton Polytechnic, where he moved to in 1990. His last e-mail message to us, which ironically we did not receive until after we had heard of his death, contained a fitting epitaph: 'The challenge for us is how to balance "statistical practice" and "statistical theory" in our presentation of the discipline of statistics.'

Teaching Statistical Concepts is dedicated to Leslie's wife, Elyane, and their daughter, Lea-Nelly, in his memory.

Anne Hawkins and Flavia Jolliffe

ACKNOWLEDGEMENTS

The authors wish to thank Joy Harterink for her contributions to the section on practicals and projects; Peter Hawkins for his patient and meticulous help with earlier drafts, and Christopher Hawkins for his help in recovering some of the source materials. The Publishers are indebted to the following for permission to reproduce copyright material:

Academic Press, Inc & the author, Arnold D Well for an adapted extract from the article 'Understanding the effects of sample size on the variability of the mean' by Well, Pollatsek and Boyce from the journal *Organizational Behaviour and Human Performance*, 47 (1990); Carfax Publishing Company for an adapted extract from the article 'Non-traditional approaches to some classical topics in probability and estimation' by K Hinderer from the journal *European Journal of Engineering Education* Vol 15 (1990), & an adapted extract from the article 'Confidence intervals or hypothesis tests?' by T Wonnacott from the journal *Journal of Applied Statistics*, Vol 14, 3 (1987); the author, Ruma Falk for extracts & an adapted extract from the article 'Conditional probabilities: insights and difficulties' from *Proceedings of the Second International Conference on Teaching Statistics* edited by Roger R Davidson & J Swift (University of Victoria, 1988); the author, Warren Gilchrist for an adapted extract from his unpublished papaer 'Teaching statistics using practicals' (1980); the author, Alan T Graham for an adapted extract from the article 'Choosing a statistics textbook' from the journal *Mathematics Teaching*, 75 (1976); the Controller of Her Majesty's Stationery Office for an extract from *DES Statistical Bulletin: Survey of Information Technology in Schools* November, 1991); Kluwer Academic Publishers for an extract & an adapted extract from the article 'Analysis of the Probability Curriculum' by A Ahlgren & J Garfield from *Chance Encounters: Probability in Education* edited by R Kapadia & M Borovcnik (D Reidel Publishing Company, 1991); International Statisticial Institute & the author, Lennart Råde for an adapted extract from *Calculators and Statistical Calculations. An International Inquiry* (1985); International Statistical Institute & the author, Mary Rouncefield for an adapted extract from the article 'Preparing the Statistics Coordinator' from *Training Teachers to Teach Statistics* edited by

A Hawkins (1990); McGraw-Hill, Inc for an adapted extract from *STATLAB: an empirical introduction to statistics* by J L Hodges et al (1975); Pergamon Press PLC for an adapted extract from the article 'Some statistical characterizations of aircraft hijacking' by R E Quandt from the journal *Accident Analysis and Prevention*, 6 (1974); Springer–Verlag & the author, K L Chung for an adapted extract from *Elementary Probability Theory with Stochastic Processes* (3rd Edition, 1979); Springer Verlag & the author, J van Brakel for an adapted extract from the article 'Some remarks on the prehistory of statistical probability' from the journal *Archive for History of Exact Sciences*, Vol 16 (1976); Statistical Association for an extract & an adapted extract from the article 'Future of Statistics' by L A Baxter from *The American Statistician*, Vol 44, 2 (1990), an extract & an adapted extract from the article 'The future of statistics in the next n years $(25<n<150)$' by T W Brailsford from *The American Statistician*, Vol 44, 2 (1990) & extracts & adapted extracts from the article 'The Planning Stage in Statistical Reasoning' by N L Chervany et al from the journal *The American Statistician*, Vol 34, 4 (1980); Sheffield City Polytechnic for our adapted Figure 1.1 from a paper *Teaching Statistics using practicals* by M Fuller at a conference on Problems of Learning Statistics in 1980; American Statistical Association for our adapted Figure 1.3, 'Brushed, linked scatterplots showing the power of EDA methods to make representations more efficient' from articles by R A Becker and W S Cleveland in *Technometrics*, Vol 29, 2 (1987), pp 127–42; Department of Mathematics, Loughborough University of Technology, and the author, David R Green for our adapted figure Figure 1.5 from *Probability Concepts in 11–16 year pupils*, second edition 1982; Mr Alan Reece and the Institute of Statisticians for our adapted Figure 1.6 'The need for course changes in response to the "microcomputer revolution"' from paper by T H Mangles entitled 'Application of Micros and the use of Computer Graphics in the Teaching of Statistical Principles' from *The Professional Statistician*, Vol 3, 7 (1984), pp 24–7, 49; Teaching Statistics for our adapted Figure 5.2 using headings from an article 'Teaching hypothesis testing as a 6-step process' by L W Johnson, in *Teaching Statistics*, Vol 3, 1981; Lawrence Erlbaum Associates Ltd and the author, J St B T Evans for our Figure 6.1 adapted from Figure 2.1 in *Bias in human reasoning: causes and consequences. Essays in cognitive psychology* (1989).

The Publishers have been unable to trace the copyright holders in the following articles and figures and would appreciate any information that would enable us to do so:

'Probability and its measurement' by R Buxton from the journal *Mathematics Teaching*, 49 (1970); 'Another definition of independence' by B W Huff from *Mathematics Magazine*, Vol 44 (1971); 'Research in Probability and Statistics: Reflections and Directions' by M J Shaughnessy (1992) in preparation.

CHAPTER 1

Statistics: past and present

THE STATISTICS CURRICULUM

Until recently, the way in which statistics developed prior to the 1960s has tended to determine both the content and the methods of this subject's teaching and assessment. Developments in statistics are still on-going and these should continue to have an impact on statistical education. It is a fairly common experience among statistical educationalists, however, that teachers and examining boards have been slow to respond to the changing nature of statistics and to recognise that it is essentially an applied subject which can, and should, be brought within the reach of all. It is not a subject only for mathematicians, in spite of its strong mathematical underpinnings. In order to convey this, a curriculum and a pedagogy which break with traditional (deterministic) mathematical values are needed;

As long as students believe there is some way that they can 'know for sure' whether a hypothesis is correct, the better part of statistical logic and all of probability theory will evade them. (Konold, 1989b)

In addressing the 2nd International Conference on Teaching Statistics in 1986, J.V. Zidek showed that, for most of its history, statistics has been an applied *descriptive* discipline, derived from many fields of application, but particularly from those where it was necessary to describe things to do with the *state*, such as economics and politics:

Statistical instruction 'really referred to the fact that numerical quantities were used in the course of instruction' [in such subjects]. (Zidek, 1988)

Nevertheless, it is statistics' relatively brief *theoretical* episode this century, stimulated by the works of Karl Pearson and R.A. Fisher, which has had a disproportionate influence on the way that the subject has tended to be taught in schools and colleges. To Zidek, the development of a satisfactory statistics curriculum has been difficult because of the lack of a suitable foundation for the subject:

There are not yet sound footings for statistical graphics, for example, nor for statistical computing and exploratory data analysis . . . In the more traditional areas of inference and decision there are lots of directions but

2 Teaching Statistical Concepts

they are all different . . . [Such difficulties] affect not only the choice of topics . . . [but also] the way we think about statistics.' (Zidek, 1988)

One accepted aim of secondary, further and higher education is to prepare our students for the real world and its needs – needs which are reflected in the mirrors of society, namely television, newspapers and radio. Even a cursory glance at media publications makes society's reliance on statistics obvious. There can be no doubt, therefore, that we must have a statistically literate population, one in which lay persons are able to appreciate statistical arguments and even produce them. People do not merely receive data arguments, they act on them, and contribute to social, political and economic decisions based on them.

Secondary education has recognised the importance of statistics and in the UK the subject has been available as an option at 'O' (now GCSE)[1] and 'A' level[2] for many years. However, in constructing statistics syllabuses, educators have traditionally resorted to the subject's theoretical basis, namely mathematics. Until recently, the highly practical nature of statistics and its applications has not begun to receive the attention in such syllabuses that it deserves. Furthermore, when statistics is taught in a mathematical and theoretical way, it places the acquisition of skills and understanding necessary for decision making out of the reach of most students.

Before the 1960s it could be claimed with some justification that meaningful practical work in the classroom was not feasible. Realistic data sets were usually too large and complex, and therefore too time consuming, to analyse. However, with the rapid development of high-speed computing facilities since the 1970s, the technology is now available to handle significant, real-life data in the classroom. This must surely give further impetus to treating *applied* statistics as a serious discipline in its own right, especially with the increasing emphasis given to practical coursework and data handling by the UK National Curriculum (see Department of Education and Science, 1989a,b). Clearly statistics has become compulsory for all, rather than an optional subject available only to a limited few.

A worrying feature that has been observed in recent entries to the UK Annual Applied Statistics Competition for Schools and Colleges of Further Education (Anne Hawkins, Institute of Education, University of London, 1982–1990) is an apparent narrowing of perspective concerning what statistics is. It seems as if the 'suggestions for coursework' derived from the UK National Curriculum have contributed to the popular misconception that 'statistics is (only) questionnaire-based social surveys', and discussions at the 3rd International Conference on Teaching Statistics in 1990 indicated that this trend was not confined to the

UK. Clearly, this is sometimes the form that statistics takes, but it is not the only one. In fact, in the past, students have entered a number of very good *experimental* and *simulation* studies for the Statistics Competition. In addition to *'Statistics is surveys'*, other misconceptions about practical statistics include:

1. *'Statistics is art'* – common among younger students who produce pages of amazing technicolour charts and diagrams, with little or no attention to methodology or interpretation.
2. *'Statistics is sums'* – common among older students who have learned a range of computational techniques and who therefore exercise these with little regard to the rationale or interpretation of their research.
3. *'Statistics is data collection'* – without rhyme or reason, simply amassing data for the sake of it.

Clearly, there is still much scope for conveying the *purpose* of statistics to our students, and it is important that a statistics curriculum should be designed to ensure that students receive practical experience of the widest possible range of statistical approaches.

Statistics is relevant to a variety of disciplines; economics, business studies, politics, geography, biological sciences, psychology, and many more. 'A'-level syllabuses for such subjects reveal more and more dependence on statistical concepts and techniques. The question to be asked is: From where are these 'user'-disciplines to derive the statistical methodologies for their subjects' needs? Is it from the traditional approach, with its inherent danger of providing a cook-book of algorithmic recipes for statistical inference? Alternatively, are teachers in these subject areas aware of the new emphasis on Exploratory Data Analysis (EDA) as a preliminary to inferential techniques, and on modelling approaches to statistical data analysis?

The syllabus of the emerging subject of *applied* statistics must address itself to some vital questions:

● How will the scope, power and relevance of statistics be communicated?
● What will be its relationship to mathematics?
● What mathematics is needed for, and in, applied statistics syllabuses?
● Given its cross- *and* multi-disciplinary nature, where should statistics fit into the curriculum?
● Can a 'core' subject of statistics be identified, or are the developing specialisms, e.g. econometrics and biometrics, such as to irretrievably fragment the subject and return it to its origins? (See Zidek, 1988.)

These questions are particularly important because of new directions being taken in statistical methodology *as practised by statisticians*, with the emphasis moving towards exploratory data analysis and more visual, graphics-based, approaches, accompanied by a loosening of its ties with formal mathematical exposition.

THE RELATIONSHIP BETWEEN STATISTICS AND PROBABILITY

Embedded in the enquiry into the role of mathematics in applied statistics is the even more urgent question concerning the role of probability. Garfield (1988) cited four issues that hinder the effective teaching of statistics, the first of which is the uncertainty surrounding the role of probability and statistics in the curriculum, the others being links between research and instruction, the preparation of mathematics teachers, and the way that learning is currently being assessed. Of course, such general curriculum questions are not confined to *statistics* education, as Shaughnessy (1992) points out. Under the recommendations of the NCTM (National Council of Teachers of Mathematics) *Curriculum and Evaluation Standards for School Mathematics* (1989), every branch of *mathematics* education must resolve such issues.

In highlighting the ambitiousness of the NCTM's proposals for the mathematics probability curriculum, Ahlgren (1989) criticised the general tendency to overcrowd *mathematics* curricula. He saw this arising because:

(a) topics are rarely dropped from the curriculum;
(b) topics are forced to lower and lower age groups, ostensibly so that more serious mathematics can be addressed in the upper grades; and
(c) recent developments in mathematics motivate the introduction of modern topics.

Ahlgren threw down the following challenge:

It is important to acknowledge that we do not yet know the best (or even a very good) way to teach students probability, and therefore need to continue to look to research when designing or choosing curricula or advocating a particular instructional approach. Far from having a guaranteed place in the curriculum, probability is in competition with many other mathematical topics to be included at school levels earlier than previously thought possible. Unless probability concepts are taught in the contexts of . . . 'real-world' matters of *real* interest, putting probability in the curriculum may not be worth the effort. (Ahlgren, 1989)

In Shaughnessy's view, an absence of appropriate materials for teaching stochastics can no longer be a reason for its absence from curricula, at least in the United States, since several projects have now produced relevant materials; e.g. the *Quantitative Literacy Series* (Landwehr and Watkins, 1986; Newman *et al.*, 1987; Landwehr *et al.*, 1986; Gnanadesikan *et al.*, 1987), the Probability Unit of the *Middle Grades Mathematics Project* (Phillips *et al.*, 1986), *Used Numbers* (Russell *et al.*, 1990) and *Using Statistics* (Travers *et al.*, 1985). In addition, technology has provided opportunities for interactive curricula on computers, for example *Hands-on Statistics* (Weissglass *et al.*, 1986) and in the Stretchy Histograms and Shifty Lines materials from the *Reasoning Under Uncertainty Project* (Rubin *et al.*, 1988). There is also an entire stochastics curriculum devoted to improving students' thinking under uncertainty (Beyth-Marom and Dekel, 1983).

According to Shaughnessy (1992), the *real* problems in the US are:

(a) getting stochastics into the mainstream of the mathematical science school curricula *at all*;
(b) enhancing teachers' background and conceptions of probability and statistics; and
(c) confronting students' and teachers' beliefs about probability and statistics.

In his view, the *gulf* between the perspectives of education and psychological researchers has more to do with the problems encountered in statistical education than the lack of relevant research. While psychological research focuses on *observing* and *describing* cognitive functioning, its 'successes' and its 'failures', Shaughnessy sees researchers in mathematics and statistics education focusing on *intervention,* changing conceptions and beliefs. He is concerned that what little collaboration there is seems to him to be one way, with psychologists paying scant attention to the work of education researchers. *We* feel that there are still many areas that are under-researched, but we would certainly support Shaughnessy's suggestion that statistical education would benefit greatly from the development of a more systematic and coherent approach to its research.

The significance of probability and the importance of understanding it are not new concerns. Pierre Simons, Marquis de Laplace (1812) said 'It is remarkable that a science which began with the considerations of games of chance should have become the *most important object of human knowledge* . . .', while the following remark has been attributed to the English philosopher and mathematician, Bertrand Russell (1929); 'Probability is the *most important concept in modern science*, especially as nobody has the slightest notion what it means.'

Clearly probability is of the utmost importance for inferential statistics, but in adopting the traditional syllabus structure;

descriptive statistics – probability – inferential statistics

these three components tend to become compartmentalised, and generally a poor balance is struck between them. For students who study statistics as a subject in its own right, little time may be devoted to descriptive statistics, particularly in the case of older students, and the time that is given to it generally focuses on the mechanics of artwork and of computing summary measures, rather than on its role in communication. Meanwhile, teachers skim through basic probability, often early on in the syllabus, in order to proceed to the 'meat' of the course, namely inferential statistics. This latter is then based on a type of probabilistic reasoning which apparently bears little or no relationship to the computational/algorithmic laws of probability encountered earlier.

Koopmans (1982) described the undesirable effects of such a programme of study:

> The escalation of difficulty [between descriptive and inferential statistics] . . . can be catastrophic to student morale. A course they [the students] had well in hand initially because it consisted primarily of trivial graphing and mindless number crunching, suddenly turns on them first with probability then immediately after with the theory of statistical inference.

Until very recently, students who did not continue with statistics as a special study in its own right, and whose only encounter with it was in a general mathematics and/or 'user'-discipline context, usually received little or no statistical inference teaching, their introduction to statistics being essentially limited to the skimped presentations of the first two components – descriptive statistics and probability.

Borovcnik (personal communication, 1990) sees these three areas as more appropriately lying under the umbrella of 'stochastics'. He advocates that students' *statistical* education should be structured by a *stochastics* curriculum. Indeed, Garfield and Ahlgren (1988) also argue for the more widespread use of the term 'stochastics' rather than 'statistics' in statistical education. It may seem to be unnecessary for *statisticians* to change to such a term because, by definition, their perception of the term 'statistics' is probably broader than that of the general public. Non-statisticians, on the other hand, might benefit from the use of the term 'stochastics' to highlight the integration of probability and statistics. Ironically, however, such integration rarely occurs in the present school level or other introductory programmes, and so the term has little chance of adoption at present. For the purpose of this book, we are taking the statistician's meaning of the term 'statistics'. In other words, we shall generally use 'statistics' to include both statistics and probability.

Since there is inherently some resistance on the part of curriculum and syllabus planners to integrating probability and statistics, readers may find it interesting to consider ways in which they might teach probability so as to enhance students' understanding of statistics, and conversely how they might teach statistics in ways that will enhance students' appreciation and understanding of probability.

There is certainly no clear and universally accepted view on the relationship between the teaching of statistics and the teaching of probability. Take, for example, the following ambivalent introduction in a book by Bassett *et al.* (1986):

The most basic division in Statistics is that between probability and inference, and accordingly we use such a division in this book. [Inference is described as a method of induction, whereas probability] . . . is the reverse process of arguing from general knowledge to special cases, a process of deduction. Since making deductions from axioms is the basic procedure of pure mathematics, probability is essentially a branch of mathematics [meaning statistics is not and probability is 'pure' rather than 'applied'?] . . . The link between probability and statistical inference is just as clear-cut as is the distinction between them [although the students may not find it so!].

Ahlgren and Garfield (1991) outline in their goals for probabilistic education, 'a coherent set of *ideas* concerning probability, *skills* in using these ideas, and *inclinations* to use the ideas and skills'. None of these is currently handled with any great success in the UK, but it is probably the last area that generally fails to feature at all in mathematics syllabuses. Despite recommending that the integrating term 'stochastics' should be adopted, Garfield and Ahlgren (1988) nevertheless argue for the relative separation of probability and mainstream statistics teaching *initially*. Probability is notoriously difficult to teach and, by treating it separately at first, they believe it can be given the prominence and attention it deserves. They are, however, opposed to the sort of mathematical formalism which, in the traditional syllabus, tends to isolate probability from the real-life world of applications.

Freudenthal (1973) also makes it clear that even if the teaching of probability is initially separated from that of statistics, it should still not be taught in an abstract fashion:

The student should learn separating mathematics and reality from each other . . . it helps the understanding both of mathematics and reality. Yet they should not be offered to him separately. He should learn to separate them himself as soon as their interrelations have grown strong enough to prevent the separation from damaging either part.

Piaget and Inhelder (1951, trans. 1975) have had a strong counter-influence on the introduction of probability at primary school level. Their findings, based on case studies, suggest that children could not really begin to grasp probability before they reached the formal operations stage – that is, until their early teenage years. Whatever one's views of the research leading to these conclusions being drawn, and it is true to say that Piaget and Inhelder's methods have both proponents and opponents, the key issue is that their studies focused largely on a search for, and a failure to find, the spontaneous emergence of formal *a priori* probability concepts in children.

Fischbein (1975), on the other hand, has taken the view that intuitions of probability, related to a child's *relative frequentist* view of the world, may be available from very early on in a child's development. This subjective probability, according to Fischbein, must be recognised, nurtured and indeed exploited from the earliest stages, as it is a crucial precursor of objective, formal, probability. In his view, the deferring of probability teaching until secondary school level, accompanied as it is by an over-emphasis on determinism, may damage existing skills and/or impede the subsequent learning and understanding of probability.

There is evidence of a groundswell of opinion towards the latter position. For example, in America, the NCTM Standards (National Council of Teachers of Mathematics, 1989) assert that probability should be taught to all students, from a very early age, throughout schooling, and that formal algebraic approaches should not, and need not, be attempted until a firm conceptual base has been established. Implicitly, some students will not progress to such an approach. In the UK also, Attainment Target 14 in the National Curriculum in mathematics is devoted to introducing probability to children throughout their compulsory schooling, that is from the age of 5 to the age of 16.

Such curricula accord with the thinking of Engel (1965, 1970) which, as Freudenthal (1973) says, suggests that it is important

to pervade all mathematics by probability at an early stage – as soon as the children get to know about fractions, not just because it is useful for future probability teaching but because this penetration brings mathematics nearer reality . . . I believe that a student who experienced probability concepts early on and intensively, can better experience, and even assimilate, mathematizations far from reality on a higher level. (Freudenthal, 1973)

While Engel is essentially showing what *should* be done, Freudenthal (1973) sets out to convince us that it *can* be done:

The demand for technically formalized mathematics in probability is very low . . . If probability is to be axiomatized, it can be done with an

axiomatic system that is the simplest that in mathematics exists. . . .
[Based largely on fractions and minimal algebraic manipulation]
probability can be applied to reality as directly as elementary arithmetic,
that is, by means of models that everybody can immediately understand.

The Schools Council Project on Statistical Education, known
as POSE, (Holmes *et al.*, 1981; Holmes, 1991) produced an
excellent example of project work for 12 year olds where the
focal concept of expected outcome integrates statistical and
probability education. The unit, entitled *Fair Play*, is based on
fairground games of chance. Students use empirical and diagram-
matic means to find ways of establishing an appropriate balance
between the charge made for playing and the likely outgoing
prize money.

In view of what has been said earlier, it is interesting to note
that the National Curriculum for mathematics has three (out of
its fourteen) Attainment Targets with the title of 'Handling
Data'. The first two are: (a) mainly data collection, processing
and computation of statistics, and survey design; and (b) mainly
constructing and reading graphical representations. The third,
probability, is therefore integrated with the former two by virtue
of sharing the overall title, while remaining separate by virtue of
having its content wholly given over to the acquisition of the
(addition and multiplication) rules of probability, etc., with no
use being made of probability in either of the other two
Attainment Targets. 'Handling Data' may be a UK entrant in the
'Find a Unifying Term Awards', but as a euphemism for
'stochastics' it has little chance of success without there being a
real underlying attempt to integrate statistics and probability.
Indeed, it is hard to see exactly how the third Attainment Target
really fits into 'Handling Data', since there is no evidence of any
data to be handled, only of events to be considered.

'REAL' STATISTICS

Whatever the problems concerning the exact interrelationship
between probability and statistics in curricula as found in the UK
and America, enormous strides are being made with respect to
what constitute mathematical, and hence statistical, activities. No
longer is it acceptable for students to be taught to perform
calculations without understanding what they are doing. Mathematics must be meaningful, and this can only be to the benefit of
statistical education.

In endorsing the NCTM Standards (1989), Kepner (1989, 1990)
underlines the significance of the intention that 'regardless of the
depth of study, the expectation is that students should interpret
and discuss their results in natural, as well as mathematical,

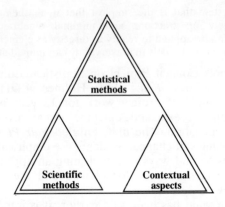

Figure 1.1 **'Doing "real" statistics'** (from Fuller, 1980)

language'. In particular, Kepner advocates 'powerful, creative mathematical thinking' as opposed to mere recall of a 'previously memorized formula' with respect to experiencing probability through simulating real situations. The UK National Curriculum (Department of Education and Science, 1987, 1989a,b) also reflects the growing expectation that skills in mathematics, and hence in statistics, should include the ability to communicate and talk about relevant ideas. However, the skills of (technical) report writing or oral presentation, whereby the results are clearly and concisely communicated in non-technical language that can be easily understood by the lay person, are not often taught, and have not been encountered in the *mathematical* context by most (school) students. Smeeton and Smeeton (1984) describe a relatively rare attempt to integrate English language and statistics teaching relevant to this.

In order to emphasize the *meaningful* nature of statistics, the Schools Council Project on Statistical Education (POSE) advocated that statistics teaching should be carried out through project work. Indeed, this is in line with much current thinking on statistical education. However, it is not without its problems. For a good discussion of these and the solution adopted by POSE, the reader is referred to the project report (Holmes *et al.*, 1981) and the teaching materials developed by the project team (Holmes, 1991). See also Chapter 7.

In 1980, Fuller portrayed statistics using Skemp's (1971) notions of *relational* as opposed to *rote learning* in mathematical education. Teaching for the former encourages the synthesis of knowledge and skills within general schema, rather than encouraging the students to see every new bit of information as an isolated entity. Figure 1.1 represents Fuller's (1980) model, based on there being three sets of schema within, and

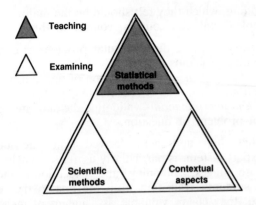

Figure 1.2 **Teaching 'statistics', but examining 'real statistics'**

schematically held together by, the overriding 'doing statistics' schema. The acquisition of all these schema, claims Fuller, is essential to the doing of 'real' statistics on any significantly sized data set.

A weakness in Fuller's model is that it makes no explicit reference to probability. Presumably it could be implicit within 'statistical methods', but that is not clear. Indeed, the diagram may well be reflecting the general failure to relate probability teaching and statistics teaching to one another, which was even more prevalent in 1980 than it is now.

What is particularly worrying in statistical education is that there is still a tendency to teach statistical methods in a relatively theoretical way, even if it is now done in a more enlightened, schematic way than was traditionally the case. Often, only the concepts in Fuller's top triangle are taught, while the other areas of 'real statistics' are neglected. When it comes to examining students, though, coursework in statistics is now considered to be important. Figure 1.2 shows the demands that this makes on the students, for which they may not have been prepared. Doing practical statistics is not in itself sufficient to ensure that the necessary practical skills in some sense 'rub off' on to the students. Any developing statistical pedagogy needs to include methods for *training* students in applied skills, and also to teach them how to link theoretical concepts with practice.

Chervany *et al.* (1980) proposed a systems approach for teaching *statistical reasoning*, which they defined 'as (a) what a student is able to do with statistical content (e.g. recalling, recognising, and discriminating among statistical concepts) and (b) the skill that the student demonstrates in using statistical concepts in specific problem-solving steps'. Their view of statistical reasoning, which they felt should be the major concern in teaching applied statistics courses, comprised three stages:

- *Comprehension* – seeing the particular problem as one of a class of similar problems.
- *Planning and execution* – the application of relevant methods for its solution.
- *Evaluation and interpretation* – validating the outcome against the original problem or question.

They argue that their approach, derived from the idea of designing an expert system, is particularly useful for teaching the second of these stages, 'planning and execution', and for facilitating the students' transition from the first to the second stage. It is also, they claim, valuable as a means of measuring 'both the students' statistical reasoning abilities and the effectiveness of the instructor's teaching' (see Chapter 6).

EXPLORATORY DATA ANALYSIS

Technological advances apart, one of the most significant influences on the practice of statistics in recent years stemmed from the publication of John W. Tukey's *Exploratory Data Analysis* in 1977. Interestingly, R.A. Fisher anticipated Tukey's ideas more than might be expected, despite his role in developing the theory of Classical Statistical Inference, whereby significance tests are carried out on hypotheses which must be specified in advance.

The preliminary examination of most data is facilitated by the use of diagrams. Diagrams prove nothing, but bring outstanding features readily to eye; they are therefore no substitute for such critical tests as may be applied to the data, but are valuable in suggesting such tests, and in explaining the conclusions founded upon them. (Fisher, 1925)

While more traditional statistics uses tables and graphs to *store* and *represent* data, in Exploratory Data Analysis (EDA) the corresponding techniques have an *exploratory* function; that is, they are tools which *develop knowledge*. Also, in the traditional approach usually one particular representation of the data is chosen. In EDA, *varying representations* are used which permit us to perceive the structure in the data, although our viewpoints are still confined to the context in which the analysis is taking place.

Tukey's approach emphasises the existence of two strands in statistical practice:

exploratory statistics – confirmatory statistics

with the teaching of EDA or (to use Chatfield's 1985 distinction) the teaching of 'Initial Data Analysis' dominating.

According to Biehler (1984), EDA is:

an experimental activity . . . which is organised by consciously optimised tools and general heuristic principles. Vague mathematical concepts play an important part in exploring displays. No theorems are proved, the ultimate justification of the tools and procedures lies in their success in practice, and it is even more important to have rich experience with applying EDA techniques than to know mathematical properties of the techniques used . . . Graphical methods play a substantial role and they do not fit into the picture of mathematics as a formal science.

Biehler still maintains, however, that EDA is a part of mathematics. For him, these informal and experimental approaches are the very aspects of mathematics which should feature in changes towards more practical and applied mathematics curricula.

In many cases, graphical displays are the only means for communicating the features discovered, which often cannot be described by analytic models and equations . . . Visualisations can become a tool for active learning, rather than being illustrative material presented by the teacher . . . Graphical displays should not only be seen as means for better teaching and learning, but the new role of graphics as research tools of mathematics should be reflected in the curricula . . .' [However, the] 'complexity of modern computer graphics calls for a more theoretical understanding as a prerequisite for an adequate use of displays . . . therefore, curricula should provide a graphical education, an education for 'graphicacy' [whereby the student learns also to guide the computer process involved in data representation]. (Biehler, 1985)

Another aim of EDA is that of *making representations more efficient*, thereby compensating for our limited capabilities to absorb and process information, and to recognise patterns within it. As well as providing valid and reliable communication, such representations should provide opportunities for us to become aware of chance variability and the more systematic influence of other potentially relevant variables, thereby opening up new perspectives on the data.

Figure 1.3 shows the technique of *brushing* a matrix of linked 2-dimensional scatterplots so that the associations between *three* variables (hardness of rubber, its strength and its abrasion loss) can be simultaneously explored by eye. Selectively highlighting points from the row 2 column 1 scattergram yields evidence of the dependence of abrasion loss on tensile strength, row 2 column 3 or row 3 column 2, for middle values of hardness, thereby permitting 3-dimensional conclusions to be drawn from a 2-dimensional representation. (The data can be found in Davies O.L., 1954.)

EDA also expands the horizons of traditional descriptive

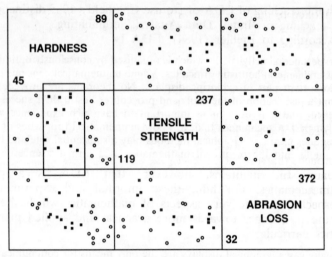

Figure 1.3 **Brushed, linked scatterplots showing the power of EDA methods to make representations more efficient** (after Becker and Cleveland, 1987)

statistics in other ways. Whereas the data manipulated by the latter is usually regarded as a random sample from some underlying population, EDA does not insist on such a requirement. It handles data from complete sets (populations) as well as sampled observations (whether randomly sampled or obtained by other means). Its techniques also apply to 'one-off' data sets and to 'dirty data' (that is, data that confront the statistician without the benefits of carefully designed collection, organisation and validation).

Biehler (1985) points to another merit of EDA:

... the methodology of EDA ... tries to regulate an otherwise unregulated 'data snooping' with computers. In this sense there may be some similarity to R.A. Fisher's important contributions to statistics, which also provided guidance to a formerly rather arbitrary practice with desk calculators in statistics.

Apart from sequential and Bayesian approaches, where some degree of retrospection is entailed, it is one of the fundamental traits of traditional statistics that the research process must be completely specified before any practical investigation commences. Hypotheses have to be formulated *before* any data are collected and examined, so that the possible range of conclusions that can then be drawn is predetermined before a single observation or measurement is taken. After gathering the data, the classic paradigm of

descriptive statistics – probability – statistical inference is invoked to perform appropriate tests of hypotheses. *Traditionally*, scientific method dictated that *hypotheses could not be suggested or generated as a result of looking closely at the data.* EDA relaxes this stringent requirement. While recognising that there will be prior knowledge and opinions about the data, it allows the data analysis itself to suggest new directions and hypotheses. Probability is then not needed until very much later and there *may* be good reasons for teaching it as a separate topic, divorced for the time being from the applied statistics syllabus, until it is needed in the confirmatory stage. The danger of this approach, that probability and statistics can come to be seen as 'separate' and 'divorced', has already been discussed and is raised again here merely to underline the persistence of this problem, irrespective of whether 'traditional' or 'modern' statistics forms the basis of the syllabus content.

MODELLING

The growing emphasis on Exploratory Data Analysis, and hence on statistical modelling, has featured prominently at successive International Conferences on Teaching Statistics (1982, 1986 and 1990), and also at the International Statistical Institute's Roundtable Conference, *Training Teachers to Teach Statistics* (Hawkins, 1990). Clearly the need to develop statistical education in this direction is a concern of educationalists internationally, and a number of research and development projects are now addressing EDA teaching methods and materials, and both initial and in-service teacher training in relevant skills.

Tukey compares the statistician exploring data to a detective searching for clues in the 'smooth' and the 'rough', these being seen as the components of data:

data = smooth + rough

The well-behaved typical data values (the 'smooth') may exhibit a pattern that is easy to visualise and interpret. The 'rough' will indicate peculiar points deserving extra attention.

The 'smooth' relationship between two variables is often modelled by fitting a 'curve' to it, which in reality generally takes the form of a straight line (after transforming the data if necessary). A straight line has many obvious advantages. It is extremely easy to

● manipulate mathematically
● construct and graph
● interpret, etc.

After modelling the 'smooth', the 'rough' is examined to see if any further pattern remains that would suggest the presence of factors making the fit to the 'smooth' inadequate. If no discernible pattern is observed in the 'rough', it is assumed that the model is acceptable. There is much scope for handling the earlier stages of data modelling visually by inspection of graphical representations. It is also possible to impose a probabilistic structure on the 'rough' (as in making distributional assumptions about the residuals in a regression analysis) and then to carry out inferential procedures on the fitted model, but a reliance on graphical procedures at first means that the more formal inference procedures can realistically be left to the later parts of a syllabus. Thus linear models play an important role in describing the 'smooth', while probabilistic models (e.g. the Gaussian distribution) are needed later for confirmatory analysis, evaluating the fit of a model and deriving contrasts and comparisons from it, etc.

Such a strategy will not be detrimental to students' statistical education. Rather, the opposite will be the case, since what is being suggested reflects the growing belief in the importance of the modelling approach to statistics in general. The more restrictive, and often less informative, significance-testing

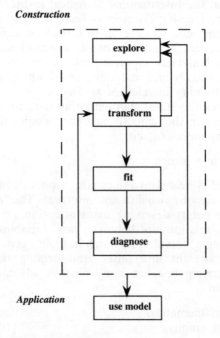

Construction

Application

Figure 1.4 **Statistical modelling**

approaches are gradually being supplemented and even replaced, by those which emphasise modelling and estimation. Where statisticians led the way, now 'user'-discipline specialists are following. For example, articles for publication in the *British Medical Journal* must now show point estimates and confidence limits rather than merely cite the *p*-values (Gardner and Altman, 1989).

The process of modelling data can be represented as in Figure 1.4, which demonstrates that a number of iterations may be required before we can obtain an acceptable model. It is this iterative nature of the modelling process, and indeed of the whole research process itself, that teachers of statistics have to emphasise. We must awaken in our students the realisation that *all models are wrong*, but that some may provide acceptable descriptions of the behaviour of the data. Students must also realise that there is *very seldom a single correct answer to a problem in statistical data analysis*. This will be contrary to the students' expectations if they see statistics only as a branch of mathematics.

Green (1982) criticised mathematics teaching for the inappropriate emphases it conveys to students about the use of models. He was particularly concerned about the failure to equip students to *construct* probability models, and the emphasis placed instead on the *manipulation* of models. In his view, the mathematics curriculum neglects the necessary skills-training to address 'real' problems, and in this sense his ideas are reminiscent of Fuller's.

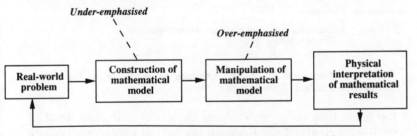

Figure 1.5 **Green's model of mathematical probability teaching**

THE ROLE OF COMPUTING IN THE STATISTICS OF THE FUTURE

In his article on the significance of the *micro-* as distinct from the *mainframe* computer, Mangles (1984) emphasised graphics and residual analyses as being the cornerstone of the '*micro*-revolution'. He criticised existing statistics courses for spending

Current Course Structure

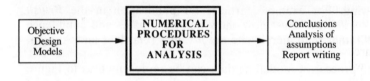

New course structure, de-emphasising numerical procedures

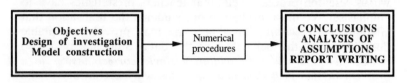

Components of the new structure

a) Defining the objective
b) Designing the investigation
c) Developing possible models
d) Supervising data collection & entry
* e) Exploratory analysis & verification
* f) Analysis
g) Interpretation of the results
* h) Analysis of assumptions
i) Feedback about the objectives/design
j) Report writing,

to which should be added;

k) Evaluating the reliability of hard- and soft-ware, and
l) Graphicacy skills

Figure 1.6 **The need for course changes in response to the 'micro-computer revolution'** (from Mangles, 1984)

too much time on giving students numerical skills, and for their continuing to artificially fragment the subject matter just because for the purposes of computation it was once easier to teach equivalent concepts, such as hypothesis testing and estimation/confidence intervals, as different entities and in different ways.

In Mangles' view, microcomputers should not only revolutionise *what* is taught (reflecting changes in statistical practice), but also *how* it is taught. He advocates a new course structure with a much reduced emphasis on the numerical procedures in statistics. The * components in Figure 1.6 are seen by Mangles to be the major areas where the impact of microcomputers should be felt.

It is glib, however, to suggest that all this can come about overnight, particularly when the availability of appropriate hardware, and software, in classrooms is still so relatively limited. In 1973, Kerridge found that the 'idea of terminals for all [tertiary level] students' seemed 'a little visionary'. Nevertheless, there are now many examples of this in practice. It is clear also that the technological revolution has accelerated since Kerridge's 'dream' and it is therefore fair to assume that, even if the resources are not currently available in the secondary classroom, they will be eventually. Just as statistics has come down the educational levels from tertiary through secondary to primary, so too will statistical computing. Furthermore, until that day, a student's own computing resources at home should not be left out of the equation.

Most teachers of statistics are now aware of the impact that the computer is making, and will make, on the **teaching** of statistics. However, in fact teachers need also to recognise that statistical computing is changing the way in which we **do** statistics. They need to be discerning in their choice of packages and to understand the underlying algorithms used in the software. They need to be clear about what a package can and cannot do for the statistician. They also need to teach their students how to evaluate and to get to know the characteristics of the computer software and hardware they use, and to recognise that statistical computing may have a role to play at *all stages of the statistical process*, from the initial planning, through the data collection, processing and interpretation, to the completion of the project. A full appreciation of this wide-ranging role of statistical computing will not be attained, however, until an equivalent view of all the many aspects of statistics itself is established.

STATISTICS AND EMPLOYMENT

The Institute of Statisticians and the Royal Statistical Society produce occasional publications relevant to the vocational prospects and training needs of students intending to become professional statisticians. Much of the focus of *this* book, however, will be on the needs of the majority of students, i.e. those who, although not intending to become specialist statisticians, may still find themselves faced with a need for statistical skills and understanding. The Sheffield Centre for Statistical Education survey report, *Statistical Needs of Non-specialist Young Workers* (Centre for Statistical Education, 1985) contains some insight into such people, and indicates a considerable 'generation gap' between management and lower grade employees.

The Sheffield study found that managers wanted their young employees to demonstrate 'common-sense' in handling quantitative material, and to have well-developed communication skills.

Job advertisements for professional statisticians often demand that the prospective candidate must be ready and able to participate in projects *as part of a team.* The amount of such teamwork in the statistics curriculum is now increasing and through it the student can gain additional and valuable experience in activities such as group interaction, group management, etc.

The variety of companies surveyed in the Sheffield report showed that there was wide-ranging use of statistics, and although the managers did not feel that their young employees were required to show much statistical initiative, the employees themselves often felt that they were. It was likely that the managers were somewhat insecure about their own statistical training, and as a result some may possibly have repressed the statistical skills of their young employees. If this is so, there is clearly a need to educate the managers, as well as their future employees, in statistics. Failure to do this could lead to serious under-usage of available techniques in commerce and industry. Perhaps hope lies in the fact that the 'New Statistics' may be more intuitively convincing and appealing to management since it emphasises the sort of 'basic' skills that they purport to want from their employees. However, the problem is that the appropriate pedagogy for teaching such skills has still to be developed and researched.

In a work context, a statistical project is generally part of a *routine* or an *on-going* process. The failure to introduce students to this type of approach precludes them from acquiring the specialist statistical skills associated with on-going knowledge acquisition, including those of literature search and research evaluation. It also encourages students to undertake invalid projects, with little or no appreciation of the real significance of their own work. Some students, as a result, will have little conviction that what they are doing is worth while. Others will have an inflated idea of the significance of their findings. Certainly, these problems are manifest more frequently than not in the entries to the UK Annual Applied Statistics Competition.

Since the current generation is not very statistically sophisticated, the need to educate future generations has serious implications for the progress of society, which now is often influenced by false quantitative premises. If more people are to be 'statistical', i.e. to 'do statistics', they must be 'good' statistically, with the same kind of professional integrity, skills and knowledge that were originally the preserve of the statistician. However, this has to be achieved without the traditional training period and content of study that a statistician receives. Appropriate pedagogy is needed that has some chance of achieving this ambitious objective. This pedagogy must focus on the reality of doing statistics today, with all the use of technology which that implies. The relevance of 'computational formulae' and the like, which used to provide substantial textbook content, are things of the past. This handbook is intended to lay a foundation for exploring how best to teach the applied skills which are currently most relevant, including the use and evaluation of statistical tools and concepts, computer hardware and software, and graphicacy.

NOTES

1. Public examinations at the end of compulsory school years in the UK, i.e. for students aged 16 years.
2. Public examinations for students aged 18 years.

CHAPTER 2

Statistics teachers, their difficulties, opinions and needs

TEACHER TRAINING AND RECRUITMENT ISSUES IN STATISTICAL EDUCATION

In 1982, the Cockcroft Committee looked at mathematics education in the UK and reported that 'some teachers, especially those who completed their degree courses some years ago, do not have sufficient knowledge of probability and statistics to teach in these areas effectively'. Furthermore, that committee found that few teachers, including those whose degree or other courses had contained statistics, had received any training in how to teach statistics.

Far from Cockcroft's recommendations resulting in an upsurge of relevant training, the succession of 'crises' in education in England and Wales has made it very difficult for teachers to avail themselves of either pre- or in-service training. The International Statistical Institute's Round-table Conference (Hawkins, 1990), *Training Teachers to Teach Statistics*, concluded that although initiatives were being taken by trainers, with few exceptions their impact was relatively localised. Centralised directives and finance are needed to change this.

At both pre- and in-service levels, statistical education suffers; either by being a part of mathematics education, where pressures of time (and inclination) marginalise it, or by being in competition with mathematics education. With more training resources and an increased demand for teachers of core curriculum subjects, students tend to opt for courses in mathematics or science education. Statistical education cannot compete with this. Difficult as it is to recruit *statistics* post-graduates, the problem is compounded in the case of recruiting non-specialist postgraduates to *statistics* or statistical *education* courses (Hawkins, 1991b). The fact that few statistics graduates take up (school) teaching is a problem in itself, but such specialists are also deterred, and in some cases prevented (if, for example, they do not have classroom experience), from moving into the academic study of, and research into, statistical education.

The failure to recruit sufficient numbers of students, and hence to justify sufficient numbers of academic staff, is a major impediment to the development of a pedagogic discipline or research basis for statistical education in its own right (Hawkins, 1991b). With more students, there are greater numbers of mathematics education lecturers, who in turn can sustain more options, encouraging more students to specialise solely in *mathematics* education rather than in *statistical* education, thus completing the vicious circle and making it very difficult for those students who want to specialise in statistical education to find enough relevant courses, resources or training support. The International Statistical Institute's Round-table Conference (Hawkins, 1990) recommended that the crisis in statistical education should be tackled first at the in-service level. Lack of finance or time allowances for in-service release make this difficult in the UK, although the cross-curricular emphasis on handling data in the new National Curriculum (Department of Education and Science, 1989a,b) may help.

It would be wrong to suggest that competition from mathematics (or other disciplines) is always to blame for recruitment problems in statistical education. For students majoring in other disciplines, some statisticians themselves contribute to poor recruitment figures when they set course prerequisites too high, or offer statistics courses that are inappropriate for the levels and needs of potential students. Also, *statistics* lecturers may be slow to practise what the statistical educationalists preach, since tertiary level teachers of statistics themselves generally receive no training in how to teach statistics.

Recruitment may be eased by distance learning programmes such as the Sheffield City Polytechnic Postgraduate Diploma in Statistics and Statistical Education. Using a combination of correspondence tuition and summer schools, this course tackles the two broad aspects of teachers' training needs, enhancing not only their statistical expertise but also their awareness of research, curriculum and pedagogic issues relating to statistical education.

Statistical education lecturers tend to be isolated within their own institutions, but so too do school teachers with an interest in statistical education. Teachers' networks, such as the Statistics Teacher Network in the United States, can help. Funded by the National Council for Teachers of Mathematics, this network produces a regular newsletter, providing a two-way communication channel between statistics teachers at all levels, researchers and policy makers.[1] Another useful network, although at present one which is more researcher than classroom practitioner oriented, is the International Study Group on Learning Probability and Statistics Concepts. This group has a tradition of informal exchanges concerning members' activities, research and relevant news items through a newsletter which is currently distributed by Joan Garfield.[2] The UK-produced journal *Teaching Statistics*[3] also provides a communication channel for the exchange of teaching ideas. With increasing computer resources being found in schools, it may well be that the problem of relative isolation could soon be minimised, and access to in-service training improved, by further exploitation of electronic communication.

One style of teacher training has been to put teachers into the role of their students. Shaughnessy (1988) describes two projects in Oregon, one for in-service teachers and one for pre-service teachers, to show them the potential of computer simulations in the teaching of probability and statistics concepts. The model used was to start with a problem situation and then to proceed from guesses through experiments to computer simulations, and finally to theoretical models. It was hoped to encourage the teachers to use the same sequence and the same experiments with their own students.

Somewhat in contrast, Schupp (1990) describes an action research programme, giving teachers responsibility for the development of curricula, teaching methods and materials. This long-term project had the merit of stimulating a commitment on the part of the teachers involved. Subsequently, these teachers became the trainers, passing on their expertise to colleagues in their schools. Such a *cascade* model of in-service training might well be appropriate in the UK, making use of Baker Days.[4] Certainly, the notion of teachers as trainers is not a new concept. Burrill (1990), for example, describes the way in which the Quantitative Literacy Project recruits and trains teachers in the United States.

A UK in-service arrangement, recommended by both the Cockcroft Committee (1982) and the Schools Council Project on Statistical Education (Holmes *et al.*, 1981), is that someone should act as a statistical coordinator in each school (or locality) who could also promote in-service statistical education within that context. This recommendation has still not been widely implemented, although the National Curriculum may now stimulate some progress. A coordinators' pack has been produced by Holmes and Rouncefield (1990) containing practical guidance and helpful references to where further resources can be found.

Students and their teachers perceive that part of the course which is examined as being the important part. Changes in *what is assessed* can therefore provide in-service training by changing attitudes towards the nature of statistics. However, what is taught and what is assessed are interdependent. The one is unlikely to change without the other, and if changes in one are not accompanied by changes in the other within a relatively short period of time, the first to be changed will revert to its original format.

Some *methods of assessment* can themselves provide a means of in-service training. Sharpe (1990) outlined a scheme for teacher consensus moderation of students' statistical coursework which, as a spin-off, provided teachers with the opportunity to meet together and hear about what was being achieved in different schools. Sharpe maintained that this was 'a powerful force for changing teachers' expectations'.

In his foreword to the Proceedings of the International Statistical Institute's Round-table Conference *Training Teachers to Teach Statistics*, Vere-Jones (1990) declared that the theme of the conference was

surely destined to be one of the major practical problems facing school mathematics in the near future. . . . [Despite the] growing acceptance of the value of statistics, in some or all of its many senses, as part of a modern school curriculum . . . the task of implementing this change on a mass basis, across all schools, and with all types of teachers, raises formidable difficulties. At the heart of these lies the problem of teacher training and retraining. Teaching statistics successfully requires different attitudes, different activities, different teaching styles, from the traditional mathematics course. Even where they are willing (and this is not always the case) mathematics teachers may not have the background knowledge or experience to tackle such challenges successfully.

The problems of introducing statistics into the curriculum in developing countries are even greater than those encountered in developed countries. Quite apart from the lack of resources, and difficulties for teachers gaining access to those which exist, in many such countries the mathematics curriculum is 'locked into place, by ill-informed bureaucracy, by stifling effects of competitive entrance examinations, and by the overriding consideration that changing curricula must take second place to extending the availability of education to a larger proportion of the population' (Vere-Jones, 1990). The International Statistical Institute, together with sponsorship from organisations such as UNESCO, is doing much to try to alleviate teachers', and hence students', difficulties in such countries, but there is still a long way to go.

A SURVEY OF TEACHERS OF STATISTICS IN THE UK

In order to find out what teachers themselves bring to their statistics teaching, a survey of teachers of statistics was carried out (Hawkins, 1989a).[5] Some of the survey findings are outlined in the following pages. The 349 respondents, drawn from primary and secondary schools, and from a handful of Further Education Colleges, included teachers of statistics in its own right, teachers of mathematics, and teachers of some 26 'user'-disciplines spanning the natural, physical and social sciences, the humanities and the arts. It is unlikely that there are any school disciplines with no statistical content, even if some teachers are not aware that when they help their students to interpret a data table, for example, they are 'teaching statistics'.

Approximately one-third of the respondents (the initial contacts in what was a linked sampling procedure) had at some time in the past expressed some interest in the Annual UK Applied Statistics Competition for Schools and Colleges of Further Education, whether or not their students had actually gone on to participate in the Competition. This would presumably tend to lead to a selection bias whereby the opinions about, awareness of, and interest in, statistics of these *initial* contacts might be more developed than those of some of their colleagues. Indeed they may have been more favourably disposed towards statistics and statistical education in general. The rest of the (linked) sample comprised colleagues of these initial contacts, up to three from each school, whose participation was solicited by the initial contacts. Selected in this way, the sample had broad coverage, but could not necessarily be considered to be wholly representative of the overall population of teachers of statistics.

Respondents' background training in statistics

Approximately one in five respondents had not studied statistics beyond school level, and 6 per cent claimed to have had no formal statistical training at all. In the main, those with lower levels of statistical training tended to be older and also more experienced teachers, i.e. with at least 10 years of experience. This is not surprising in view of the developments in statistical education in recent years, leading to its recognition and introduction at earlier levels and in more subject areas. It is by no means clear, however, that time served teaching can necessarily compensate for the lack of relevant training in the subject matter.

Grouping the teachers by the context and by the highest level at which they were currently teaching, Table 2.1 shows that more than a third of the primary school teachers had had no college-level training in statistics. The proportion was similar for lower secondary teachers of 'user'-disciplines. At upper secondary level, the picture was as might be expected, with teachers having had college training closely associated with their current teaching. Some statisticians, and many 'user'-discipline specialists, may be a little unhappy with the relatively high proportion of mathematics-

Table 2.1 **Does their own statistical training equip teachers to teach the statistics demanded of them?**

Statistical training and its context	Respondents' teaching level and its context (%)							
	Primary	Lower secondary			Upper secondary			
		Stats	Maths	User	Stats	Maths	User	Overall
None	5.2	10.3	7.7	0	8.5	4.5	4.8	6.0
School level only	**31.0**	3.4	11.5	**34.8**	6.8	18.2	11.9	15.8
College: User	25.9	3.4	7.7	**39.1**	5.1	2.3	**56.0**	22.9
Maths	22.4	**37.9**	**44.2**	8.7	**35.6**	**50.0**	6.0	27.8
Stats	15.5	**44.8**	28.8	17.4	**44.1**	25.0	21.4	27.8
Per cent	100	100	100	100	100	100	100	100
(Column total)	(58)	(29)	(52)	(23)	(59)	(44)	(84)	(349)

Table entries show numbers of respondents expressed as percentages of *column* totals, with large or otherwise noteworthy entries highlighted in bold typeface. 'Primary' level means teaching students aged 11 and under. 'Lower secondary' means teaching students in the 11–16 years age-group. 'Upper secondary' means teaching students in the 16–19 years age-group.

trained respondents who are teaching statistics, and may assume that this training background lends itself less well to the more applied aspects of the subject, or may not stimulate the necessary empathy with less mathematically inclined students. One particularly serious point, and one that is often overlooked, is that many teachers who have been 'statistically trained' (as per the 1989 survey definition, i.e. they have studied statistics as a subject in its own right) will have studied mathematics as well. The converse is not necessarily true. To be entered in the 'mathematics-trained' category does not necessarily imply much statistics training, although it may do.

For the purposes of the 1989 survey, the term 'college-trained statisticians' referred to those respondents who claimed to have studied statistics as a subject in its own right as opposed to combined with mathematics or within a 'user'-discipline. Clearly, though, 'statistics in its own right' does not guarantee any particular level or depth of study. Hopefully, however, it does imply a commitment and philosophy appropriate to statistical education on the part of those training the respondents. Similar concern might be expressed, of course, about the variety of levels and depth achieved in combination with mathematics and 'user'-disciplines. This wide disparity between courses, both within and between school and college courses, is one of the things that makes this sort of research into statistical education particularly difficult.

In view of the problems associated with identifying the nature of teachers' background training in statistics, it may be useful to consider the respondents' perceived in-service needs, shown in Table 2.2, although these will of course reflect, in part, their

Table 2.2 **Respondents' perceived in-service requirements**

Requirements*	Frequency	%
Theoretical statistics	43	11.7
Applications	172	46.9
Teaching statistics	141	38.4
Use/management of technical resources	169	46.0

* More than one 'need' could be indicated by the survey respondents.

teaching needs (and their willingness to participate if in-service provision were to be provided). More training in theoretical statistics was not felt by most of the respondents to be a priority. Presumably, then, most of them felt able to cope with the statistical *techniques* encountered within their teaching.

Those who had not studied much theoretical statistics themselves did not wish to, and those who had already studied it did not feel the need to do more. It is debatable whether this is as satisfactory as it sounds pragmatic. If statistics were seen to be a mainstream subject in its own right, its teachers would certainly be expected to have a stronger coverage of the theoretical underpinnings of the discipline than was evidenced by the levels of background training reported in this survey.

Respondents' own difficulties with statistics

The survey also explored specific areas of difficulty for teachers (and their students) based on Fuller's model of 'doing *real* statistics' shown in Chapter 1 (Figure 1.1). Table 2.3 shows teachers' ratings of the amount of difficulty that they personally experienced with each of Fuller's three areas of statistics: namely techniques, applications and research design/scientific methods. It is undoubtedly the case that the respondents' perceptions were in part influenced by the demands of their current teaching.

The respondents were provided with an appropriate scale point to signify 'no difficulty'. Therefore, at least some of those teachers who specified 'not applicable' *or who left the questions unanswered* were saying something different from 'no difficulty'. The response 'not applicable' and the non-responses imply that certain aspects of statistics are erroneously considered to be *non-relevant*.

With the exception of 'user'-discipline teachers, *applications* and *scientific methodology* seem to pose more problems for the teachers than the statistical *techniques* themselves. These problems were fairly consistent irrespective of the teachers' training backgrounds, with a slight lowering of perceived problems for those with no formal training. Possibly the teaching level of such

Table 2.3 **Teachers' own perceived difficulties in 'doing statistics'**

Degree of difficulty reported	Respondents' teaching level and its context (%)								Areas of difficulty reported
	Primary	Lower secondary			Upper secondary				
		Stats	Maths	User	Stats	Maths	User	Overall	
Non-response	22.4	10.3	7.7	8.7	8.5	4.6	11.9	11.2	Technique
	20.7	6.9	5.8	8.7	8.5	4.6	11.9	10.3	Applications
	24.1	10.3	19.2	21.7	18.6	29.6	23.8	21.8	Sci. meth.
Some difficulty	27.6	13.8	23.1	**52.2**	8.5	25.0	**47.6**	28.7	Technique
	41.4	**55.2**	42.4	**52.2**	44.1	50.1	59.5	49.3	Applications
	51.7	**65.5**	44.3	34.8	45.8	54.5	47.6	49.0	Sci. meth.
No difficulty	39.7	75.9	69.2	34.8	83.1	70.5	39.3	57.9	Technique
	27.6	37.9	51.9	34.8	47.5	45.5	28.6	38.4	Applications
	13.8	24.1	34.6	39.1	23.7	13.6	27.4	24.4	Sci. meth.
Not applicable	10.3	0	0	4.4	0	0	1.2	2.3	Technique
	10.3	0	0	4.4	0	0	0	2.0	Applications
	10.3	0	1.9	4.4	11.9	2.3	1.2	4.9	Sci. meth.
Per cent (Total)	100 (58)	100 (29)	100 (52)	100 (23)	100 (59)	100 (44)	100 (84)	100 (349)	

See footnote to Table 2.1.

respondents was lower and therefore less demanding. However, it may also be the case that they have a narrower perspective on what is really needed in statistical education.

The most worrying aspect was the relatively high reporting of scientific methods as being 'not applicable' or the ignoring of this item. Scientific methodology is not only to do with how data are collected. It must also be taken into account when data are evaluated and processed. If teachers consider this to be 'not applicable', where are the students to acquire this awareness and understanding? Methods and materials are needed that will incorporate this aspect of statistics into all areas of statistical education. However, unless a more realistic view of statistics can be encouraged – one that is shared by examination boards and teachers – progress will not be made in this respect.

Attitudes towards teaching statistics and probability

It is important to know not only something about whether teachers have difficulty with the subject matter, but also about their attitudes towards teaching statistics and probability. Table 2.4 shows the extent to which respondents reported that they enjoyed teaching statistics and probability, classified by the teachers' most statistically demanding current teaching level, and its context. Most respondents were found to enjoy teaching statistics. Many enjoyed teaching probability too, especially

Table 2.4 **Do teachers differ in the extent to which they enjoy teaching statistics and probability?**

Enjoyment of teaching	Primary	Lower secondary			Upper secondary			Overall	Areas of enjoyment reported
		Stats	Maths	User	Stats	Maths	User		
Non-response	3.5	0	9.6	4.4	1.7	2.3	4.8	4.0	Statistics
	5.2	0	9.6	30.4	1.7	2.3	20.2	9.7	Probability
Yes	81.0	96.6	80.8	65.2	96.6	86.4	60.7	79.7	Statistics
	55.2	86.2	80.8	8.7	84.7	86.4	25.0	60.2	Probability
No	0	3.5	7.7	13.0	1.7	11.4	28.6	10.9	Statistics
	6.9	13.8	7.7	17.4	10.2	11.4	16.7	11.7	Probability
Not applicable	15.5	0	1.9	17.4	0	0	6.0	5.4	Statistics
	32.8	0	1.9	43.5	3.39	0	38.1	18.3	Probability
Per cent (Total)	100 (58)	100 (29)	100 (52)	100 (23)	100 (59)	100 (44)	100 (84)	100 (349)	

See footnote to Table 2.1.

college-trained mathematics and statistics specialists. It should be remembered, however, that the sampling strategy may well have led to a selective bias towards those more favourably disposed towards statistics. Differences shown in Table 2.4 confirm the separation of attitudes towards statistics and probability, despite the fundamental role of probability in statistics.

There was fairly consistent enjoyment for all teaching levels of statistics, and a lower, but still consistent level for probability. Too many primary teachers saw probability as not applicable, rather than considering themselves to have an important role to play, in accord with Fischbein's (1975) views, in developing the precursors of probabilistic reasoning. This situation must change if the National Curriculum in mathematics, with probability teaching for all children aged 5 to 16, is to succeed.

'User'-discipline teachers showed less enjoyment of both statistics and probability teaching than did mathematics and statistics teachers. In particular, their enjoyment of probability was replaced by their feeling that it is not relevant to them, especially at the lower secondary level. As has already been stated, this is potentially a very worrying state of affairs, and one that is likely to perpetuate a weak representation of what statistics really involves, its scope and its power.

The impact of changes in statistics and statistical education

As Chapter 1 shows, there have in fact been a great many changes in the way statistics is practised. Most teachers (59.9 per cent), however, did not report any changes, and 10.1 per cent actually said that there had been 'no changes'. The equivalent percentages for the teachers' perceptions of changes in the *teaching* of statistics, 39.8 per cent (non-response) and 8.7 per cent (reporting no changes had occurred) are less indicative of a 'blinkered' outlook. Firstly, they are lower, and secondly, they probably do reflect a real lack of change in teaching statistics in certain subject areas. They are nonetheless worrying.

The main changes reported in the way in which statistics is practised were those relating to applications, wider accessibility and the impact of computers. Mathematics-trained teachers were proportionately more aware of the change towards an increased number of applications than were the other respondents. This *may* reflect inferences based on their observed teaching changes, rather than direct knowledge of changes in statistical practice.

Table 2.5 shows the extent to which the teachers were aware of changes having taken place in statistics teaching during the past ten years, classified by their own most statistically demanding current teaching level, and its context. Respondents were free to record as many changes as they wished. Few recorded more than one. The main teaching changes reported were similar to those reported as changes in doing statistics; more applied work, accessibility to more non-specialist students, the impact of computers and a greater prevalence of statistics in many different 'user' areas. It should be noted that these observations are somewhat at odds with the fairly widespread view that scientific methodology is 'not relevant'.

Table 2.5 **Of what changes in teaching statistics are teachers aware?**

Awareness changes in teaching statistics	Respondents' teaching level and its context (%)							
	Primary	Lower secondary			Upper secondary			Overall
		Stats	Maths	User	Stats	Maths	User	
Blank	34.5	37.9	32.7	**60.9**	18.6	**47.7**	**50.0**	39.8
None	8.6	6.9	11.5	4.4	5.1	4.6	10.7	8.7
Applications	13.8	37.9	32.7	8.7	**50.8**	25.0	13.1	25.8
Lay use	8.6	3.5	5.8	4.4	1.7	2.3	3.6	4.3
Computer	17.2	6.9	3.9	13.0	5.1	11.4	7.1	8.9
Prevalence	12.1	6.9	9.6	4.4	0	6.8	9.5	7.5
Per cent	100	100	100	100	100	100	100	100
(Total)	(58)	(29)	(52)	(23)	(59)	(44)	(84)	(349)

See footnote to Table 2.1, but note that infrequently reported changes have not been included.

It would appear that teachers of statistics in its own right, and in the context of mathematics, have experienced the greatest changes in its teaching. This is not particularly surprising since the main changes seem to be related to applied work, and 'user'-discipline teachers started out with the applications already *in situ.*

Any expansion of statistics within the curriculum seemed to be felt in the areas of statistics in its own right, and within mathematics, at the upper secondary level (69.5 and 61.4 per cent, respectively). There were few teachers who felt that statistics has contracted within the curriculum (overall 6.3 per cent) and many who felt that it is expanding (overall 53.6 per cent). There was some suggestion that it is contracting as a subject in its own right at lower secondary level, but this may be seen in part to be a response to the increased statistical content in the (GCSE, National Curriculum) *mathematics* context. Clearly, such figures will be particularly sensitive to the most recent curriculum policy statements.

Respondents' opinions on where and how statistics should be taught

Table 2.6 shows respondents' opinions about the appropriate context for the teaching of statistics, classified by the teachers' most statistically demanding current teaching level, and its context. Initially, their responses were made without differentiating between 'statistics' and 'probability'. Considerable support was found for saying that mathematics is the context in which statistics should be taught, although 'user'-discipline respondents did not favour this. They firmly advocated that statistics should be taught in a 'user'-discipline context at both secondary levels.

Table 2.6 **Opinions about the appropriate context for the teaching of statistics**

Preferred context for teaching statistics	Respondents' teaching level and its context (%)							
	Primary	Lower secondary			Upper secondary			
		Stats	Maths	User	Stats	Maths	User	Overall
Non-response	13.8	10.3	9.6	21.7	11.9	15.9	10.7	12.6
Statistics	3.5	24.1	17.3	4.4	11.9	4.6	9.5	10.3
Mathematics	29.3	31.0	23.1	8.7	23.7	31.8	6.0	20.9
'User'	39.7	3.5	25.0	52.2	8.5	11.4	41.7	26.9
Combination	13.8	31.0	25.0	13.1	44.0	36.4	32.1	29.2
Per cent (Total)	100 (58)	100 (29)	100 (52)	100 (23)	100 (59)	100 (44)	100 (84)	100 (349)

See footnote to Table 2.1.

The table also shows that overall, nearly 30 per cent of the respondents advocated a combination of contexts, which is probably an expression in support of the *status quo*. As we shall see from the next section, this may well reflect teachers' perceptions about the divided nature of statistics. The only real support for statistics being taught as a subject in its own right came from teachers already teaching it in that way. It is particularly noticeable that statistics teachers, and most upper secondary mathematics teachers, did not want 'user'-disciplines as the principal context for statistics teaching.

Respondents' opinions on who should teach statistics and probability

There has been a long-standing debate as to who should teach statistics and/or probability, and to which students (see, for example, the Mathematical Association of America, 1979). Table 2.7 shows the views of respondents in the 1989 survey about who should teach statistics and probability classified by the teachers' most statistically demanding current teaching level, and its context. Mathematics teachers favoured mathematicians for teaching both statistics and probability. Many 'user'-discipline teachers would accept a mathematics teacher teaching probability, but not

Table 2.7 **Views on who should teach students statistics and probability**

Preferred teacher	Primary	Lower secondary			Upper secondary			Overall	Aspects of stochastics
		Stats	Maths	User	Stats	Maths	User		
Non-response	8.6	0	1.9	4.4	5.1	4.6	4.8	4.6	Statistics
	10.3	0	1.9	21.7	5.1	4.6	15.5	8.6	Probability
Mathematician	19.0	51.7	30.8	26.1	27.1	50.0	17.9	28.9	Statistics
	27.6	79.3	65.4	43.5	61.0	84.1	46.4	55.9	Probability
'User'-specialist	25.9	3.5	17.3	21.7	11.9	2.3	32.1	18.6	Statistics
	20.7	0	5.8	4.4	5.1	0	14.3	8.9	Probability
Combination	12.1	31.0	44.2	34.8	40.7	38.6	41.7	35.2	Statistics
	8.6	6.9	19.2	26.1	18.6	9.1	22.6	16.3	Probability
Class teacher	32.8	0	0	0	0	0	0	5.4	Statistics
	32.8	0	0	0	0	0	0	5.4	Probability
Other, including statistician	1.7	13.8	5.8	13.0	15.3	4.6	3.6	7.2	Statistics
	0	13.8	7.7	4.4	10.2	2.3	1.2	4.9	Probability
Per cent (Total)	100 (58)	100 (29)	100 (52)	100 (23)	100 (59)	100 (44)	100 (84)	100 (349)	

Respondents' Teaching level and its context (%)

See footnote to Table 2.1.

statistics. Although approximately one-third of the respondents advocated a combination of teachers for teaching statistics, only 16.3 per cent overall felt that this would be appropriate for the teaching of probability.

In fact, approximately half (46.4 per cent) of those who advocated a 'user'-discipline specialist to teach statistics actually recommended that probability should be the domain of the mathematics teachers. The same was true of those who recommended a combination approach of mathematicians and 'user'-discipline teachers for statistics. 48.4 per cent of these recommended that a mathematics teacher should teach probability. Clearly, much progress has to be made if the integration of probability and statistics is seen to be important for the greater understanding of statistics.

IN CONCLUSION

In this chapter, we have considered some of the issues that may impede progress in statistical education. Evidence from educationalists around the world indicates that these are not exclusively UK problems, although the precise nature of the difficulties may show variations between and within different countries, according to how far the statistical curriculum has developed and the extent to which it is governed by traditional views of statistics. It is clear from teachers' own responses to the Hawkins' (1989a) survey that despite recent advances in curriculum in the UK apparently establishing statistical education on a firmer footing, the infrastructure for doing this in a meaningful way is still underdeveloped. One anxiety which we have is that the overt appearance of a 'Statistics for All' philosophy in the UK National Curriculum (Department of Education and Science, 1989a,b) will result in a complacency towards the very real problems that we still see in its implementation.

APPENDIX: TEACHERS' VIEWS ON A RESEARCH AGENDA FOR STATISTICAL EDUCATION

The following topics for necessary research were suggested by respondents to Hawkins' survey (1989a), some of which indicate the personal needs of the respondents in their teaching contexts.

How to teach data handling, statistical ideas
How much to involve computers and how
Use of software, development of user-friendly software
Statistics project material development

Development of teachers' handbook with resource information
Development of concept teaching materials
Statistics teaching methods and materials for different abilities or
    age-ranges
Materials and methods for primary school
Integration between cross-curricular and mathematics coverage
Cross-curricular and vocational needs
Development of teaching materials of a vocational kind
Employers' perspectives on statistics
Student perceptions of statistics
Student problems and misconceptions
Statistics as a cognitive development
How to aid probabilistic reasoning
Appropriate assessment methods and instruments
How to raise confidence and motivate students
Use of resources other than computers
Raising teachers' awareness of the statistics they do
Role of statistics coordinator
Ethnic and gender differences and their relevance to statistical
    education
How to teach research design
How to develop relevant problems
How to link theory with practice
Level of statistical literacy among non-mathematicians, non-
    scientists

Some of these areas are, of course, already at least partially
researched by projects in the UK and overseas, and are
addressed elsewhere in this book. There has, however, been
much emphasis in these projects on the *development* of teaching
materials, and it is significant that the teachers themselves are
advocating *research* as well as development.

NOTES

1. Contact John Kinney, Mathematics Department, Rose-
   Hulman Institute of Technology, 5500 Wabash Avenue,
   Terre Haute, IN 47803, USA. (e-mail; kinney@rosevc.rose-
   hulman.edu)
2. Contact Joan Garfield, University of Minnesota, General
   College, 106 Nicholson Hall, 216 Pillsbury Drive
   SE, Minneapolis, Minnesota, MN 55455, USA. (e-mail;
   pqa6031@umnacca.bitnet)
3. Sponsored by the Applied Probability Trust, the Institute of
   Statisticians, the International Statistical Institute and
   the Royal Statistical Society. Publication details available

from The Centre for Statistical Education, Department of Probability and Statistics, University of Sheffield, Sheffield, S3 7RH.

4. Baker Days are days in the school calendar, which are set aside for in-service teacher training, often on an in-house basis, and when the students do not attend.

5. Supported with a contribution from the University of London Central Research Fund.

CHAPTER 3

The first hurdle: teaching descriptive statistics

INTRODUCTION

The model for the statistics syllabus, as described in Chapter 1:

descriptive statistics – probability – statistical inference

provides a useful starting point for a discussion of the challenges and problems facing teachers who actually have to deliver the concepts in the classroom. The traditional view was that these sections represented hurdles to be cleared in order to achieve the aim of sound statistical reasoning and practice. All three areas contribute to, and are necessary for, the art of statistical reasoning and all three present both teacher and student with their own conceptual peculiarities.

Popular paperbacks such as *How to Lie with Statistics* (Huff, 1954) have already brought the strange nature of statistical reasoning to the attention of a wider public. More recently, several books in the Popular Statistics Series published by Marcel Dekker have been on a similar theme, in particular Hooke (1983) and Jaffe and Spirer (1987). The implication for teachers is that we must be constantly aware of these conceptual problems.

The following list of general misconceptions, derived from Landwehr (1989), provides some idea of the sort of difficulties that will confront most teachers of statistics in their classrooms:

(a) any difference in the means between two groups is significant;
(b) there is no variability in the 'real world';
(c) unwarranted confidence in small samples;
(d) insufficient respect for small differences in large random samples;
(e) the size of a sample should be directly related to the population size;

to which Shaughnessy (1992) added

(f) a lack of awareness of regression to the mean in everyday life.

With respect to people's understanding of *randomness* and *variability* (and its assessment), Lopes (1982) compares the type of judgements made by subjects penalised in tests of probabilistic understanding with those of the so-called experts who exposed Burt's possible fraudulent research results:

Burt's critics were clearly statistically more sophisticated than the average person; consequently, they were sensitive to problems in the data that were probably too subtle to be noticed by naïve persons. But their intuition that reasonable amounts of random error are to be expected in all empirical work is no different in principle from the intuition of naïve subjects that games of chance ought to show trial-to-trial variability in outcome.

Rubin *et al.* (1990) observes that students have difficulties in understanding what it means for something to *represent* another thing. She draws a distinction between the way in which a histogram is meant to represent a sample *accurately*, and the way that a sample is meant to represent a population *probabilistically*. The former is evaluated in terms of *correctness* or *usefulness*, while confidence in the latter representation will depend on the *randomness*, or *unbiasedness*, of the sampling technique, and the *size of sample* drawn. Students tend not to distinguish these two types of representation, with the result that they expect '*sample = population*' and if it differs they believe that the experimenter has made a mistake. This also leads them to assume therefore that there should be no sampling error, i.e. no variability.

Another observation that Rubin *et al.* (1990) make is that

Although students often carry out surveys of their own in class, they do not generalise their insights about the importance of the details of data collection to problems from a textbook.

This certainly concurs with the view expressed by Hawkins (1991a) based on observations of entries to the Annual UK Applied Statistics Competition. Furthermore, students tend to see 'the purpose of explanation to be persuasion . . . no matter what the data showed' (Rubin *et al.*, 1990).

For the purposes of our discussion we shall, in this and the next two chapters, look in more detail at the traditional statistics syllabus and highlight those areas in descriptive statistics, probability and statistical inference which do indeed generate common misconceptions.

NOTATION

It is fair to say that the notation used in textbooks is not 100 per cent consistent, and this can contribute to the student's difficulties. We have tried to adopt the more conventional notation for the purposes of this book, but it should be noted that the 'rules' for notation within statistics do not always follow common-sense dictates, so inconsistencies will be found. These are particularly problematical for those students who do not have facility with mathematical symbols, but we would advocate that statistical concepts should never be presented exclusively by symbolic, algorithmic means to *any* students, whatever their level of mathematical attainment. We have adopted the following general principles:

1. We use capital letters X, Y, etc., to denote random variables. Usually words describing the variable, for example 'age', can be substituted for X, etc.
2. We use lowercase letters x, y, etc., to denote observations on random variables. In the case of quantitative variables x, y stand in for numbers.
3. We tend to use Arabic letters to denote sample statistics, and Greek letters to denote population parameters. A parameter is a constant, but is often unknown. Inconsistencies, such as p for a population proportion, abound however, as will be noted elsewhere in this text.

MISCONCEPTIONS IN DESCRIPTIVE STATISTICS

The section on descriptive statistics in most syllabuses will deal with:

*   the collection, organisation, tabulation and graphical representation of data;
*   summary statistics corresponding to measures of location and dispersion;
*   the search for modal groups or other patterns in data (activities which feature strongly in the initial phase of statistical analysis as EDA, Exploratory Data Analysis – investigating straight line relationships in bivariate data is typically such an activity).

The following are some of the topics that are often problematic from the student's conceptual point of view.

Populations and samples

One of the first difficulties faced by the new student is that of understanding the statistician's use of the terms *population* and *sample*. To the lay person, the word 'population' refers to people living in some area, whether it be as large as a continent or as small as a hamlet. The word 'sample' has a wider general interpretation, being met in such contexts as a *sample* survey (considered to be a sample of people), free *samples* of consumer goods and *samples* of blood and urine in medical investigations. Population and sample can mean such things to the statistician too, but much more as well. A *population* is the complete group of persons, objects or measurements in which we are interested. On the other hand, a *sample* is part of that population, and is implicitly meant to be a representation of that population.

Even this apparently simple statement has hidden traps for the unwary. Some populations are finite, even if very large, but others are infinite and to some extent imaginary. For example, the results of an experiment might be considered to belong to a population of results of experiments of that type, both those already executed and those that might be done in the future. Some populations, such as a person's blood, are *continuous* in nature, in the sense that they are regenerating. Furthermore, what is at one time a sample might at another time take the role of a population. For example, on occasions we might wish to consider a sample of schools within an education authority's population of schools. On another occasion, we might wish to look at a sample of students selected from a school's population of students. Only the context of the investigation in hand can determine what the relevant population is, and indicate what might be an appropriate sample to draw from it.

The mental picture of a sampling process is often one of taking a sample of *physical* elements. However, in statistics it is the measurements on the sample (or population) that are studied, and the terms 'population' and 'sample' are taken to refer to collections of *observations* or *measurements*.

Almost before the student has come to terms with that mental step, the realm of the random variable has been entered, where populations (and samples) are defined in terms of distributions, the population being described by its *parameters* and the sample by its *statistics*. Close on the heels of these concepts comes the idea of *sampling distributions*, being the derived distributions of statistics from repeated sampling from population distributions. It is hardly surprising that students regularly confuse these three kinds of distribution, especially when their descriptors have so much in common, μ and X-bar to describe location, both being referred to as *means*, and σ^2 and s^2 the *variances* of population and sample, respectively. The nightmare really begins, however, with the introduction of the term standard *error* to represent the standard *deviation* of the sampling distribution. There is much to be said for a presentation that colour-codes population, sample and sampling distributions, and which emphasizes the distinctive use of the terms 'parameter' and 'statistic'.

As we shall see in Chapter 5, the ideas underlying the descriptions of samples and populations become more confused when the student is faced in classical inference with data from two or more samples, known to have been meticulously drawn from the *same* population (considerable teaching time having generally been devoted to the drawing of such random, possibly matched samples, etc.) but about which the inference procedure suddenly requires judgements about 'whether or not they are likely to have been drawn from the same population'. The problem is one of conveying to students the idea of *hypothetical* or *imaginary populations*, the characteristics of which are first estimated and then compared. This jump from describing the concrete evidence of the samples drawn to the imaginary world of the population parameters is not at all easy, and great care and ingenuity are needed on the part of the teacher to convey these ideas. Of course, underlying them is classical inference theory which pretends that many samples have been drawn. The student, however, knows that this is not the case, and is now expected to imagine the outcomes of samples that might have been taken, and furthermore to imagine that something is known about the population, namely its variance, on the basis of the limited amount of sampled data in front of the student. The whole classical approach is then based on an assumption about the population parameter which the student believes is unknown, and to be discovered. It is not uncommon for this step to leave students wondering why the research is being done at all if this parameter is already known to the teacher! It is certainly not easy to convince them at this stage that statistics really can tackle the unknown.

Types of data

One of the first topics that we introduce in the section on descriptive statistics deals with types of data. Classification usually proceeds in accord with Figure 3.1.

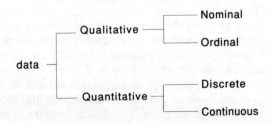

Figure 3.1 **The classification of data types**

A major distinction is drawn between the qualitative and quantitative types of data. Basically with qualitative data the 'values' are essentially words to identify defining categories. With quantitative data, values are numerical attributes. Qualitative data are often given numerical codes, but any arithmetic done with the codes will be meaningless, as will generally become obvious when one returns to the words behind the codes. For example, type of dwelling ('detached', 'semi-detached', 'terrace', etc.) is qualitative (nominal). The 'values' might be coded '1', '2', '3', etc., but although we can add '1' and '2', adding 'detached' and 'semi-detached' has no meaning, and certainly does not result in 'terrace'!

The term 'ordinal' is used when there is an underlying continuity behind the words. For example, the responses to a question asking 'How often do you have problems getting to sleep?' might be labelled 'every night', 'most nights', 'sometimes', 'rarely' and 'never'. The correspondence between these words, although clearly graded in order, and their position on the continuum scale is incompletely defined, as are in this example the 'distances' between the different labels.

An example that is often cited as *nominal* is that of 'the gender of the respondent' which is then generally treated as falling into one of two discrete categories, 'male' or 'female'. In fact, this apparently straightforward example can generate a great deal of interesting, and informative, discussion. For example, the World Health Organisation's *European Non-Aggregate AIDS Data Set* (released quarterly) defines gender categories as 'male', 'female' and 'unknown', but adds a footnote on the definition of 'transexual' which is sometimes used in the UK, but does not have a standard interpretation internationally. 'Bi-sexual' is another such term.

Although categorical data are by their nature discrete in the sense that the categories are separated entities, the issue of whether sexuality, for example, is a discrete or continuous dimension may be addressed, demonstrating that sometimes we base our distinction between 'discrete' and 'continuous' upon statistical or social convention as much as on the underlying nature of the variable concerned.

Perhaps the most robust distinction to cultivate is that qualitative data may yield frequency *counts* for the categories, while quantitative data may also, but tend rather to be treated as *measures* or *scores*. Quantitative (numeric) data may be discrete (for example, 'the number of children in a family') or continuous (for example, 'the height of an experimental subject in cm') but new students often think of discrete numeric data and categorical data as being of the same type. This misconception is bolstered by the fact that these two types can have similar graphical representations, namely some form of bar chart where the bars are separated to indicate the different categories or the discreteness of the numeric values.

To overcome this confusion and emphasise the distinction between categorical and discrete data, we might well refer to the graphical representation of the former as a 'bar chart' while for the latter we could reserve the term 'line *chart*', (the term 'chart' being used so as not to confuse it with the form of diagram used by nurses for plotting successive body temperatures and known as a 'line *graph*').

While a line chart is reserved for discrete data, a stem-and-leaf diagram can be used for either discrete or continuous data in raw form. Before his untimely death, Glickman was pioneering a distinction between the two using a broken, '_ _ _ _', or a continuous, '_____', stem, respectively (see Glickman, 1992). A histogram, although generally regarded as the device to be used for the graphical representation of continuous data, can also be used for either discrete or continuous data in grouped form. A box plot is also a useful summary diagram which can be used to portray the distributional characteristics for any quantitative data. Conventions vary, but the important principle to grasp is that the choice of representation does say something about the underlying assumptions concerning the variable. Providing there is not a contradiction between these two things, there may well be room for choice between different forms of graphical presentation. We feel that the impression given by some examination boards of there being 'one right way to illustrate a particular kind of data' belies the genuine *art* of statistics.

Teachers should emphasise that in line charts, bar charts and bar graphs it is height or length that is proportional to frequency, while in a histogram it is *area* that is proportional to frequency, that is, the heights of blocks *of equal width* in the histogram are proportional to frequency density. This will help students to understand properties and manipulations of probability distributions that they encounter later.

A distinction often drawn by teachers and textbooks is that 'discrete means *whole*' numbers', whereas 'continuous can mean fractions and decimals'. Clearly, however, this distinction is worthless. Take, for example, the case of the 'numbers of questions answered correctly in a test of spelling'. This will be represented by 'whole' numbers, and therefore may serve to confirm the distinction being made. However, represent the same data as the '*proportion* of correct answers' and the misconception is exposed, for it is clear that 21 correct answers out of 30 is a discrete value that may nevertheless be represented as 0.7 when it is the *proportion* of correct answers that interests us. A better distinction is that *discrete* applies when all possible values are separated from each other by impossible values, while *continuous* applies when the possible values vary so that with fine enough measurement there would be no values within the range that were not possible. In reality, however, continuous variables are inevitably expressed by discrete versions of the continuous phenomenon.

The definition taken must rest on whether, *for the purposes of the present investigation*, it is relevant to consider that there might exist an infinite number of intervening values for the variable in question, should we care to use a sensitive enough measure to expose them. Students' personal beliefs in this may be a matter of judgement from situation to situation, sometimes influenced by the way in which the data have been collected and recorded as much as by conventional views of the underlying distribution of possible values for the variable. Clearly some variables make for less uncertainty than do others, but as we shall see, 'age' and 'income', for example, can prove very difficult. It is important to realise that it is this skill of judgement which must be taught, not least because a different judgement on the part of our students may lead to radically different ways of illustrating the data, and to different approaches to the calculation, and understanding, of derived variables such as the arithmetic mean. It may help to encourage students to follow the good practice of declaring the assumptions that they are making about variables, in order to justify their choice of treatment of them. This is an important, and general, lesson for students who are often over-focused towards finding 'hard and fast rules as to what to do', which rarely exist in statistics. In fact, it may be that there are more hard and fast rules about what *not* to do!

Many introductory statistics courses include methods for use on data which are tacitly assumed to be at least at the level of sophistication of *interval* scales, *ratio* scales being extremely rare. Interval data imply equally discriminating units across the relevant range and hence the property of additivity, which is of paramount importance for computing derived statistics such as the arithmetic mean. A classroom practical for demonstrating the properties of ordinal and interval scales, and leading into the principles underlying comparability of data, transformations and standardisations, is to be found in Hawkins (1985). Indeed, this practical provides an easy way of introducing the distinctions between the branches of statistics known as *parametric* (depending on assumptions concerning the population distribution as described by its parameters) and *non-parametric* (based on inference procedures which are free of many such assumptions about population parameters) by giving a basic intuitive understanding of the types of assumptions that can or cannot be made about population distributions, and the possible errors that can arise when such constraints are violated. Although the particular example features the normal population distribution, there is scope for introducing more general intuitive ideas about differently shaped parent distributions.

Observation and frequency

Some students find it difficult to make a distinction between *observations* on a variable and the *frequencies* of those observations, erroneously manipulating the frequencies instead of the observations. This confusion is reinforced by the fact that in a tabulated frequency distribution there is normally a column for the observations and a column for the frequencies. Both columns are used in subsequent calculations and both may come to be regarded by the student as having equal status.

This blurring of the boundaries between observation and frequency is compounded when students come to measures of location. Barr (1980) points out that, after their first encounter with the median and mode, students are left with what he calls 'surface' concepts of these measures. Superficially, the median is thought of as the 'middle value' and the mode as the 'most frequent value'. But the middle value of what? The most frequent value of what? When applying these concepts to a frequency distribution, students are still liable to choose the 'middle' *frequency* or the 'largest' *frequency* instead of the appropriate *observation*.

The confusion between observation and frequency also appears when students draw diagrams of cumulative distributions. One of the authors set an examination question involving a real distribution, as shown in Exhibit 3.1. This non-standard presentation of a distribution with 'columns in reverse' appeared to 'throw' the students and many of them cumulated the pounds figures under the *Males* and *Females* columns, whereas what was required of the students was the manipulation of the percentages to represent frequencies.

Exhibit 3.1 **An examination question that caused problems**

Distribution of gross weekly earnings	Males	Females
10% earned less than (£)	117.9	85.3
25% earned less than (£)	150.1	103.8
etc.		

Source: New Earnings Survey, Department of Employment (1987)

Consistently emphasising the difference between an *observation* and its *count* (frequency) will help students when they encounter two-way contingency tables in which the cells contain *counts* (frequencies) which may be analysed by the chi-square method. There are tables where, although superficially similar in appearance, the cells contain *observations* or *measures*, in which case a two-way analysis of variance might be an appropriate method of analysis. Often, though, as a result of confusing observation or measure with frequency, students will perform a chi-square calculation in a two-way ANOVA situation and vice-versa.

If these distinctions are not adequately developed, related problems will also arise in work involving applications of the Central Limit Theorem, where students experience great difficulties distinguishing between the distributions of the *original* data and those of *derived* statistics and hence fail to grasp the distinction between a standard *deviation* and a standard *error*. (See also Chapter 5.)

SUMMARY STATISTICS OF LOCATION AND DISPERSION

Measures of central tendency

In investigating an understanding of the arithmetic mean, a common finding is that students tend to use mechanically an incompletely developed algorithm which fails to deal with *weighted* as opposed to *simple* arithmetic mean problems. So when faced with a example along the lines of

There are three ballet dancers who have an average weight of 90 lb and five rugby players whose average weight is 190 lbs. What is the average weight of these people over all?

students will often merely add 90 plus 190 and divide the result by 2, whereas the investigators want them to compute 3 times 90, plus 5 times 190, divided by 8. Just exactly why researchers should want students to do such a meaningless calculation in the first place is highly dubious, since they are essentially expecting students to provide a single *representative* value for what should be treated as two separate distributions.

A more meaningful weighted average problem would be one involving more homogeneous sets of data where the single derived representative value could be seen to represent something useful. The following serves as such an example:

A student doing casual work during the vacation earns £80 per week for 8 weeks and £110 per week for 4 weeks. What was the student's average weekly earnings over this vacation period?

Research in this area – for example, that by Myers *et al.* (1983) – has tended to make use of first-year undergraduate psychology students, assuming them to have 'no previous exposure to probability or statistics'. The present authors feel that it is unlikely that there would have been students with *no* previous knowledge in the 1970s and 1980s, and although we applaud the intention behind the studies – and a number of related studies concerned with the understanding of probability (e.g. Myers, 1983), and the design of instructional materials (e.g. Hansen *et al.*, 1985, and Mayer and Greeno, 1972) – namely, to explore statistical cognition using classical experimental paradigms, we feel that there are nevertheless a number of methodological shortcomings which make it necessary to treat the research findings with caution. We feel, however, that there is now scope for building on these foundations and developing further, and better, research studies. In general, however, this is not the type of research in which statistical educationalists currently engage, which is a pity because it is an area where the divide between educationalists and psychologists can be bridged, with very real potential for providing insight into the teaching/learning process, the different levels and types of understanding required by learners, and the design and use of relevant teaching materials.

Variation, the variance and the standard deviation

Figure 3.2 seems to suggest that it is an easy task to convey to our students what is meant by the concept of variation; two distributions can have the same mean and symmetry of shape and yet differ in their spread (about the mean). Nevertheless, students still find it difficult to absorb the notion of variation and the related measures, the variance and the standard deviation.

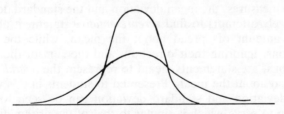

Figure 3.2 **Data distributions may be characterised by their variation as well as by their point of central tendency**

In the first section of the traditional statistics syllabus dealing with descriptive statistics, we present a diagram such as that shown in Figure 3.2 and assume that our students have learned the relevant lesson. We are then surprised to find later, when discussing random variables, that students still believe that the variance operator acts like the expectation operator. Just as

$$E(X-Y) = E(X) - E(Y)$$

so students expect that

$$\text{Var}(X-Y) = \text{Var}(X) - \text{Var}(Y) \text{ as distinct from } \text{Var}(X) + \text{Var}(Y)$$

(assuming that we are dealing with independent random variables, X and Y). The students' misconceptions of what is a variance (and a variation) have not disappeared. Their grasp of variance as a *representative* value is as weak as their grasp of that characteristic, namely representativeness, of measures of location or central tendency.

Variation is one of the fundamental ideas, if not the most important concept, in statistics. One barrier to the ready acceptance of the notion of variation must be the almost immediate introduction (early in the syllabus in the section on descriptive statistics) of the formula for the variance of a set of data, and the failure to provide adequate answers to the inevitable questions that follow: 'Why squared deviations?' 'Why divide by $n-1$ (which seems to be the prevalent practice)?' As teachers, the answers are perhaps clear to us, for we know that we are laying down an investment against the time when we need these forms of variance (and the standard deviation) for use later in the inference section of the syllabus.

This is, of course, no answer to give our beginners. However, since the variance (and standard deviation) of the *sample* do not require the use of a divisor of $n-1$, it is hard to see why this should be introduced so early, and so illogically. As for the idea of squared deviations, this can be presented as an alternative way of evaluating 'amount of spread' which allows it to be aggregated, as does the use of $|\text{deviation}|$ in computing the mean deviation.

Both measures, the mean deviation and the standard deviation, are merely attempts to find a *representative* statement about the *typical* amount of spread about the mean, while the sum of deviations, ignoring their direction, and the sum of the squared deviations, are statements meant to represent the *overall* amount of spread about the mean. Presented to students in this way, the mean deviation and standard deviation can be seen to have a function to serve which is similar to that of the arithmetic mean. Students can thereby be alerted to those characteristics of data (e.g. extreme outliers) which may make either derived statistic less than helpful, especially the standard deviation where squaring the distance from the mean can seriously distort what is meant to be a *typical* value.

In approaching the standard deviation via the mean deviation, a common approach, we base our introduction on the property that the sum of deviations about the mean is always zero. The students may not, however, already have the necessary firm grasp of this principle from their earlier introduction to the arithmetic mean, and consequently methods which depend on eliminating the 'nuisance' effects of negative signs in order to aggregate overall amount of variation may not register with them. It is important to emphasise the fact that *distance* from the mean is the criterion of variation, and not the signs attached to the direction of its measurement. At this stage it may also prove instructive to present an example of a set of measurements taking negative values (for example, a collection of sub-zero temperatures) and work through the calculation of their variance. In addition to gaining more insight into the distance criterion underlying the variance, students will then more readily accept the fact that $Var(-X) = Var(X)$.

When we describe and summarise our results we must, of course, present our findings in terms of the units in which we measure the phenomena under investigation. Thus, dividing by n in the case of the mean deviation, and dividing by n [or by $n-1$ if a population parameter is to be estimated] and then taking a square root for the standard deviation are means of re-establishing equivalence with the original units. Otherwise, with the variance, our measure of deviation would end up based on squared units, e.g. minutes^2 or kg^2, which might have no real meaning in the context in which we are working. Taking the square root of the variance in order to obtain the standard deviation is a means of 'returning to the norm', but the significance of this is often missed by our students, who may just see this as a further complication in a string of complicated computational procedures. It is debatable as to what role a calculator or computer may take in dispelling such confusion since, unless handled appropriately, such aids merely conceal the underlying principles. As always, the answer lies with the professional qualities of the teacher and, in turn, with that teacher's own grasp of the underlying statistical principles.

As indicated, the above problems for teachers and their students pale into insignificance when compared with the confusion caused by the dispute over whether n or $n-1$ should be used as the divisor in the formula for the variance, s_n^2 or s_{n-1}^2. As has already been said, provided the variance is introduced purely as a (sample) descriptive statistic, then the confusion should not arise. The use of $n-1$ can be deferred until inference to a population is required. At this point it is fair to say that the methods of demonstrating the need for $n-1$ *rather than* n may not help the less mathematically inclined student, but it should be possible to remove *confusion* as such. If 'proof' of the appropriateness of $n-1$ is required, an empirical demonstration of the characteristics of the variance with the n denominator as opposed to the $n-1$ denominator, for example using pebble-sampling or some other concrete context within which to do repeated sampling, should satisfy both those who are mathematically gifted and those who are less mathematically able.

At the very least, distancing the concepts of $s_n{}^2$ and s_{n-1} can be helpful in minimising *confusion* between the two, even if we can only justify the $n-1$ divisor to our students by telling them in an informal way that

> we use $n-1$ instead of n as divisor because 'on the average' (i.e. in the long run) we obtain a more accurate estimate of the *population* variance.

Here we are assuming that the data have been collected as a *sample* for *inferential* purposes related to the underlying population. Division by $n-1$ gives us an *unbiased* point estimator, s_{n-1}^2, of the population variance. In the case of classical inference under normal distributional assumptions, it also allows us to write Student's t-statistic as:

$$\frac{(\bar{X} - \mu)}{s_{n-1}/\sqrt{n}}$$

in a form analogous to the z-statistic;

$$\frac{(\bar{X} - \mu)}{\sigma/\sqrt{n}}$$

which usually precedes Student's t-test in the syllabus. If we had used division by n in computing the sample standard deviation, the t-statistic would need to be written in the more confusing form;

$$\frac{(\bar{X} - \mu)}{s_n\sqrt{(n/(n-1))}}$$

In this adjusted t-statistic there is a waste of effort in dividing by n to get s_n and then multiplying back again. Also rounding errors can creep in as well as possible errors in the square rooting of n.

We normally do not tell students that s_{n-1} is *not* an unbiased estimator of the population *standard deviation*. They therefore come away with the illusion that the properties of s_{n-1}^2 apply to s_{n-1} as well!

Lately, statisticians have been turning their attention to exploratory data analysis where they investigate batches of data without the intention of proceeding to the confirmatory (inferential) stage. Here, there may be an argument for using $s_n{}^2$ (the ordinary average of the squared deviations). A further justification for this is that there is also a revival of interest in that lesser known measure of spread, the MAD (the Mean Absolute Deviation), a particular case of which was referred to earlier as the mean deviation:

$$(1/n) \ \Sigma \ |x_i - \bar{x}|$$

Farnum (1988) and Ehrenberg (1982, 1983) both point out the real life importance and applications of this neglected measure. More generally, we can look at the mean absolute deviation from an arbitrary value c. It is known that 'c = median' minimises

$$(1/n) \ \Sigma \ |x_i - c|$$

and there are a number of proofs of this fact that are suitable for classroom use (see Arbel, 1986, and Farnum, 1988).

The median tends to be highlighted more in EDA than in traditional descriptive statistics, and in such a setting one would prefer to compare the properties of

$$(1/n) \ \Sigma \ |x_i - \text{median}|$$

with

$$(1/n) \ \Sigma \ (x_i - \bar{x})^2$$

than with

$$(1/(n-1)) \ \Sigma \ (x_i - \bar{x})^2$$

As a compromise in the division by n versus division by $n-1$ controversy, we still suggest that n should be used in exploring data where no inferential analysis is required. $n-1$ is to be used in the more traditional inferential statistics where the set of data is a sample from an underlying population and where hypothesis testing and/or estimation of population parameters will follow the initial data analysis.

BIVARIATE TECHNIQUES

Correlation versus regression

In basic statistics courses the initial investigation of bivariate data is based upon the techniques of correlation and regression. There is a serious misconception as to the relationship between these two techniques. Students may regard the topics as being two sides of the same coin. A high correlation would indicate a strong linear relationship between X and Y. On the basis of this, we could proceed to a regression of Y on X (or X on Y). There is, however, a fundamental distinction between a correlation and a regression analysis which makes such reasoning erroneous. The distinction reflects the predictive modelling nature of regression.

Both regression and correlation are seen to deal with bivariate data, typically denoted as (X,Y) pairs of observations. One of the fundamental assumptions of classical regression is that the explanatory (independent) variable X is measured without error; that the experimenter is able to fix or control X. In practice, this is an ideal that is difficult to achieve, but nevertheless we usually make this assumption and proceed with the analysis. A simple regression model is written in the following form:

$$Y = \beta_0 + \beta_1 x + \text{error}$$

with x in the lower case to emphasise that it is no longer a random variable.

In terms of distributional assumptions, we look only at the univariate distribution on the response (dependent) variable Y, for given values of the independent variable (or on the error component in the model).

Strictly speaking, a correlational analysis applies to (X,Y) with a *joint* bivariate probability distribution. To obtain a meaningful regression analysis in the case of Y on X, for example, we need to condition on X (Chaterjee and Price, 1977), a point that is not often explicit in an introductory course in statistics. Indeed, such a theoretically advanced discussion would be out of place at the level intended by such a course.

The formula for Pearson's correlation coefficient is symmetric in X and Y. That is,

$$r_{XY} = r_{YX}$$

But while a regression of Y on X is legitimate if the underlying assumption (of X measured without error) holds, an algebraically derived regression of X on Y will be meaningless unless X and Y are perfectly correlated.

These confusing subtleties do not aid the teaching of regression and correlation and their presentation in the textbooks. There is a school of thought which believes it to be more reasonable to retain at the introductory level material that involves univariate distributional assumptions (regression) and to defer until a later part of the course, or text, material which requires joint bivariate distributional assumptions (correlation). Such a teaching strategy would be counter to the implied ordering of typical syllabus and textbook contents. Certainly there would have to be a marked shift towards acknowledging that correlation is not the easy topic that it is often suggested to be, before such a change of strategy could be widely adopted.

The present authors are not alone in making this suggestion. For example, Well *et al.* (1988) say that

We believe that future efforts should be directed away from the question of whether subjects can produce numerical judgments that reflect the correlation coefficient or some other measure of covariation and toward developing a better understanding of what information about the relationship between two variables people are sensitive to and how this information is used and represented. To this end, what people learn about event covariation and how they use what they have learned can probably best be investigated by developing process models and comparing the predictions of these models to the data of human subjects.

They are of the opinion that when a subject is confronted with a correlation question 'two reasonable but quite different inter-pretations of the strength of relationship between X and Y are (1) how much, on the average, one variable changes as the other changes and (2) how predictable one variable is from the other'. Instructions to subjects make a great difference as to how the task is perceived.

Regression involves the exploration of bivariate relationships with a heavy dependence on graphical methods (e.g. scatterplots, residual plots). It therefore fits naturally into a modern introductory course on data analysis where the emphasis is on modelling and representing data, and can therefore be included relatively early in the course content. EDA regression is gaining in popularity (see Marsh, 1988) and median fits leading to resistant (robust) regression are available as procedures in packages such as MINITAB. Rather than mention the correlation coefficient (which may not have a formal meaning in the regression paradigm), it is preferable to introduce the coefficient of determination which describes quantitatively the proportion of explained variation (see Draper and Smith, 1981):

$$\text{Coefficient of determination} = \frac{\Sigma(Y_{\text{predicted}} - \bar{Y})^2/}{\Sigma(Y_{\text{observed}} - \bar{Y})^2}$$

We can present it as a meaningful measure of linear fit, relying initially on graphical evidence, and later derive the correlation coefficient from it using

Correlation coefficient $= \sqrt{}$(Coefficient of determination)

with the appropriate sign (see Freund, 1988).

Correlation, causation and association

It is important to clarify the notion of co-relationship as distinct from causation. Indeed, many textbooks make this point. There is, however, a related source of confusion which is rarely addressed, namely that which describes 'association' as 'correlation', thereby demonstrating an underlying confusion between frequency and score data. Although it is true that there are correlation coefficients to deal with dichotomous variables, these will not have been encountered by our students, and permitting such sloppiness in terminology generally does them no service.

Geoffrey Rose, in his lectures to trainee medical statisticians and epidemiologists at the University of London School of Hygiene and Tropical Medicine, uses an interesting teaching example to provoke consideration of 'association', 'causation' and 'correlation':

At the beginning of the 1970s, the Samaritan counselling services were introduced to a number of cities in the UK. After a short period of time, the suicide rates in those centres fell, and the 'cause' was attributed to the 'association' with the availability of the Samaritans' support. Subsequently, a statistician observed that the suicide rates had fallen in exactly the same way in other areas where there was no 'association' with Samaritan counselling support. On further investigation, it was found that the decline in suicide rates coincided with the introduction of Natural Gas to all these areas, and it was then inferred that the more likely 'cause' of the decline was the removal of one formerly readily available method of committing suicide.

The moral of this story, as far as Geoffrey Rose is concerned, is that 'You can't exclude the explanation that you haven't considered!' Both the above explanations of the suicide decline were plausible. Who knows whether there were other equally compelling, but unrecognised, explanations; changes in (social) climate, diet or government, etc.? The situation is bound to have more complexity than our teaching strategies generally acknowledge, as Gnanadesikan (1977) states:

Most bodies of data involve observations associated with various facets of a particular background, environment, or experiment. Therefore, in a general sense, data are always multivariate in character.

It may be that the intuitive grasp of associated occurrences may provide an intermediary means of breaking through the misconception of spurious correlation which is often cited in textbooks but rarely taken to heart by their readers. This misconception involves attributing a causal dependence between two variables, X and Y, say, as a result of a high correlation between the two. The literature is replete with examples of spurious correlations where one variable is highly correlated with another simply because each is correlated with a hidden third underlying factor. A common example of this phenomenon occurs when both X and Y are time series data. There may be a high correlation between 'language ability' and 'height', for example, only as a consequence of the fact that both are increasing with 'age' (the third underlying factor).

Notice here that our view of correlations is also dependent on the context in which we measure them, which in turn depends on our perception of what are possible 'extraneous' variables (see also Chapter 6). So, for example, if we have a model of intelligence which implies a certain generalisation across abilities, then we might expect 'mathematical ability' and 'language ability' to be correlated, free of the effects of 'age'. One approach to investigating this might be to restrict the age-range, to hold it constant, but this would *not* eliminate other possible influences, nor would it overcome test effects that might result from the design of tests which are highly discriminating over a narrower age-range, without which it is unlikely that a correlation would be found.

To dispel these types of misconception, the teacher should really delve into the more advanced topic of *partial* correlation, something which, in a formal mathematical way, is not really feasible at the introductory level of our subject matter. In fact, some intuitive inroads to partial correlation *may* be made by graphically presenting subgroups identified on overhead transparency overlays, or by recourse to the better kinds of graphics software packages that allow subgroups of data to be 'toggled' on and off the screen. The effect is less good if the software clears the screen and re-draws new, possibly re-scaled, diagrams each time a subgroup is added in or removed from the display.

The (simulated) data set[1] given in the appendix to this chapter provide an example of an exercise for such treatment. The data comprise both categoric and numerical variables, e.g. gender, age (11 to 13 years, say, with an element of rounding for discussion), IQ and language ability scores. Operationalising the questions to be answered, and recognising the role of the statistician in establishing exactly what the consultee wants to find out – in this case, evidence that his catchment is 'different' – provide interesting insights into what may and what may not be legitimate, and the statistician's responsibilities in this respect.

Although intended to be used in an *exploratory* and not an *analytical* way by students, teachers may find it useful to know that the data were simulated from normally distributed populations with bivariate correlations of age : IQ, approximately 0.2 (low), IQ : language, approximately 0.9 (very high), and age : language, approximately 0.7 (high). From the students' point of view, *looking at a scattergram*, that for IQ : language, however, appears to be considerably lower than 0.9 (i.e. not very tightly clustered about a hypothetical line of best fit) unless the influences of age and gender are first controlled for. More details of the data set's characteristics, and its classroom use, may be found in Hawkins (1984).

Preliminary exploratory analysis by frequency distribution diagrams encourages an *intuitive* approach to comparisons of sample and population distributions, and the concepts of location, dispersion, the ideal of normal symmetrical spread, and discussion about the underlying principles of test development, standards and norms. 'Language ability' should show up fairly clearly as being bi-modally distributed with respect to gender, suggesting the need to treat the two genders separately to establish whether there is a correlation between 'IQ' and 'language ability'. Any outliers will also become visible, and their effects on summary, representative, statistics can be used as the basis of a discussion of whether to include or exclude them subsequently. Finding that the location of the distributions of 'language ability' scores seem also to change with increasing 'age' suggests by analogy the need to consider further subgrouping, and some interesting strategies for such subdivisions should emerge for consideration. Finally, visual inspection of the kind of scattergram distributions of 'IQ' by 'language ability' for the separate subgroups allows intuitive comparisons of whether the story is the same for all groups, in other words gives some experience of the processes of confirmatory as opposed to aggregate analyses.

CONCLUSIONS

It is in descriptive statistics that the student first encounters types of data, their graphical representation, summary measures and ideas of variability. The latter, especially, can take a long time to percolate in students' minds and are easily prone to misconceptions. With the emphasis now on initial (exploratory) data analysis teachers have the opportunity to devote more time to the presentation of such basic concepts. The opportunity therefore exists to overcome the impediments to teaching good data analysis.

APPENDIX: EDA EXTENDS STUDENTS' PERCEPTIONS WITH MULTIVARIATE DATA

Background information

Correl Street School is a Secondary Comprehensive School. It has been suffering slightly from a decline in numbers of pupils entering the First Form. Last year, there was a five-form entry. This year, the entry was down to only four forms. There is no streaming until the third year, and on entry to the school in the First Form, children are allocated to classes in alphabetic order according to their surnames.

Mr O'Statsy, the headmaster, has recently been on a refresher course on pupil assessment at the local Education Institute. He has decided to test a theory that he heard, while on the course, that language ability is related to intelligence.

In recent years, there have been changes in the district in which Correl Street School is situated. Mr O'Statsy is therefore also interested in checking whether the resulting social mobility may have led to a change in the ability levels observed in his intake of pupils now compared to those of his intakes in previous years. This is particularly important to him because, with the decline in pupil numbers, there has been a greater opportunity for parents to choose whether they want their children to go to Correl Street School or to the nearby school where Mr O'Statsy's rival for teaching resources, Mr MacAdemia, is headmaster.

Mr O'Statsy decides to carry out a small study. He selects a random sample of 100 children from the first two year-groups in his school. The resulting sample of 52 girls and 48 boys are each given a standardised IQ test for which the manual states the norms as being: mean = 100 and standard deviation = 15. The children are also given a language test which, for the age-group concerned, has a mean of 17 and a standard deviation of 6, although the manual does not give further details of how these values were obtained.

All the testing was carried out on one day in the Spring term, and the children's ages at the time of testing were recorded, correct to the nearest three months. Having arranged for the class teachers to carry out the testing, Mr O'Statsy now finds that 'his pressure of work is too great' and so he looks to you to answer his research questions for him. The (simulated) data follow:

Data: Column 1 – Pupil number   Column 2 – Gender
          Column 3 – IQ   Column 4 – Language ability
          Column 5 – Age (in years and months, to nearest 3 months)

1	2	3	4	5	1	2	3	4	5
1	F	100	21	12.25	51	F	92	15	12.5
2	F	93	18	11.75	52	F	89	19	12.75
3	F	114	21	12	53	M	110	19	13
4	F	85	17	12	54	M	106	12	11.75
5	F	113	27	13	55	M	93	14	12.5
6	F	93	18	12	56	M	117	21	13
7	F	88	17	12	57	M	90	7	11.25
8	F	108	27	12.75	58	M	94	11	11.75
9	F	100	16	11	59	M	101	14	12
10	F	97	22	12.5	60	M	96	13	12
11	F	106	26	12.75	61	M	81	10	12
12	F	77	18	12	62	M	106	19	13
13	F	116	20	11.75	63	M	97	28	11.75

Data: Column 1 – Pupil number   Column 2 – Gender
      Column 3 – IQ   Column 4 – Language ability
      Column 5 – Age (in years and months, to nearest 3 months)

1	2	3	4	5	1	2	3	4	5
14	F	75	10	11.25	64	M	105	12	11.5
15	F	92	23	12.75	65	M	94	7	11
16	F	84	16	11.75	66	M	106	15	12
17	F	103	26	12.5	67	M	86	11	12
18	F	112	27	13	68	M	95	12	12
19	F	114	22	12	69	M	116	12	11.5
20	F	118	23	12	70	M	113	13	11.75
21	F	97	17	11.75	71	M	88	7	11.25
22	F	125	24	12	72	M	118	12	11
23	F	114	25	12.5	73	M	92	18	13
24	F	91	18	12	74	M	104	12	11.5
25	F	119	27	13	75	M	108	16	12
26	F	89	15	11.25	76	M	95	4	11
27	F	112	19	12	77	M	81	10	12
28	F	109	17	11.25	78	M	111	16	12
29	F	93	19	12.25	79	M	92	13	12
30	F	124	25	12.5	80	M	83	5	11.25
31	F	108	21	12	81	M	101	9	11.25
32	F	121	29	13	82	M	81	8	11.5
33	F	132	23	11.75	83	M	108	17	12.75
34	F	103	19	12.25	84	M	84	12	12.25
35	F	99	25	13	85	M	98	10	11.5
36	F	112	20	11.25	86	M	127	20	12.75
37	F	110	17	11.25	87	M	89	9	11.5
38	F	96	20	12.25	88	M	128	18	12
39	F	99	21	12.25	89	M	133	20	12.25
40	F	144	29	12.75	90	M	115	18	12.5
41	F	93	21	12.5	91	M	97	16	12.75
42	F	56	12	11.25	92	M	112	18	12.5
43	F	135	29	13	93	M	78	9	12
44	F	108	18	11.25	94	M	102	16	12.5
45	F	106	17	11.75	95	M	103	15	12.25
46	F	99	23	12.75	96	M	96	10	11.75
47	F	111	20	11.5	97	M	80	14	12.5
48	F	98	19	11.75	98	M	85	11	12.25
49	F	103	22	12	99	M	106	14	12.25
50	F	93	18	11.75	100	M	91	4	11.75

NOTE

1. Data generated using techniques described in Naylor, T.H., Balintfy, J.L., Burdick, D.S. and Chu, K. (1966) *Computer Simulation Techniques*, Wiley. Caution should always be exercised with the use of simulated data, since students and their teachers are apt to treat findings based on such data as though they had real-life significance. Ironically, the more 'real' the data appear, the more dangerous this may be.

CHAPTER 4

The second hurdle: teaching probability

INTRODUCTION

From Chapter 1 it is evident that how, when and where probability is to appear in the statistics curriculum are controversial issues. The fundamental importance of this field of study and the care which is needed in clarifying probability concepts for our students, however, is not in question.

People's whole conception of 'chance', 'luck' and 'random' or unpredictable events may well be highly suspect. This has far-reaching consequences for how they behave, and of course it has implications for the teaching of statistics which is so dependent on sound reasoning in this area. Wagenaar (1988) makes the following observation:

Chance is not a cause itself, but only alludes to the fact that the physical causes are unknown. In the minds of many people luck and chance often seem to act as real causes.

Wagenaar feels that the 'erroneous' biases and heuristics that people adopt are a direct consequence of their understanding of 'chance' as cause. When chance breaks down in the face of apparently non-random events (e.g. a long sequence of reds in roulette) then 'luck' is invoked as a second causal factor, operating independently (and possibly interfering with) the first causal factor, 'chance'. According to Wagenaar, gamblers feel that they are influenced by chance, skill *and* luck, and they have difficulty deciding whether 'luck' is more like 'chance' or more like 'skill'. To them it seems as if you must wait until luck appears (therefore it is like chance), but since you must also use it wisely when it happens, it is like skill.

By getting people to judge 80 stories (40 representative of 'chance' and 40 of 'luck') in terms of where certain aspects were on scales between 'not applicable' and 'totally applicable', Wagenaar reports the following clusterings as respectively discriminating between the perception of 'chance' and 'luck' events in daily life:

{Chance, surprise, fun, coincidence, social contact}

{Luck, level of accomplishment, important consequences, escape from negative consequences}

'Probability' showed up as a 'neutral point' between the two, with 'Emotions' and 'Long-term consequences' being not particularly close to either group. Such research into the underlying semantics of daily life usage of terms which are interpreted by statisticians as technical has serious implications for teachers.

In general, people seem to be able to separate 'chance' (the statistical rules of a game) from 'luck' which they perceive can either favour them or not. Superstitious reasoning seems to make people more inclined to interpret the outcome as caused by chance, i.e. the outcome looks more like a coincidence, more surprising. 'Luck', it is believed, can influence the bettor's choice, but not the performance of the random device. Wagenaar suggests that the basic fallacy of gamblers could well be a belief in 'luck', a belief that through 'luck' future outcomes may determine their choices. The existence of such beliefs and their robustness in the face of challenge may well produce classroom problems analogous to those cited in Garfield and Ahlgren (1988) concerning conflicts with belief systems in the areas of science teaching. There are a number of notorious probability problems which provide interesting ways of stimulating such conflicts. 'Monty's dilemma' (Shaughnessy, 1992) and the 'problem of the three prisoners' (Mosteller, 1965; Bar-Hillel and Falk, 1982) are popular examples.

Probability is indispensable to the learning and understanding of statistical inference. Often, however, the students come ill-equipped to handle the probability theory needed. The fact is that, with existing syllabuses, too little time is spent on teaching elusive probability concepts before the inference section, which actually needs sophisticated ideas based on probability (for example, sample statistics as random variables, significance levels, probabilities of type 1 and type 2 errors, etc.).

It is probably true to say that the transmission of probability concepts to our students remains our greatest challenge. Probabilistic ideas are notoriously counter-intuitive and are easily prone to misunderstanding. We must admit that not only our students but we ourselves can succumb to incorrect thinking in probability. Charles Sanders Pierce, a nineteenth-century American philosopher, is credited with the following statement;

This branch of Mathematics [Probability] is the only one, I believe, in which good writers frequently get results entirely erroneous.

It must also be realised that it is not only at the pedagogic level that misconceptions about probability exist. There are deep-seated psychological fallacies concerning the notions of chance and randomness. Kahneman *et al.*'s (1982) review is a good introduction to the research into these deeper misconceptions. See also Chapter 6.

RANDOM EXPERIMENTS

The concept of a random experiment is the fundamental notion on which a probability calculus must be built. However, at all levels of probability teaching little time is spent on discussing probabilistic experiments and comparing and contrasting them with deterministic experiments. A deterministic experiment is regarded as behaving as follows: given the same initial conditions at every repetition of the experiment, the same outcome will manifest itself. In the case of a probability experiment, at every repetition the totality of possible outcomes (the *sample space*) is known, but the actual outcome is not known until the results of the experiment are finally observed.

It should also be pointed out to our students that, even in the realm of the experimental sciences (where so-called deterministic laws govern phenomena), variation and randomness are present. In the practicals it is difficult to ensure that the initial conditions are exactly the same as last time. The results from one experiment to another do not conform exactly with the law given in the textbook. Students might welcome this revelation. If we really want to stir things up and the students are sufficiently advanced, we could introduce the idea of measurement error at this point (see Barford, 1985).

Of course students of all ages will have experience of the effects of uncontrolled variation. One example is in cooking – these days no longer something done only by girls. Even if the recipe or the instructions on the packet are followed 'exactly' the same way as last time, the resulting dish may still be noticeably different. Another common example is that of journey times. Here the variation is noticed most when the journey time is extra long. The student will say 'I left the same time as I do every day, Miss' on arriving late for school.

Even very young children will be aware of instances when something that 'always' happens does not happen; a clock whose strike develops a fault perhaps, or electronic equipment that starts doing odd things. Adults too can be taken aback by experiences of this nature. We should build on all these experiences of randomness. It is not difficult to think of examples. It *is* difficult, however, to think of deterministic examples.

There are two important aspects to a probability experiment:

formulation and *enumeration*. There is the description (formulation) of the experiment itself and there is the identification of all the possible outcomes that constitute the sample space (enumeration). With few exceptions textbooks do not elaborate on the significant role of formulation in the treatment of probability. Clearly enumeration depends on formulation. If the statement of the experiment is misinterpreted, then an erroneous sample space ensues.

The source of many misconceptions can be traced back to these two aspects of a probability experiment. We have not yet mentioned probability measures or the probability calculus, but have concentrated on the importance of carefully describing a probability experiment. Teachers and textbooks need to devote more time and space respectively to such concepts *before* turning to the usual discussions of probability measures, random variables, distributions, etc.

This emphasis on the description of a probability experiment was stressed as long ago as 1693. In a communication to Isaac Newton, Samuel Pepys requested his help in finding certain dice probabilities. Pepys phrased the problem as follows:

A – has 6 dice in a box, with which he is to fling a 6;
B – has in another box 12 dice, with which he is to fling 2 sixes;
C – has in another box 18 dice, with which he is to fling 3 sixes;

Q[uestion] – Whether B and C have not as easy a taske as A at even luck?

Schell (1960) has this to say about Newton's reply to Pepys:

Nearly any practicing statistician will feel a high degree of kinship with Newton in his stress on formulation in his reply. He is mostly concerned with whether he has understood the question. Are A, B and C to throw independently? Are *exactly* 1, 2 and 3 sixes involved or *at least* 1, 2 and 3 sixes? Is it understood it is 'expectation' that is involved and not the outcome of a particular throw? [*sic*]

Teachers and students of probability are well advised to read the actual correspondence between Newton and Pepys (see Tanner, 1926).

The 'birthday problem' (Mosteller, 1962) is another famous example where the actual experiment in question is often misconstrued. Many students, when presented with this problem:

What is the least number of people (*n* say) in a room for the probability to be at least 0.5 of two or more having the same birthday?

immediately but perhaps not consciously, translate it into the 'birth*mate* problem':

What is the least number of people (n say) in a room for the probability to be at least 0.5 of two or more having the same birthday *as mine*?

Under appropriate assumptions the answer to the *latter* problem is $n=183$ (i.e. approximately 0.5 * 365). Students are therefore surprised to learn that the answer to the original birthday problem is $n=23$.

Coins, dice and urns with tokens are popular devices for demonstrating probabilistic ideas. They serve another useful but less emphasised purpose; we can employ them to model real-life random phenomena. The modelling process itself forces us to examine the experiment carefully and to formulate it precisely. In most cases the ambiguities inherent in the natural language description of an experiment can be removed by translating the original formulation into a more 'tangible' coin, dice or urn model.

We can reformulate the above 'birthday problem' in the following manner;

An urn contains 365 tokens numbered 1 to 365 (denoting the 365 distinct dates in a non-leap year). n tokens are drawn at random and with replacement. What is the least value of n so that the probability that two or more tokens with the same number are drawn is at least 0.5?

The birthmate problem now appears as follows:

An urn contains 365 tokens numbered 1 to 365 (denoting the 365 distinct dates in a non-leap year). n tokens are drawn at random and with replacement. Fix attention on one particular number. What is the least value of n so that the probability that two or more tokens with that same number are drawn is at least 0.5?

Plummer (1940) observed that:

apparently plausible reasoning may lead to different solutions of a problem. When this happens it will be found that the conditions of the problem have been so ill-defined that the same statement covers in effect a variety of problems. This is particularly liable to be the case when a question is formulated in abstract terms for the defect is then less easily detected. *A concrete form is greatly to be preferred* [current authors' emphasis].

Coins, dice and urns provide these concrete forms. A well-known illustration of Plummer's observations is the 'family with two children problem':

A child from a family of two children is seen to be a boy; what is the probability that the other child is a boy?

This problem can have a number of interpretations and important simplifying assumptions have to be made before any solutions are attempted (see Glickman, 1982). There is a clear discussion of this problem, about which much has been written, and some similar problems, in Bar-Hillel and Falk (1982). If we know that Mr Smith has two children and we meet him in the street with a boy whom he introduces as his son, is it reasonable to assume that Mr Smith randomly chose which child to take out with him? If Mr Smith tells us that he has two children and at least one is a boy this is different from us discovering by observation that one of his children is a boy. We see that it is not just that the experiment has to be fully described, but also that the wording of the experiment has to be crystal clear.

Many of the misunderstandings in probability occur because the language of probability is different from our usual conversational language. One example of difficulties caused by language is when referring to the union of events E_1, E_2, . . ., E_n which is sometimes described as 'either E_1 or E_2 or . . . or E_n' we actually mean the occurrence of *at least* one of the events $E_1, E_2, . . ., E_n$.

Another example is the failure of our language to distinguish adequately between the probability that both A and B occur and the conditional probability $P(A|B)$. For example, the phrase '80 per cent of persons having a particular illness recover' implies that Prob(recover|have the illness) is 0.8, but might be misinterpreted by some as meaning Prob(have the illness and recover) is 0.8. Here natural language has had the effect of suppressing the conditional nature of a probability statement.

The attempt formally to define the notion of a probability measure has resulted in deep philosophical controversies, subjectivism versus objectivism being a case in point. To emphasise the ease with which such a variety of different opinions could have arisen, an interesting list of 26 probability statements has been given in the appendix to this chapter. Each of these, according to Van Brakel (1976), has been used at least once to support or oppose some philosophical point of view about the interpretation of the probability concept. It is not our intention to discuss these issues here, but rather to look at some definitions of probability and their relevance to the teaching of probability. The founding fathers of probability analysed various games of chance; games involving dice, roulette wheels, cards, etc. The symmetry assumed to be inherent in these devices led to the use of the equally likely approach in determining (usually) simple probabilities. It led to the classical definition of probability:

Consider an experiment with a finite number of mutually exclusive outcomes which are equiprobable (that is, equally likely because of the nature of the experiment). Then the probability of the event A is defined as the fraction of the outcomes in which A occurs and is denoted by $P(A)$. More formally,

$$P(A) = N(A)/N$$

where N is the total number of possible outcomes and $N(A)$ is the number of outcomes leading to the occurrence of A.

The equally likely approach seems to be a natural starting point for the study of probability, especially where young children are concerned. Many children experience the ideas of 'chance', 'luck' and 'fairness' in the framework of their play with games of chance (Hirst, 1977). They might therefore be reasonably receptive to the *equally likely* development of probability concepts. However, research has shown that children do not necessarily believe wholeheartedly in equal likelihood. They may see the '6' as a difficult number to throw on a dice, having a preference for 'lucky' numbers when asked to predict outcomes, etc.

The exact reasons for such behaviour and/or misconceptions are open to discussion, and so too is the exact nature of children's capabilities in the realms of probability. Some of the relevant research studies of Piaget and Inhelder (1951, trans. 1975), Fischbein (1975), Falk (1983), etc., will be considered in Chapter 6. However, it would certainly seem sensible for teachers to try to build on the framework of children's experience, but to do so in the knowledge that they may well have to break down misconceptions which they hold in spite of their experience. Unfortunately, the research studies that should be able to show teachers how to do this are not as prolific or helpful as would be hoped.

Coins and dice dominate as devices used in the presentation of elementary probability but, as Hirst (1977) points out, such experiments are usually of a contrived nature. Nevertheless, while the symmetry in the equally likely approach is intuitively self-evident, some reinforcement through actual practical experimentation in the classroom is desirable in preparation for future developments when coins and dice may be used to simulate more realistic phenomena. The Sheffield Centre for Statistical Education, for example, devised a simple simulation of this kind related to the game of tennis. Tossing coins and rolling dice can also begin to provide insight into the relative frequency definition of probability, which will be discussed later.

By its very definition, the equally likely approach relies heavily on combinatorial techniques. Such techniques are often thought to be notoriously difficult for the beginner – see the section on combinatorial naïvete below. Indeed, Piaget and Inhelders (1951) view would be that they are not available until the stage of Formal Operations is reached, i.e. not until mid-adolescence. In contrast, however, Engel *et al.* (1976) describe a number of games which can be very effective for introducing the necessary concepts to children much younger than this.

If the important role that probability plays in modelling the real-life world outside the classroom is to be stressed, then clearly the *equally likely* approach will not suffice, since equal likeli-hoods rarely, if ever, pertain. Indeed, there are risks in over-emphasising this definition of probability in the classroom. As Green (1982) demonstrated, there is a (well-known) danger that a student reared on an 'equally-likely diet' will always attach a probability of 0.5 to each of two mutually exclusive and exhaustive events based on *any* probability experiment, irrespec-tive of how different the events' probabilities really are. Jolliffe and Sharples (1991) also noticed, in studies of undergraduates in the United Kingdom and in New Zealand, a tendency for subjects to choose the 'events are equally likely' option. However, Konold (1989b) argues that some individuals reason according to the outcome approach in which they try to predict the outcome of individual trials and use a probability of 50 per cent to mean that no prediction can be made.

The following simple exercise, adapted from Buxton (1970), will reveal even to the young beginner in probability the inadequacies of our present definition:

The student is to stand at a checkpoint in a road and to count the number of vehicles that pass this checkpoint in a 5-minute interval. The student is to assess whether the outcomes 'no cars passing in this interval', 'one car passing in this interval', 'two cars passing in this interval', . . . '20 cars passing in this interval', . . . '100 cars passing in this interval' are equally likely.

It should not be too difficult for the student to realise intuitively that in such a situation some events will be rarer than others. It should also be immediately obvious that the number of possible outcomes is in a sense open-ended, being only bounded by the possible speed of the traffic. Thirdly, the student should agree that time of day is the underlying factor which influences the assessment of probabilities for the above outcomes. Clearly, empirical investigation over a reasonably long period of time, etc., is required in order to *estimate* the probabilities of these outcomes. It is worth remarking that this particular exercise is a good example of integrating the consideration of probability and statistical ideas.

Next we discuss the relative frequency approach to measuring probability. The formal definition is as follows:

An experiment is repeated an infinite number of times. The probability of a particular outcome is defined as the limit of the proportion of those outcomes in the first *n* trials when *n* tends to infinity. (It is assumed that such a limit exists.)

Indeed, some people *have* tossed coins a *very* large number of times, e.g. Kerrich (see Freedman *et al.*, 1978b). In reality, probabilities are estimated by relative frequencies obtained from a *finite* number of repetitions. Teachers may find that use of the word 'proportion' as a step towards 'probability' makes the meaning clearer for students.

Clearly this definition opens up the possibility of investigating a wider spectrum of probabilistic experiments. Although the student is generally confined to the classroom, devices such as urn models and computer-aided simulation can effectively describe realistic experiments within the context of the probability lesson.

The following (the 'Decaying Pennies problem') is an example of how simple games in an *equally likely* framework can lead the student to investigations of more realistic phenomena in a *relative frequency* framework. The problem starts with the following simple formulation:

Three fair coins are tossed. Those that come up 'heads' are removed. The remaining coins are tossed and again those that come up 'heads' are removed. This process is continued until there are no coins left to toss. Of interest here is the number of turns (waiting time) until all the coins have been removed.

It is not too difficult to describe both verbally and diagrammatically the possible outcomes of this experiment. Additionally, the problem lends itself to an easy simulation on the computer. The teacher can then proceed to the following game:

Five fair dice are rolled three times. The student must attempt to roll as many 6's as possible. After each roll, all the established 6's are left while the non-6's are rolled again, hoping to roll some more 6's. The game continues until all the dice have come up 6.

Given that some students do not consider 6 to behave in the same way as the other faces of the dice, it may also be worthwhile letting them experiment with a number other than 6. The similarity to the coins experiment is clear. In fact this game is one possible strategy in a popular dice pastime called *Yahtzee* (Litwiller and Duncan, 1982). The event in which all five dice show the same specified face (6 in the above example) is actually called 'Yahtzee' and it is of interest to determine the probability of achieving 'Yahtzee'.

A generalisation of 'decaying pennies' type problems can be achieved by means of urn devices.

There are n urns and each contains w white tokens and r red tokens. A token is drawn at random from each urn. If the token is red, the corresponding urn is removed. If the token is white, the token is replaced and a token is again drawn at random from each of the remaining urns. Urns are removed again according to the same criteria and the experiment continues for a predetermined number of trials or until all urns have been removed.

Alternatively the generalisation can be obtained as an extension of the game with three fair coins, described earlier. Starting by throwing n coins, each coin having a probability p of 'heads' where p now does not necessarily equal 0.5, i.e. the coins are not necessarily unbiased, those coins coming up 'heads' are removed from subsequent throws until no coins remain. Again, the interest is in how many throws this will take.

The teacher can now present the students with the following real-life situation concerning *redundant systems* (Weiss, 1962). The operation of a redundant system can be described as follows: a system of components performs a given task repetitively at discrete times. Each component is considered to have the same probability of ceasing to function (becoming redundant) and it is assumed that these components are *failure-independent*, that is, that the failure of one component has no effect on the performance of another component. The system need not be attended to (*serviced*) until all components have *decayed*.

Students should be able to see how the 'decaying pennies' can effectively model such systems and computer-aided simulation can then be applied to investigate characteristics of these systems. The following applications of such systems are among those to be found in the literature and may be useful. Von Neumann (1952) discussed a mathematical model of the brain which uses redundant elements to control error. Lundberg (1955) suggested the applicability of such a redundant system to the study of aircraft wing fatigue and failure. Råde (1983) relates the 'decaying pennies' model to reliability problems.

By investigating further, the teacher may be able to find empirical data based on applications of such systems and thus enable the students to estimate various parameters of the systems and to compare them with results obtained from simulation studies.

Subjective probability is a measure of a person's *degree of belief*. Buxton (1970) emphasises that a subjectivist assigning a probability to an event does not ask 'How likely *is* this event?' but rather 'How likely do I *think* this event is?' Besides being at the centre of philosophical controversy, this approach suffers from a major practical problem; namely, how to obtain a precise and universally accepted statement of a (subjective) probability of an event.

Nevertheless, this area of probability cannot be avoided since it is part and parcel of both students' and teachers' everyday experiences. Witness questions such as:

What do you think your chances of getting the job are?

What do you think your chances of getting the job are, now the
  interview is over?
How probable is it that your teacher likes you as a student?

It may well be that teachers should *introduce* the study of
probability by confronting students with their differing estimations of the probabilities of the same events, for example by
asking them to place terms like 'impossible', 'probable', 'certain',
'highly likely', etc., on a scale of 0 per cent to 100 per cent (see
Ernest, 1984). Not only will this show up differences in personal
probability scales, it will also provide some challenging data for
analysis.

Given this sort of approach, both the *equal likelihood* or
frequentist probability derivations, and their subsequent manipulations, should be seen against the backdrop of subjective
probabilities and intuitions of probability. Chapter 6 contains
further discussion about some of the research findings that may
give guidance on how to handle subjective probability and how to
assess its influence on the formation of formal, or *objective*,
probability.

Green (1982) reports that there are individuals who seem to be
'instinctively' able to judge formal probabilities very quickly. He
warns against ignoring the silence of other students which may
meanwhile be hiding not only ignorance of the 'correct' solutions,
but also great confusion and conflict based on personal beliefs as
to whether the given answer is in fact 'correct'.

There is a fairly thin borderline between subjective probability
and estimation based on relative frequencies. A degree of belief
is normally a reflection, in some way, of past experiences. In the
case of the relative frequencies estimation, the 'past experiences'
are confined to those observed in the defined experiment. In the
case of subjective probability, the 'past experiences' are more
widespread, and less defined, and the ways in which they are
perceived and stored are less consistent both between and within
people.

In the areas of risk taking and insurance, and even in weather
forecasting, probabilities are based on a combination of subjective beliefs and relative frequencies. The mathematical method of
combining the two uses Bayes' theorem, but people do not
always adjust probabilities according to Bayes' rule. (See Navon,
1978, who reports conservative revision of probabilities which are
smaller than Bayes' but still in the appropriate direction.)

The current authors agree with Margenau (1950), cited in Van
Brakel (1976), that

General discussions of the meaning of probability by philosophers have
lately shown little evidence of agreement upon any common view, and
the literature is becoming progressively more confused.

As far as teachers and the teaching of probability are concerned, the safest course is to adopt the mathematical approach to probability, beginning with a set of axioms (common to any interpretation of probability) and formally constructing deductions from those axioms. However, there is a price to pay for taking this route – namely, that results based on mathematical probability may clash with the intuitive notions that our students have of probability. Careful explanation with well-chosen examples is therefore needed at all points in the probability syllabus.

We now look at some further problems that students encounter in basic topics in probability.

PROPORTIONALITY ARGUMENTS

The typical beginning student enters the environment of probability theory after being exposed to arithmetic (and/or geometry) where ratio and proportion arguments are important. The student may therefore try to import intuitive notions of proportionality into the new world of probability. Such action may lead to conceptual problems. The classic example of mistakenly applying proportional arguments to probability calculations comes from the early history of probability when, in 1652, the Chevalier De Mere discussed with Blaise Pascal the following problem, which we pose in modern dress:

> What is the probability of obtaining at least one six in 4 throws of a single die? What is the probability of obtaining at least one double-six in 24 throws of two dice?

By the time of De Mere (that is, by the middle of the seventeenth century) rules of proportion were well established. Such a rule, which had flourished for a long time in gambling circles would demand the following of the above exercise: if when throwing a single die (with 6 possible outcomes) repeatedly the probability of success (i.e. a six) in 4 throws exceeds 0.5, then when throwing two dice (36 possible outcomes) repeatedly, the probability of success (i.e. double-six) in 24 throws should also exceed 0.5 since

$$4 : 6 = 24 : 36$$

De Mere was confused by the fact that his observed results did not conform to the above rule. Our formal calculations today reveal that the probability of at least one six in 4 throws of a single die is

$$1 - P(\text{no six in 4 throws of a die}) = 1 - (5/6)^4$$
$$= 0.5177$$

(to 4 decimal places)

while the probability of at least one double-six in 24 throws of two dice is

$$1 - P(\text{no double-six in 24 throws of two dice}) = 1 - (35/36)^{24}$$
$$= 0.4913$$
$$(\text{to 4 decimal places}).$$

Proportional rules give misleading results!

The problem which Samuel Pepys sent to Isaac Newton in 1693, and which we discussed in the context of the section on random experiments, is another classic example of the fallacy of proportionality. We repeat the statement of the problem.

A – has 6 dice in a box, with which he is to fling a 6;
B – has in another box 12 dice, with which he is to fling 2 sixes;
C – has in another box 18 dice, with which he is to fling 3 sixes;

Q[uestion] – Whether B and C have not as easy a taske as A at even luck?

In modern terminology the question being posed by Pepys and its underlying assumptions read as:

Since 1 : 6 = 2 : 12 = 3 : 18, surely the probabilities of the three events A, B and C are equal?

Again, simple binomial calculations show that the probabilities are indeed *not* equal, which is contrary to proportionality expectations.

COMBINATORIAL NAÏVETY

When describing probability experiments, especially those based on devices such as coins, dice, urns, etc., the first step is often to enumerate all possible outcomes that constitute the sample space as well as those outcomes in the event whose probability we are trying to calculate. If a coin is tossed three times or if a die is rolled twice, then it is easy to list the outcomes in the corresponding sample space. If, however, the number of trials is increased the counting processes can become very complex indeed.

Students who have taken a traditional advanced level (or high school) course in Pure Mathematics will have touched upon counting methods under the headings of 'Permutations' and 'Combinations'. These two are often presented as respectively 'taking order into account' and 'ignoring order'. On the other hand the notions of counting 'with replacement' and 'without replacement' possibly do not receive the same attention in the school syllabus. Whatever the case may be, 'Perms and Combs' are notoriously difficult to handle.

For the student of probability and statistics an alternative strategy (see Hamdan, 1978) is to model counting methods by performing n drawings of m numbered tokens from an urn. There are essentially four such sampling procedures: with replacement and with order, without replacement and with order, without replacement and without order, with replacement and without order. The attempt to describe a particular combinatorial probability experiment by one of these models will force the student to look carefully at the mechanisms underlying the experiment. This in itself will not guarantee that the counting will be done correctly – combinatorial complexity will still remain a formidable barrier but hopefully such an approach will prevent students from claiming, for example, that

. . . with two dice it is as feasible to throw 12 points as to throw 11; as the one and the other can only be achieved in one way; . . .

Such an erroneous statement was made by no less a famous intellect than Gottfried Leibniz (1646–1716) (see Glickman, 1990). He made the common mistake of not taking order into account and assumed only (6, 5) as a partition of 11 while ignoring (5, 6).

To alleviate difficulties in a student's attempt to solve a counting problem, Chung (1979) suggests four *heuristics*:

(a) If the problem is not clear, try some particular case with small numbers (but not too small so as to trivialise the problem). This may assist in clarifying in the student's mind what is to be counted and pinpoint any duplicates or omissions.

(b) Break up the problem into smaller, more manageable 'pieces'.

(c) Do not try to reason step by step if complications begin to accumulate.

(d) If there is ambiguity in the natural language statement of the problem, as a first step try all possible (non-trivial) interpretations.

In addition the current authors suggest the following.

(e) Wherever possible, employ diagrams to assist in the counting process.

Relating counting to sampling methods and implementing the above hints are not universal remedies, but they will make combinatorics more relevant to the area of probability and statistics.

CONDITIONAL PROBABILITY

Falk (1988) has identified three main areas of difficulty associated with conditional probabilities. The first involves the interpretation of conditionality as causality. Falk presents a typical example:

An urn contains two red tokens and two white tokens. From this urn two tokens are drawn at random one after the other without replacement. The first question is: what is

Pr(White token at second draw|white token at first draw)?

Secondly, what is

Pr(White token at first draw|white token at second draw)?

Falk suggests that while beginning students will easily accept the first answer as 1/3, the majority will claim 1/2 as the answer to the second question (although the correct answer is again 1/3). The typical argument put forward is that before the first draw the second draw has not yet been performed and 'the first token doesn't care whether the second is white or red'.

According to Falk, students do not perceive these two problems as being symmetrical from the point of view of their informational content. Psychologically the students are reasoning causally, and they therefore believe that, while the result of the second draw depends causally on the outcome of the first, the reverse is not true. Further psychological investigations of causality and conditional probability can be found in Tversky and Kahneman (1980).

A second area of difficulty lies in the definition of the conditioning event. In addition to ambiguities that may arise out of natural language usage, there is also what Falk refers to as the problem of conditioning on an inferred event. The following example will highlight this problem.

There are three cards in a hat. One is blue on both sides, one is green on both sides, and one is blue on one side and green on the other. A card is drawn at random and put on a table as it comes out. It shows a blue face. What is the probability that the hidden side is also blue?

Students will probably answer 1/2 by conditioning their calculations on the event that the double green card is 'out' and each of the two remaining cards is equally likely to be the one on the table. But the event 'double green is out' is an inferred event; the immediate event given as information in the above problem is that 'blue side is up'. The experiment described in the problem has six equally likely outcomes; the six faces of the three cards. The conditioning event is 'blue side is up' and there are three outcomes satisfying this criterion. Two of these outcomes have blue on the hidden side and one has green. So the correct conditional probability is 2/3.

The third problematic area in conditional probability has been designated by Falk as the 'confusion of the inverse', that is, a lack of discrimination between the two directions of conditioning, $P(A|B)$ and $P(B|A)$. Such confusion often occurs in medical contexts, where the probability of a disease given a positive test result is incorrectly equated with the probability of a positive test result given the disease. (See discussion in Eddy, 1982, and in Milton and Corbet, 1982.) A similar problem also occurs in legal contexts where the probability of actually being guilty of a crime given a verdict of 'guilty' is confused with the probability of the verdict 'guilty' given that the defendant is actually guilty. As an exercise teachers should ask their students to read carefully the article by Hille (1978/79) in an attempt to reveal the 'confusion of the inverse' hidden in the discussion.

Another misconception that needs to be brought to the attention of students is that it does not make sense to refer to $A|B$ as the 'conditional event', although as we have seen, the term 'condition*ing* event' does have meaning. Realising that there are only conditional probabilities, and not conditional events, will help students to grasp the notion of stochastic independence as a *probabilistic* concept. See the discussion below.

MUTUAL EXCLUSIVENESS AND INDEPENDENCE

Many students feel with some conviction that mutually exclusive events must be independent events. This fallacy may have its roots in the natural language interpretation of the 'independence of two entities' as meaning 'separation from' or 'non-contingent upon'. This is reinforced by a pictorial representation of two mutually exclusive events (or sets) A and B, say, as in Exhibit 4.1, where the 'separateness' is forcibly projected on to the viewer's mind.

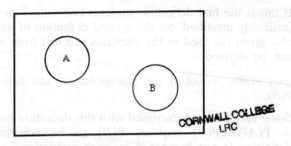

Exhibit 4.1 **Mutually exclusive events**

To overcome the persuasiveness of these arguments it will be worth while to concentrate in the classroom on three separate concepts:

(1) mutual exclusiveness of two events (sets) A and B as indicated in Exhibit 4.1;
(2) intuitive independence of A and B which says more or less the obvious: the occurrence of one of these events has no effect on the occurrence of the other; and
(3) stochastic independence of A and B, a formal definition from probability theory, which requires $P(A|B) = P(A)$, that is, the *probability* of event A is not affected by the occurrence (or non-occurrence) of B.

Mutual exclusiveness is purely a *set-theoretic* concept, while stochastic independence is a *probabilistic* concept where the independence of events depends on the probability measure assigned to the sample space. Szekely (1986) has provided some useful and illustrative examples which demonstrate that two events can be intuitively independent but not stochastically independent, and *vice-versa*.

Looking at Exhibit 4.1, the only conclusion at which we can arrive is that the events are mutually exclusive. We cannot at this stage make any statement about the independence or otherwise of A and B. Once we know that neither $P(A)$ nor $P(B)$ is zero, we can then conclude that these events are stochastically dependent since $P(A) > 0$ while $P(A|B) = 0$.

CONDITIONAL PROBABILITY AND INDEPENDENCE

When presenting the notion of stochastic independence to students, the definition usually takes the following form:

Two events A and B are independent if and only if $P(AB) = P(A)P(B)$.

If this is the first definition students encounter, then they will be justifiably mystified. So the second definition of independence is also given (as used in the previous section) from which the first can be derived:

Two events A and B are independent if and only if $P(A|B) = P(A)$.

Some care must be exercised with this definition because $P(A|B) = P(A \cap B)/P(B)$ requires $P(B)$ to be non-zero. The first definition is not hampered by such restrictions.

When we elaborate informally on these definitions to our students, we often state something like:

Two events A and B are independent if the probability of A occurring is unaffected by whether or not B occurs.

In the light of such practice, Huff (1971) has suggested an alternative definition:

Two events A and B are independent if and only if $P(A|B) = P(A|B')$ where B' is the complement of B. Again we assume no division by zero is allowed.

It should be noted that here only conditional probabilities are involved. The previous definitions can be deduced from this one. It can prove useful in cases where it is easier to derive conditional probabilities than unconditional ones. Also, in addition to matching our informal explanations to students, it emphasises what has already been said above, that stochastic independence is a probabilistic concept, not a set-theoretic one.

THE NOTION OF A RANDOM VARIABLE

Traditionally probability is introduced against the background of a sample space and events. Teachers employ the algebra of sets either formally or pictorially (Venn diagrams, for example) to state the general laws of probability. But subsequently this set representation fades away in favour of a formulation involving random variables. In introductory courses the emphasis is usually on binomial and Poisson probabilities which respectively refer to random variables 'numbers of successes' and 'numbers of events per unit time or space'. Seldom is there a need to discuss these distributions with the aid of set theory and associated algebraic operations. It does seem, as Hinderer (1990) claims, that random variables are a more natural and convenient representation of events.

The concept of a random variable is a subtle one. It is a numerically valued function with the sample space as domain. To define it properly requires a mathematical level of sophistication we do not really expect from our beginning students. Hinderer concludes that a unified approach to events and random variables is desirable and that indicator (binary) variables provide an appropriate mechanism. An event A can be formulated as an indicator random variable I_A;

$$I_A(\omega) = \left\{ \begin{array}{ll} 1, & \omega \text{ in } A \\ 0, & \omega \text{ not in } A \end{array} \right.$$

While this is an attractive proposition, it again introduces a formal notation and approach which are not really appropriate in an introductory course. But Hinderer's general recommendations are sensible; namely, start with the definitions of a sample space and events, and at the same time also introduce random variables even before the definition of 'probability'. In addition we suggest that set-theoretic notions should be used sparingly and informally via Venn diagrams, say, and that the 'random variable' formulation of events should dominate.

THE ALL-PERVADING INFLUENCE OF THE NORMAL DISTRIBUTION

The normal distribution plays a dominant role in a basic statistics course. Its prominence stems from the Central Limit Theorem and the fact that hypothesis testing and estimation (both point and confidence interval) based on normal distributional assumptions are widely known and easily implemented.

This all-powerful image of the normal distribution can become the starting point for a range of misconceptions relating to probability distributions and statistical inference. These will be discussed in detail below. For the moment we give a simple illustration as to the effect of 'normality' on a student's thinking.

At an early stage in a statistics course we introduce our students to the concept of a transformed, or more particularly a standardised score, sometimes known as a z-score. Such scores will play an important role in the inference section of the syllabus. While eventually being able to calculate and manipulate z-scores, Huck *et al.* (1986) claim that students still retain widespread misconceptions about the maximum value that z can assume. One group of students feels that z-scores always range from -3.00 to $+3.00$, while others think that they can vary from negative infinity to positive infinity.

The cause of these misconceptions is the emphasis on standardisation in the normal distribution. The first group of students sees a picture of the standard normal curve lying within three standard deviations of the mean; the second sees a normal curve with its tails asymptotic to the horizontal axis and reason that a z-score can lie anywhere in the infinite interval.

As mentioned above, one reason for the dominance of the normal distribution in statistics is the Central Limit Theorem. Although the proof of the theorem is beyond the scope of introductory courses, it is reasonably easy to state (in an informal manner) and it is equally easy to demonstrate the consequences of the theorem via computer-aided simulation.

We give the following careful (and correct) formulation of the Central Limit Theorem (as found in Freund, 1980):

If $X_1, X_2, \ldots, X_n$ are independent random variables having the same distribution with mean μ and variance σ^2 and moment generating function $M_X(.)$ then if $n \to \infty$, the limiting distribution of

$$Z = \frac{\bar{X} - \mu}{\sigma/\sqrt{n}}$$

is the standard normal distribution.

Even this statement is probably too formal for our beginning students. However, as Brewer (1985) demonstrates, an informal approach leaves the Central Limit Theorem and the normal distribution open to abuse.

We do not wish to undervalue the consequences of the above theorem. It confers upon the normal distribution an importance that it deserves. However respect should not turn to blind adulation. The use of the normal distribution based only on the fact that one has a large sample can lead to imprecise if not faulty statistical practice.

In some cases students meet the normal distribution for the first time as an approximation to the binomial distribution. There has been a long-standing debate concerning the inclusion of the continuity correction in this approximation. Addelman (1976) argues persuasively for the correction to be used at all times even if the sample size is very large. He gives an example where the sample size is 200 and where the discrepancy between the approximation with and the approximation without the correction factor is substantial, the former being nearer to the true distribution.

The use of the correction could be supported for another, more basic, reason; namely that the student must be made aware at all times of the distinction between the discrete (binomial in our case) and continuous (the normal distribution, for example) in statistics. The term 'correction factor' should always be referred to as the 'correction for continuity'. By doing so, we impress upon our students that a continuous distribution is being employed to give approximate probabilities for a discrete one. Such a policy will always result in a more appropriate and therefore more precise statistical analysis. Statistical computing packages will usually incorporate the continuity corrections where relevant, but students should still be aware of the underlying reasons.

One needs to balance the above arguments in favour of a continuity correction against the extra complexity involved by actually introducing it into formulae which beginning students must manipulate. It will confuse (and may depress) them. With possibly the exception of the normal approximation to the binomial distribution, continuity corrections should not be discussed at an introductory level.

Some formulations of the Central Limit Theorem include the 'magic' number 30 (sometimes 25), stating that the normal approximation is good if the sample size is greater than 30. A typical consequence of this is that the normal distribution comes to be used by students if n (the sample size) exceeds 30, even when the exact distribution is available. Student's t-distribution is a case in point. For situations where the sample size is greater than 30, students are often advised to construct a 95 per cent confidence interval, say, for μ when σ is unknown by using the well-known z (standard normal) value 1.96 instead of the appropriate t-value for which tables are available even for large degrees of freedom.

The majority of statistical computing packages now provide procedures like probability plots for checking normality, justifying and making possible fuller consideration of the relevant issues and assumptions. Before their advent, however, most teachers and textbooks would warn their audience that the classical methods of inference required that the underlying populations being sampled followed normal distributions – yet these assumptions were rarely put to the test. The classic chi-square goodness-of-fit test was cumbersome to implement especially for the normal case, just as the manual construction of probability plots was tedious, and more often than not the whole issue was quietly forgotten. Some of the blame must also be placed at the door of the Central Limit Theorem. A large sample implied a normal approximation so assumptions were not checked.

Traditionally the normal distribution dominated the probability section of the syllabus. Nevertheless students still proceeded to the inference section with an incomplete grasp of the notion of a sampling distribution and of the Central Limit Theorem and its implications. As we shall see in the next chapter this lack of a firm foundation in probability only adds to the confusion and misconceptions inherent in hypothesis testing and estimation.

APPENDIX: VAN BRAKEL'S LIST OF PROBABILITY STATEMENTS

1. Smith will probably come to the party.
2. Probably the train goes at 10.23.
3. It is very improbable that someone with testimonials as good as these will fall into dishonesty.
4. The probability that a child being born is a boy is 0.51.
5. Of the children born, 51 per cent are boys.
6. The probability that a man of 30 will survive his 31st birthday is 0.995.
7. Statistics indicate that if a wounded man is treated immediately with penicillin the probability of his escaping sepsis is more than 9 : 10.
8. A snow storm in New York during January is more probable than one during November.
9. It is probable that there will be rain before the day is over.
10. It WAS probable that it would rain.
11. The probability that a normal coin will present a head after being tossed is 1/2.
12. The probability that this particular die will fall five uppermost is 1/6.
13. The probability of the prediction 'The relative frequency of cases in future series of throws of this die will be in a certain small interval' is high.
14. The probability that a positive integer is square-free is $6/\pi^2$.
15. The probability that a molecule of hydrogen has a velocity in the interval between v_1 and v_2 is p.
16. The probability of a 10 degrees deflection of an alpha-ray passing through this film is 1/4.
17. The probability of this radium atom's disintegrating within 1700 years is 1/2.
18. The intensity of a spectral line is determined by the probability of the corresponding quantum transition.
19. The probability that, on the basis of the evidence in 1938, the electronic charge e has a value in the interval:
    $(4.770 \pm 0.005) \times 10^{-10}$ e.s.u
    is 0.67.
20. It is probable that the sun will rise tomorrow.
21. Relative to our present evidence the theory of light quanta has a probability which is greater than its probability relative to the evidence available in 1920.
22. We cannot assign high probabilities to the generalisations

made in sociology because the number of cases in which we are able to confirm them is not very large.

23. The theory of evolution has a higher probability on the evidence than the theory of special creation.

24. The evidence makes it highly improbable that Aristotle composed all the work attributed to him.

25. It is probable, had Cleopatra's nose been half-an-inch longer, the course of the Roman empire would have been different.

26. We know now that the stories which Marco Polo told on his return to Venice were true, however improbable they may have been for his contemporaries.

CHAPTER 5

The final hurdle: teaching statistical inference

INTRODUCTION

Statistical inference as taught in the school curriculum, and at introductory tertiary levels, means essentially simple point and confidence interval estimation and hypothesis testing based on normal or large sample assumptions (see Chapter 4). It is this section of the statistics syllabus that is probably most prone to misconceptions.

Estimation and hypothesis testing revolve around the difficult concepts of random variables, sampling distributions and conditional probability. We have suggested before that these ideas have had little time to percolate in students' minds, especially when descriptive statistics and probability theory are regarded as stepping stones to be skipped over quickly on the way to the 'meat' of the syllabus, namely, inference.

To appreciate fully the traditional methods of statistical inference the student must have a firm grasp of the notion of a sampling distribution of a statistic. This usually means the sampling distribution of the mean, $\bar{X}$ (uppercase X). Whereas a few weeks (or chapters) ago the student was busy calculating a descriptive statistic called $\bar{x}$ (lowercase x) with a specific numerical value, $\bar{X}$ is now a sample statistic, that is, a random variable with a probability distribution of its own. It is true that in the typical syllabus the student will have covered the topic of sampling distributions together with some simple exercises bolstered by (computer-aided) simulation. Nevertheless the concept of a random variable in general, and a sample statistic in particular, needs a great deal more absorption time than it is usually given.

In the initial section of the statistics syllabus dealing with descriptive methods, the difference between a population *parameter* and a sample *statistic* is treated as rather superficial. The former is based on a complete set of measurements; the latter on a subset of measurements taken from the complete set.

In the context of inference, the student must view the value of a sample statistic as a realisation of a random variable. On the other hand, the true population parameter (for example, the mean μ) is a constant (whose value is unknown and about which we wish to infer certain things). So there is an intrinsic difference between population parameter and sample statistic in addition to the superficial one mentioned above.

A lack of understanding of these essential differences leads to the common errors perpetuated by beginners in statistics. For example, in confidence interval estimation we encounter students making such statements as:

* $P(75 < \mu < 85) = 0.95$ – treating a constant μ as a random variable;
* the confidence interval for $\mu = \bar{x}$ plus/minus, etc. – here the 'equals' sign offends;
* the confidence interval is plus/minus its half width – with no indication of the limits of the confidence interval being given, and
* calculating confidence intervals for sample means centred on μ.

Students will readily accept that $\overline{X}$ is the sample mean and μ is the corresponding population parameter. However, they will not immediately see why one cannot set up hypotheses about random variables or why one cannot make probability statements about fixed constants (for example, μ). We assume that Bayesian ideas are not part of the introductory syllabus being discussed here, otherwise *prior* and *posterior* distributions for μ would allow us to associate probabilities with events determined by μ.

In the case of confidence interval estimation it is difficult to talk to the beginning student about a *sample interval* as a *random variable*. It is much easier to simulate 100 confidence intervals, say, and show that approximately $100(1 - \alpha)$ per cent contain the parameter where $(1 - \alpha)$ is the confidence level. However, in spite of the evidence from simulation exercises, we feel that the concept of a random variable remains fuzzy in the mind of the student.

Hypothesis testing (probably even more than estimation) must be regarded as a major source of confusion and misconceptions. Additionally, there are controversies as to the role of hypothesis (or significance) testing in the scientific method in general. We shall touch upon these later. The first important point to stress when presenting hypothesis testing is that the setting up of hypotheses and the decision-making criterion must come *before* the actual collection of data and any statistical analysis. This might be obvious in the real world, but in examples used with students the data are usually given as part of the example, and often the hypotheses are given as well. This means that students will pay little heed to warnings about the order of steps in a test. Remember that we are discussing the treatment of inference in the *traditional* statistics course, and ignoring temporarily the relaxation of these principles in newer approaches like EDA. Possibly a more imaginative approach to examples is needed, splitting the stages into separate parts. Thus the first stage might be a discussion of research problems and a formulation of hypotheses with no reference to data.

If this stage is successful, a commonly occurring formulation of hypotheses such as

$$H_0: \overline{X} = 80; \quad H_1: \overline{X} > 80$$

where 80 is the observed *sample* mean, is immediately seen to be inadmissible. Sometimes students write hypotheses in terms of $\overline{X}$ simply because they are using the wrong notation for the population mean μ, but in some cases they do so because hypothesis tests are a complete mystery to them, and they write statements down blindly in the hope of hitting on the correct formulation by luck.

At a deeper level, hypothesis testing involves subtle conditional probabilities whose correct manipulation is essential to the correct interpretation of results. Confusion related to these conditional probabilities leads to major errors and misconceptions. To elaborate on this, consider the representation of the hypothesis testing process shown in Figure 5.1, which is a useful diagram to keep in front of our students throughout the treatment of hypothesis testing as it allows us to stress the following points:

1. The value of a population parameter is unknown. We postulate two hypotheses relating to the parameter, but we cannot be certain as to which is the correct one.
2. The statistician has to decide which is the correct state of the population. This can only be done on the basis of partial information represented by a sample of observations taken from the population. The statistician can therefore err.
3. From Figure 5.1 we see that two types of error are possible; if the statistician decides to reject H_0 when H_0 is true, this is a type 1 error; if the statistician decides not to reject H_0 when H_1 is true, this is a type 2 error.

We note that events such as 'type 1 error' and 'type 2 error' are possible outcomes of the decision-making process and as such may have probabilities associated with them. Thus:

Pr(Type 1 error)

is also known as the 'significance level' of the hypothesis test and is usually denoted by α. (The 'significance level' is often quoted

Statistician's decision based on
sample of observations

		Do not reject H_0	Reject H_0
True state of population	H_0	Correct	Type 1 error
	H_1	Type 2 error	Correct

Figure 5.1 **Classical statistical inference**

as 100α per cent.) Sometimes the terms 'type 1 error' and α are considered erroneously as being the same thing. Even if it is realised that α is a probability, its description as

$$\Pr(\text{Type 1 error})$$

tends to obscure the conditional nature of this probability. Looking at Figure 5.1, it is clear that we should write

$$\Pr(\text{Reject } H_0 \,|\, H_0 \text{ is true})$$

for α.

It is important to keep in mind that students may find difficulty with the classical hypothesis testing approach because their intuitions lead them to seek confirmatory instances, rather than to try to negate a proposition. Evans (1989) suggests an alternative explanation for this difficulty, namely that the confirmation bias may result not from a tendency to seek confirmations, but rather from the inability to formulate negative tests.

Perhaps because of such difficulties, hypothesis testing is an area to which the 'cook book', almost algorithmic, approach seems to be most readily applied. Textbooks and teachers often present it systematically by reference to a 'recipe'. Johnson (1981), for example, suggests teaching hypothesis testing in six steps, as shown in Figure 5.2.

For the student who will eventually use hypothesis testing as part of a classical scientific method of investigation, these may be sound guidelines in the sense, for example, that they will ensure that the hypotheses are set up before the data are collected and thus provide a protection against 'data-snooping'. However, they wrongly suggest that the process is mechanical, and the level of significance chosen at step 2 (often one of the 'magic' values of 5

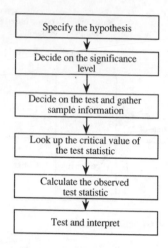

Figure 5.2 **A framework for hypothesis testing**

and 1 per cent) tends to become the sole indicator of whether a hypothesis should be retained or rejected. In many ways, quoting a p-value (the probability that a result as, or more, extreme than that observed could have arisen by chance) is to be preferred, and the facility for doing so is available in many statistics packages. A small p-value suggests that the null hypothesis should be rejected. However, it is not always obvious how to proceed in two-sided tests (Gibbons and Pratt, 1975) and students can be puzzled by the inconclusive nature of this method of presenting a result.

The one area where some form of mechanical approach may be recommended is in the decision-making process leading to the choice for a statistical hypothesis test or procedure for a particular set of data. Even for the most basic of hypothesis tests there are so many questions to answer, so many assumptions to be checked: are we dealing with one or more populations? Which parameter is under investigation? Can we assume the underlying populations to be normally distributed? Is the sample size 'large'?, etc. As we shall see in Chapter 6, Chervany *et al.* (1980) have researched a teaching strategy which, they believe, forces the students to address all these important questions, and helps them to acquire an appreciation of good statistical practice.

STATISTICAL SIGNIFICANCE VERSUS PRACTICAL IMPORTANCE

As Gardner and Altman (1989) point out, a process such as the six-stage hypothesis testing procedure outlined above represents an inadequate state of affairs. What is more important than whether or not results are *statistically significant* is whether they are *meaningfully significant* or are of *practical significance*.

When we carry out a hypothesis test and reach the decision step in our six-stage 'recipe' described above, we may conclude that our test statistic is *significant* and reject H_0. We often refer to these tests as tests of significance. In its natural language form the term 'significant' has the connotation of 'important' and our students immediately associate a significant test result (usually a significant difference) with a result that suggests a strikingly important difference in the wider (research) context.

Practitioners have been warned for some time in textbooks and journals (Daniel, 1977a,b) to differentiate carefully between *statistical* significance and *practical* significance. It is perhaps useful at this stage to remind ourselves that the aim of hypothesis testing is to come to a conclusion about a population on the basis of evidence found in a sample from that population.

Daniel suggests that we distinguish statistical significance from practical significance as follows. A statistical hypothesis test will reveal *statistical significance* which is applicable to sample results. It cannot detect *practical significance* which applies to conditions existing in the population. He proceeds to warn us *not* to use the word 'significant' when stating the null hypothesis, as in

H_0 : There is no significant difference between . . .

Many researchers who do this seem to be asking the subsequent statistical test to indicate the presence or absence of practical significance – something which the test cannot do! Always remember that *null hypotheses are statements about populations*, a point we have already emphasised above. They must contain no reference to the samples!

The implications for our students are that they, as statisticians, will generally be carrying out an analysis either at the behest of, or in conjunction with, users from other disciplines. While the statisticians can determine the statistical significance or otherwise of a hypothesis testing procedure, they cannot normally be the sole judges of the practical importance of the results. Consultation is needed between the statistician and the user. A statistically significant result may not be practically important, and vice versa! At this point we can remind our students once more that in statistical analysis there may not be a unique (right or wrong) answer to the question under investigation.

CONFIDENCE INTERVALS VERSUS HYPOTHESIS TESTS

The first types of hypothesis test that our students meet involve a single parameter:

$$H_0 : \mu = \ldots$$
$$H_0 : \sigma^2 = \ldots$$
$$H_0 : \mu_{\text{difference}} = \ldots$$

and so on. Instead of performing the standard hypothesis testing procedure, we could find the classical, Neyman–Pearson, $100(1 - \alpha)$ per cent confidence interval and reject the null hypothesis at the 100α per cent level if the interval excludes the null value because, as Wonnacott (1987) points out, in the framework of the Neyman–Pearson theory confidence intervals and hypothesis tests are theoretically equivalent. In this case is there any reason for preferring one approach to the other? Yes, says Wonnacott, who points to two major practical advantages, especially where the inference relates to a single parameter: in its form of estimate ± error, a confidence interval

(a) is certainly easier to explain to the 'customer' and easier for the 'customer' to understand;
(b) provides a point estimate and therefore more information;
(c) emphasises how large a parameter is and therefore emphasises practical (scientific) significance as well as giving some idea of statistical significance (see our previous discussion of practical versus statistical significance).

To sum up: the *confidence intervals*, related to the particular value of the *point estimate*, are more informative than the results of significance tests.

In the research literature, a growing number of journals now insist that, in addition to *p*-values, confidence intervals must also be quoted in relevant papers. As we saw in Chapter 1, for example, this is now the policy for contributions to the *British Medical Journal* (see Gardner and Altman, 1989). The result has been the generation of yet more pressure for emphasising confidence intervals in teaching courses at introductory and undergraduate levels.

It is a fact, however, that the general intuitive understanding of *confidence* is rather poor, as Oskamp (1965) points out:

. . . as information is added in a probabilistic inference task, confidence increases rapidly, whereas accuracy increases only minimally, if at all. The base-rate fallacy is a demonstration of how new information may actually lead to a *decline* in predictive performance, by suppressing existing information of possibly greater predictive validity. In the mind of the human judge, more is not always superior to less.

A further confusion is now exposed relating to the understanding of *statistical* confidence, with respect to the nature of the size or width of the confidence intervals, i.e. to the degree of *precision* of estimation. The design of studies is still crucial to the obtaining of meaningful results. As Moore (1990) points out, a frequently misunderstood concept with non-statisticians is

that the precision of the estimate formed from a sample is not primarily determined by the *percentage* randomly sampled from the population – rather it is the *size* of the sample itself that determines precision. Well *et al.* (1990) echo this theme:

The appreciation that naïve subjects have been shown to have for the law of large numbers often does not result from in-depth understanding of the relation between sample size and variability. Rather, correct answers may result from the application of low-level heuristics such as 'bigger is better'. Performance will be poorer on some problems because they do not map well on to the correct heuristics or because they elicit inappropriate heuristics such as representativeness or the 'extreme score' heuristic.

In general, Well *et al.* feel that it is very difficult to determine what is students' understanding of sample characteristics, sampling distributions, sample size, typicality of statistics and likelihood of occurrence of extreme values, and their ability to make appropriate statements about central points or tail ends of samples, etc.

There is certainly widespread confusion as to what *precision* means. To many of our students, it is often semantically indistinguishable from *accuracy*. In reality, of course, *accurate* means that, in the long run, the sample estimates of a population parameter would form a distribution from which a confidence interval could be constructed that would contain the *true* parameter value. *Bias*, the antithesis of *accuracy*, implies that the method (or statistic) being used would not yield an accurate estimate.

In designing a survey or an experiment, *precision* can be manipulated, and *should* be, if *statistical* and *meaningful* or *practical* significance are to be equated. Take, for example, the confidence interval from the sampling distribution of the mean. The population parameter, its mean, μ, is said to lie within plus and minus 1.96 standard errors of the mean (estimated by $s/\sqrt{n}$) from the sample mean, $\bar{X}$ [at the 95 per cent confidence level]:

$$\bar{X} - 1.96 \, (s/\sqrt{n}) < \mu < \bar{X} + 1.96 \, (s/\sqrt{n})$$

Notice that for example by investigating in a more homogeneous context (reducing s), or more importantly by increasing n (the sample size), the *precision* of the estimate may be improved and the width of the confidence interval decreased (see Figure 5.3). Given a biased sampling method, a more precise estimate is less

Precision, accuracy and confidence

Comparison of population parameters

$$\mu_1 \qquad\qquad \mu_2$$

$$\overline{X}_1\!+$$
$$-\;-\;-\;-\;-\;-\;-\;-\;-\;-\;-\;-\;-\;-$$
$$+\,\overline{X}_2$$

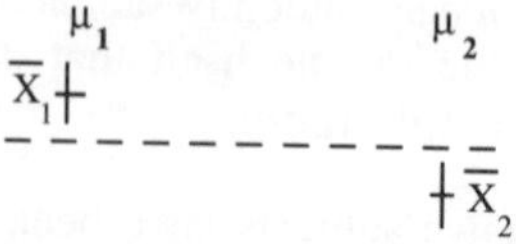

For each of the two populations, the parameter μ shown above lies within the confidence interval range shown about the relevant sample mean, $\overline{X}$. If the confidence intervals around the sample statistics are reduced, so too is the difference between the point estimates that is necessary for a conclusion that a statistically significant difference exists between the population parameters.

In the presence of biased sampling techniques; resulting in a systematic distortion of the sample's location, improved precision can make the outcome "less accurate" in the sense of "less correct" because narrower confidence intervals are more likely to exclude the true parameter.

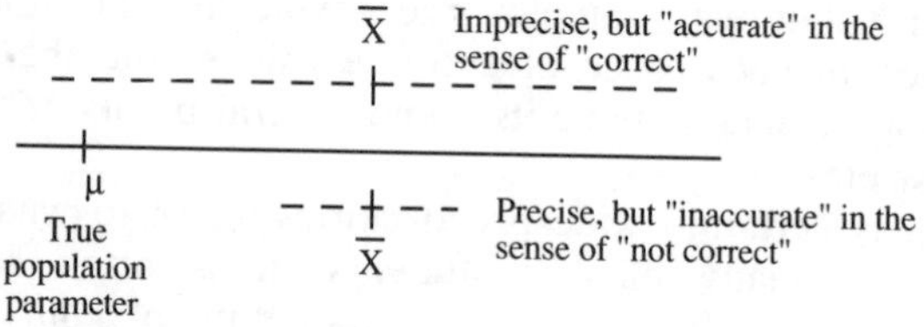

$$\overline{X}$$ Imprecise, but "accurate" in the sense of "correct"
$$-\;-\;-\;-\;-\;-\;-\;+\;-\;-\;-\;-\;-$$

μ
True
population
parameter $\overline{X}$ Precise, but "inaccurate" in the sense of "not correct"

Random and biased sampling from a Normally distributed population

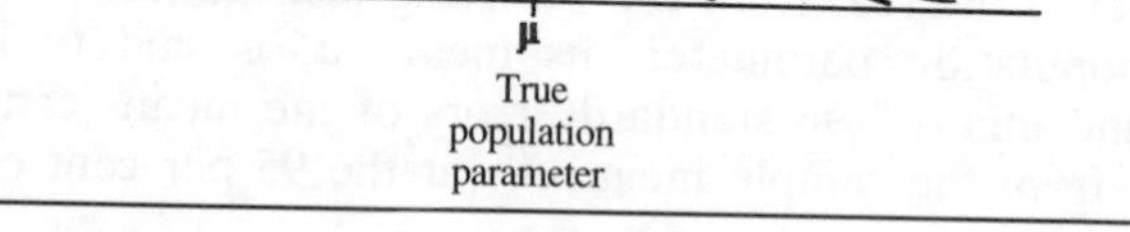

Random sampling   *Population*
Extreme effects
swamped out by   *Biased sampling*
more likely units'   As *n* increases
as *n* increases   the bias is
                                           accentuated

μ
True
population
parameter

Figure 5.3 **Precision, accuracy and confidence**

likely to be 'accurate' in the sense of 'correct' since there will be less scope for including the true population parameter from a 'false' starting point than if the estimation were to be less precise.

Furthermore, if a hypothesis about a difference between two populations is being tested, the observed difference is found to be statistically significant if daylight can be seen between the two estimation bounds, i.e the two confidence intervals do not overlap. The spurious precision caused by exceptionally large sample sizes will then make it more likely that the investigator will find the results to be *significantly* different, though not *meaningfully* so or of *practical significance*. Our students generally have enough information on the relationship between sample size and precision by the time they reach the level of Sixth Form work. Nevertheless, they do not appear to appreciate its *practical* value in the pre-planning stages of their projects.

A further misconception with respect to sampling concerns why an unlikely extreme observation in the sample does not markedly affect the sample statistic if a reasonably large sample is selected by random methods. Students tend to assume that its effect will be *cancelled out* by the drawing of a compensating extreme observation from the other end of the spectrum. What actually tends to happen is that the sample builds up comprised of more of the 'more typical' observations, and the effect of the extreme observations is *swamped out*, not cancelled out.

This illustrates a fundamental principle of probability that students also seem to find difficult to grasp. A rare or unlikely occurrence, such as an extreme value, has a small probability of happening. To obtain two extreme values, to compensate each other, will therefore have a $(\text{small})^2$ probability of occurrence, i.e. *very* unlikely indeed.

Of course, with a biased, as opposed to random, sampling method, the mechanism does not operate in this manner, as the distribution is no longer symmetrically balanced, and the so-called 'extreme' values can no longer be assumed to be extreme in the original sense. Swamping of their effects will no longer take place as the sample size is increased. Rather, the effect of the bias will become more pronounced with the selective sampling method, and indeed their effect will become worse with the increased precision bestowed on the resulting biased estimator by the increase in sample size.

THE SIGNIFICANCE TEST CONTROVERSY

From the discussions above about the 'mechanical and magical' properties of levels of significance such as 5 and 1 per cent levels, about the important distinction between statistical and practical significance, and about the rivalry between confidence intervals and hypothesis tests, it should come as no surprise that significance testing has been a controversial area of statistics for some time. It is not our intention to enter into a deep and philosophical investigation of this area. The reader is referred to

Morrison and Henkel (1970) for a suitable introduction. We shall merely mention one unsatisfactory aspect of hypothesis testing highlighted by Falk (1986). A researcher using significance testing in some scientific experimental work may reject H_0, the null hypothesis. The probability of rejecting H_0, given that it is true, Pr(reject $H_0 | H_0$ is true), is *alpha*. This result seems to represent to many researchers and teachers the probability of 'making a mistake' and therefore it is to be kept as small as possible, 5 or 1 per cent! But the real question of importance to the scientist relates to the more interesting and vital 'probability of error', i.e. to the probability that H_0 is true given that it has been rejected, Pr(H_0 is true | reject H_0). In the classical Neyman–Pearson framework this is a question that really cannot be answered. The role of hypothesis testing in the scientific method must therefore be looked upon with suspicion.

It has taken the teaching community some time to realise the fundamental problems inherent in significance testing. But there is a greater awareness of these now and the signs are that in the realm of statistical inference and its two major areas, hypothesis testing and estimation, emphasis is turning to the latter.

CHI-SQUARE TESTS

Goodness-of-fit and contingency table tests are popular topics in the introductory statistics syllabus. The former allow us to check whether data come from certain specified distributions (the binomial, Poisson and normal being typical) while the latter investigate association in two-way tables.

We have already mentioned that in contingency tables our attention is focused on frequencies (observed and expected) and their manipulation. Frequencies are not to be confused with measurements, which may require an analysis of variance type of approach.

The chi-square statistic is based on the expression

$$\Sigma \, [(O - E)^2/E]$$

where O denotes 'observed frequency' and E 'expected frequency'. The idea of some form of 'distance' between O and E is appealing as a measure of goodness-of-fit or of association. But there are a number of complications which accompany this test statistic. The student must be aware of the following points when performing a chi-square test.

It is recommended that all expected frequencies in a chi-square test should be greater than 5. If not, row and/or column categories should be combined until all expected frequencies satisfy this criterion. Often students are just given this rule without the explanation that a small E-value can inflate the chi-square value in an undesirable way. They then tend to combine rows and/or columns mechanically without checking whether such combinations give rise to new categories that are meaningful.

Associated with the chi-square test are its degrees of freedom. For the simple contingency tables which students meet initially, the number of degrees of freedom can be explained as being the number of cells not determined by row and column totals. However, in a goodness-of-fit exercise, where the parameters of the fitted distribution have to be estimated from the data, we lose one degree of freedom for each such parameter. Justifying this procedure is more difficult than before and the tendency is simply to give students the rule

subtract one degree of freedom for every parameter estimated

without any explanation.

We must remember that the above test statistic has a distribution which is only approximately chi-square with the appropriate degrees of freedom. If the degrees of freedom for a particular chi-square test turn out to be one, then a *continuity correction* (Yates' correction) is often recommended (see Freedman *et al.*, 1978b). This introduces some additional computational complexity and must detract from the simplicity underlying the basic chi-square procedure.

When applying the goodness-of-fit test to continuous distributions (especially the normal distribution), the calculations involve grouping the data and are quite tedious. As mentioned before, such heavy computation deters students (and teachers) from checking whether normal distributional assumptions hold in the classic inference setting thus leading to less than sound statistical practice.

The chi-square test is essentially a non-parametric procedure and in the case of goodness-of-fit there are probably superior contenders from this area of non-parametric methods. The Kolmogorov–Smirnov type of tests and their graphical derivatives involving the use of Lilliefors paper (see Iman and Conover, 1989) deserve more consideration at introductory level than they have received.

Frequencies that appear in tables of the type discussed above are often reported as proportions or percentages. Students must be reminded that a chi-square test cannot be performed when only percentages in category classes are provided. It is the actual (raw) frequencies that are required. Teachers can highlight the danger of ignoring this by pointing to the following example taken from the research literature. In a section of an article on aircraft hijacking, Quandt (1974) tested the null hypothesis that hijackers showed no preference to flights on any particular day of the week, in other words that there was no association between hijacking episodes and the day of the week on which they occurred. Examination of USA flight timetables revealed that the percentage of flights on Monday to Friday was 16 per cent each day, and on Saturday and Sunday it was 10 per cent each day. From a total of 296 hijackings Quandt calculated the percentage of hijackings by day of week and obtained:

Sunday	10 per cent
Monday	16 per cent
Tuesday	11 per cent
Wednesday	18 per cent
Thursday	12 per cent
Friday	23 per cent
Saturday	10 per cent

Comparing these observed values with the hypothesised values based on percentages of flights, Quandt arrived at a chi-square goodness-of-fit value of 5.9, which was not significant at the 5 per cent level and so the null hypothesis was not rejected, i.e. it was concluded that there was no association between hijacking episodes and the days of the week on which they occurred. Had the actual frequencies been used in the analysis, a test value of 29.9 would have been obtained and the null hypothesis would have been rejected (at the 5 per cent level) leading to a conclusion that hijacking episodes were associated with particular days of the week. Here incorrect use of percentages in a chi-square procedure has led to an incorrect conclusion!

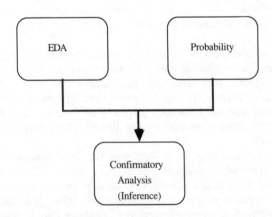

Figure 5.4 **A proposed form of syllabus for statistics**

CONCLUDING REMARKS

The teaching of statistical inference is at a disadvantage in the sense that it has to cope with the students' misconceptions that have been carried forward from the first two sections of the syllabus, especially probability. To alleviate some of the impediments to a clear presentation of inference, time and care must be devoted to delivering descriptive statistics and probability. The growing emphasis on exploratory as opposed to confirmatory methods provides a possible approach to the structuring of an effective syllabus, as shown in Figure 5.4. Here EDA and probability are taught in parallel and separately. Just how and when they merge to provide the basis for confirmatory analysis (inference) are fundamental questions requiring a great deal of careful research in the future.

CHAPTER 6

Research into statistical education

In contrast to other chapters in this book where the results of research studies are cited in order to illustrate or support other points, this chapter concentrates on the actual nature of the research. A number of research studies will be outlined in order to show the sort of directions that research into statistical education has been, and is, taking. The examples given, which are grouped into sections according to statistical topic, should not be considered to be a comprehensive review of all relevant research in the area. Although the findings of the studies may themselves be of inherent interest, it is intended that the reader should also begin to gain a critical appreciation of the research methodology adopted. The examples given here and elsewhere in this book may also act as stimuli for those readers who want to undertake their own research studies.

EXPERIMENTAL EVALUATION OF TEACHING METHODS AND MATERIALS

Because it can be hard to control for other factors that might affect the outcomes, it is difficult to do valid research on teaching methods and materials. Consider, for example, the comparison of an innovatory method of teaching with the method usually employed. The research strategy of using one method one year and the other method the next, with the following cohort of students, would not be very satisfactory. For example, the subsequent year's students will be different in all kinds of ways from those of the previous year, such as having different prior experience of statistics, or having followed different syllabuses and teaching in their other subjects. In addition, if the same teacher is involved in both years there will be an experience factor that could affect the quality of the teaching, and hence the learning outcome. This experience effect might be especially influential if the method is really innovatory, initially requiring the teacher 'to get the wrinkles out of it', for example!

A better design would be one with two classes of a similar mix of students taught in the same academic year where one method is used with one class and a different one with the other class. However, if the two classes are in the same school there is a chance of contamination in that the students might discuss their lessons with one another (but if two schools were to be involved it would, of course, be even more difficult to isolate the effect of the method under investigation from other competing variables). If the two classes are taught by different teachers then teaching method and teacher effects are confounded. Alternatively, if both classes are taught by the same teacher, the teacher would not necessarily be equally comfortable using each method. Furthermore, it would be difficult to rule out experimenter effects since it would be unlikely that the teacher would not know which method was innovatory. In other words, it is difficult to implement double blind experimental designs in educational research.

Problems can also arise because of difficulties in operationally defining the characteristics of the teaching methods or materials to be compared. See, for example, the studies by Myers *et al.* (1983) and Hansen *et al.* (1985), both of which were attempts to investigate the effectiveness of different instructional methods. It is extremely difficult to define, and constrain, the exact characteristics of an instructional method, and also to evaluate the cognitive responses in a way that is equally appropriate to each instructional method.

In the UK, a reasonable attempt to do a controlled study comparing teaching methods was undertaken at the University of Essex with students on a first-year introductory probability and statistics course (Harding *et al.*, 1981). Four matched groups were given a course comprising either lectures only, or lectures followed by tape slides, or tape slides followed by lectures, or tape slides only. No differences were found between the groups on examination results, attitudes and so on but, costed over a five-year period, the lectures alone were found to be slightly cheaper than the other methods.

When comparing two methods of instruction, it can also be difficult to isolate the factors that have *caused* an apparent difference in outcome. A change of method, for example to one where the students are encouraged to participate more in class, might also involve a change of text or instructional content and a change in the sequence of presenting the topics. Conclusions concerning changes have to relate, therefore, to the complete teaching–learning package and not just to a single 'causal factor' which is assumed to be *the* influential factor.

Related studies by Pollatsek *et al.* (1981) and Hardiman *et al.* (1984) serve to highlight some of the difficulties inherent in designing and interpreting such research, particularly those associated with the need to infer something about cognitive processing on the basis of relatively scant external representations of it. The degree to which the research approach predetermines possible responses from the subjects will inevitably influence the likely outcome of the study. For example, the choice of closed as opposed to open questions to evaluate the students' understanding must be a major consideration when designing research. So too must be the choice of evaluation items. For example, weighted mean questions to test for understanding of *average* when some subjects have been *set* to use simplistic (unweighted) rather than realistic (weighted) algorithmic understanding will introduce a tautology that may undermine the whole research project.

On the whole, more studies of teaching methods have been done in higher education than at school level, and many of these have been in North America or Australasia where classes are very large so that subdivision into smaller groups for some activities is already likely to occur, a fact that can be put to good effect in research studies. Indeed, it is partly because of the need to find non-labour-intensive methods of teaching statistics to very large groups (in excess of 500 students) that some of the experiments into teaching methods have taken place.

FIELD-TESTING

Rubin *et al.* (1988, 1990) describe how some new teaching materials were field-tested in a number of schools. In major projects carried out by the Centre for Statistical Education in Sheffield it has also been usual to test resource material in schools, often presenting it later in in-service courses and then publishing it. At the time of writing, the latest such project is on using databases and spreadsheets to teach data handling and statistics. Information about these projects can often be found in *Random News*[1], and *Teaching Statistics*.[2]

A possible weakness in some research and development projects is that the teachers volunteer their students to take part. This may well produce a selective bias because the material is then developed in schools where teachers are already interested in, and possibly committed to, the developments. Such schools might be different in important respects from those schools that do not become involved. Ironically it is the non-volunteer schools which probably have most need of the materials being developed, yet because material is less often field-tested in these schools it may not ultimately be ideal for their use.

Even where new developments are field-tested, their evaluation is often based on rather anecdotal evidence with little reliable or valid comparative investigation of the relative merits and de-merits of different materials. Sometimes, for example, field-testing largely comprises trying out the materials on teachers rather than on their students. In other studies, the teachers' opinions about the materials are all that are obtained.

RESEARCH INTO STATISTICAL THINKING

Just as it is difficult to do research on the effectiveness of a teaching method, so it is difficult to do research into people's statistical thinking and into how people learn statistical concepts. If more was known about the latter, research into teaching methods would almost be unnecessary because the knowledge of the learning process would more or less determine the teaching method. As Garfield and Ahlgren say, however, in their 1988 review of literature related to difficulties that students have in understanding probability and statistics and of associated research '. . . little empirical research has focused on the effectiveness of the different instructional methods or teaching approaches in developing statistical and probabilistic reasoning'. There is also a lack of research on the development of instruments designed specifically to measure statistical understanding and reasoning. Some discussion of the assessment of understanding is given in Chapter 10, and work in related areas is presented in Jolliffe (1991).

Part of the problem is that little is known about the statistical reasoning process or about how students assimilate statistical ideas. Evans (1989) is 'sceptical of the view that thinking can be taught as a general skill and [feels that] it is quite clear that verbal instruction in general principles of reasoning is unlikely, in itself, to provide protection from biases arising in specific situations'. He advocates an expansion of experience-based training in the domain of application, speculating that simulation software should be useful, allowing experiments with different parameters and feedback.

Research into deductive reasoning looks at people's ability to recognise the validity or otherwise of arguments of a formal logic kind. Inductive inferences, and more particularly intuitive statistical inferences, however, are not supported by formal logic, so the major interest in this context would concern the soundness of the strategies used to formulate, test and eliminate alternative hypotheses. To avoid the danger of only discovering differences rather than similarities between these types of reasoning because of the use of different experimental paradigms, Evans (1989) believes that the possibility of a *common* theoretical approach to research into behavioural decision theory and statistical inference should be explored. Traditionally they have been quite distinct.

His suggestion that research into reasoning may be more difficult than into memory or perception would not necessarily be universally accepted. Cleveland (1987), for example, would probably find the criteria and measurements for research into graphical perception just as difficult to determine, and as open to controversy, as Evans asserts they are in reasoning research. However, it is certainly the case that research into reasoning can be very difficult to design, to conduct and to interpret.

The model of statistical reasoning suggested by Chervany *et al.* (1977), and touched on briefly in Chapters 1 and 5, may provide useful insights into the cognitive processes involved and provide a basis for research. Their model has ten steps between 'Request for problem solution' and 'Report solution' which are grouped into the three stages of 'Comprehension', 'Planning and execution', and 'Evaluation and interpretation'. Chervany *et al.* (1980) report on students in an introductory statistical methods class being asked to *construct* a decision-tree structure as a project, in order to force the students to work out for themselves the relevant stages in solving a statistical problem. In order to evaluate the effectiveness of the project, correlations between scores on the project and scores on examination questions were calculated for 35 students. There were high correlations between scores on the project and on the two examination questions which required statistical reasoning, but low correlations with scores on two essay questions. Chervany *et al.* conclude that the *construction* exercise is a very useful pedagogic approach. They do not advocate that students should be *given* the decision framework. As with many published articles on statistical education, however, Chervany *et al.*'s emphasis is on describing a theory or idea, with less attention being paid to the rigorous evaluation of its effectiveness, the evidence tending to be rather anecdotal. There was no control group, for example, because *a priori* the decision-tree project was thought to be too worth while to withhold from some of the students.

Lee (1989) claims that although statistics is a rational subject, students do not always learn in a rational way but tend to learn in a pattern-forming mode and, for example, recognise problems (not always correctly!) as being similar to ones met previously. He gives anecdotal evidence to support this, and suggests that teachers should present material in a way that would take advantage of the pattern-forming mode of learning. Again, there is a need for such views to be put to a more formal empirical test, but Lee's idea would accord with the first of Chervany *et al.*'s (1980) stages: 'comprehension – seeing the particular problem as one of a class of similar problems'.

In a study reported by Allwood and Montgomery (1982), ten students on a first-year statistics course were asked to think aloud while solving two problems, having first been given a problem-solving manual which suggested various ways of checking solutions. To be really useful, studies of this nature require much larger numbers of subjects and when, as here, some new feature such as the problem-solving manual is involved, there should also be a control group.

Research into statistical reasoning about everyday problems, as opposed to problems presented in a statistical framework, is an interesting line of approach. Nisbett *et al.* (1983) report some experimental work done to find out if and when people reason statistically, and the factors that influence this. The problems given to subjects essentially had no standard method of solution or no known answer. For example, in one study subjects were told to 'imagine you are an explorer who has landed on a little known island in the south-eastern Pacific'. Subjects were then posed such questions as 'Suppose you encounter a new bird, the shreeble. It is blue in colour. What percent of all shreebles on the island do you expect to be blue?' Nisbett *et al.* assert that statistical procedures were part of their subjects' intuitive equipment, which would be in accord with Fischbein's (1975) view. If this is so, then statistical training has a basis on which to build. It can be argued that people with statistical training will be more likely to take a statistical approach to everyday problems and to obtain a better 'statistical' solution than persons without statistical training, a view that would be supported by Fong *et al.* (1986).

The debate about whether Man really is an Intuitive Statistician, which to a large extent grew out of the hypothetico-deductive view of *Man the Scientist*, subsequently developed into a debate about what sort of statistician he might be. Clearly, Man's judgements did not accord with those indicated by the rules of formal probability, as Kahneman *et al.* (1982) have been at length to point out. The view of *Man the Bayesian Statistician* stimulated a number of empirical studies to find out whether this view of Man could resolve some of the discrepancies, and the notion of *coherence*, i.e. people's ability or otherwise to estimate the probabilities of an exhaustive set of alternative events so that their sum equalled unity, became a fashionable area of study. Peterson and Beach (1967) give a review of the foundation studies in this area, and Lindley *et al.* (1979) provide another source of ideas concerning research possibilities.

Wonnacott (1986) discusses people's facility with Bayesian and classical hypothesis testing, suggesting that the Bayesian approach is easier to teach and understand. He reports briefly on a study with 44 students who had been taught the classical but not the

Bayesian approach and comments on their differential abilities to minimise the long-run costs in 'guessing' critical values. For a very different but nevertheless interesting approach, readers should look further at Eddy's (1982) literature-based research into probability misconceptions in Bayesian decision-making in medicine (also mentioned in Chapter 4).

STATISTICAL AND PROBABILISTIC UNDERSTANDING

As has been said, Kahneman *et al.* (1982) provide a good review and starting point for those interested in research into statistical and probabilistic understanding. Most of the studies reported deal with adult subjects, however, and they should not automatically be assumed to be directly relevant to younger students' understanding. Nor should they be accepted uncritically. Fiedler (1983) provides some helpful insight into potential weaknesses of some of the work – for example the failure to distinguish between retrieval and judgement effects – as does Shaughnessy (1992). Indeed, one problem is that the style of research often involves question and answer techniques where the questions are extremely complex, well beyond the capabilities of the subjects even if they were afforded the opportunities of paper and pencil, or calculators, etc., which they are not. Such research, which is based on anticipating the nature of subjects' errors, also prejudges the range of cognitive strategies that could be found, precluding the discovery of other possibly more correctly identified strategies.

The two classic texts pertaining to children's understanding in this area are those by Piaget and Inhelder (1951, trans. 1975) and Fischbein (1975). The former is a description of a series of 'experiments' with selected transcripts of the young children's responses to questions asked of them about various contexts which manifested chance or probabilistic events. The latter is an extensive review of research, with four reprinted papers of Fischbein *et al.*'s own research studies. Piaget and Inhelder's work is mainly concerned with the existence or non-existence, and the development, of *a priori* probability concepts in children aged from about 3 to early and mid-teenage. In a sense, Piaget and Inhelder's studies are completely constrained to finding what children are *not* capable of, whereas Fischbein is looking for evidence that children do have useful precursors of formal probability, in the form of intuitions. Indeed, some of the evidence for these is found in the subsequent mis-application of the precursors, leading to erroneous intuitions and probabilistic judgements.

On first reading, there may appear to be a very wide gulf between these two standpoints. In a sense, however, they may be 'different sides of the same coin', each having a basis in developmental psychology, but primarily concerned with very different types of probabilistic understanding. The rigour of Piaget's 'experimental' methods has been questioned by a number of researchers not espoused to his 'ages and stages' model. However, we would like to suggest that some of the harsher criticisms should actually be levelled at Piagetian disciples who over-exaggerate the principles of Piaget's model of intellectual development. Nevertheless, there is potentially a major weakness in an approach that seeks to confirm an existing general model of this kind.

Fischbein saw probabilistic reasoning as a fundamental skill, which is based on intuitions of *relative frequency*, and which is necessary for Man's adaptation. His view, that probabilistic reasoning can be socially mediated and modified, is far more useful to the teacher since it contrasts with the message that comes from Piaget's work about what not to teach children because they are not able to do it. Fischbein discusses where to start from and how important it is to recognise existing precursor skills, to exercise and to develop them in order to provide a firm basis for more formal probabilistic ideas. In common with Evans (1989) he favours experience-based learning rather than verbal instruction as a means of modifying probabilistic reasoning.

The tasks developed by Piaget are clearly described in Piaget and Inhelder (1951, trans. 1975) and have been used by many other researchers in ever more complex and finely discriminating forms, particularly the 'beads in an urn' type of studies where the child has to state a preference for one rather than another configuration of coloured beads in two different urns. This stated preference is intended to be a behavioural manifestation of the child's awareness or otherwise of which urn provides the best chance of drawing a bead of a particular stated colour. The developments of these experiments include configurations to differentiate between children choosing on the basis of things like preferred colour, larger number of beads overall, smaller number of wrong colour beads in one, the other, or both urns, proportion of beads, ratio judgements, etc. (e.g. Falk, 1983; Falk *et al.*, 1980).

Predicting where individual, and collections of, snowflakes will fall on a grid representing a tiled roof is another frequently used research task, sometimes given for the children to *produce* random events, or sometimes given for children to *discriminate* between what does and does not appear to be random. Of course, such studies raise difficult philosophical issues as to what is 'random'. In a sense, for an event to be random any possible outcome is permissible. However, outcomes of experiments on randomness invariably depend on the experimenter's decision that some outcomes are 'not random', being too systematic for his or her liking. The problem is that there is a fundamental contradiction between random as *anything possible might occur* and random as *only the 'untidy' outcomes are permissible within the definition.*

Lopes (1982) questions whether we can define randomness at all, distinguishing between questions where it is the randomness of the *process,* and those in which it is randomness of the *product* that is of interest. Wagenaar (1972) also addressed the issue in describing fifteen experiments on subjective randomisation. In his opinion, randomness is easier to disprove than to prove, there being many different ways of measuring *non*-randomness. What he feels is needed is a uniform definition of mathematical randomness, and better controlled experiments based on this definition.

Spencer Brown (1957) discussed some of these more philosophical issues surrounding the concept of randomness. He distinguished *primary chance* or randomness applicable to *discrete events* from *secondary chance* or randomness applicable only to *series of events*. The only relevant criterion of primary randomness is that we are able to guess. It can only apply to a future event. A random series is a series with no discernible pattern. Neither concept of randomness can be inferred from the other and they are incompatible.

The essence of randomness has been taken to be the absence of pattern, but in a sense the absence of one pattern may logically imply the presence of another. So if two observers look for different kinds of pattern, they will disagree upon their impression of whether or not randomness is present. Even after all this time, research studies have not managed to overcome the problems associated with the elusive nature of randomness, and the constructive, inventive pattern-imposing way in which subjects approach situations that are resistant to the identification of 'obvious' pattern still serves to confound insights into people's understanding of, recognition of, or ability to produce, random phenomena.

Green (1979) in a paper and pencil test of probability concepts in students aged 11 to 16 years, used a number of Piagetian-type tasks presented in symbolic form, including versions of the snow-flake example and the beads in urns problems. Not surprisingly then, Green's interpretations of his findings have a rather Piagetian 'ages and stages' ring to them, which is dangerously near tautology. However, Green's work represents a different type of research study in that it is a *large-scale psychometric* study, which demonstrates the importance of field-testing questions, the extreme difficulties of wording questions in an appropriate non-biasing way, and the difficulties that are encountered when the experimenter is remote from the respondent. Of course, at the other extreme, Piaget is criticised for being too involved with his subjects, but he did have the advantage of being able to capture, and query, any data *which he felt to be of interest*, which Green only really experienced during the pilot stages of his study.

Piaget and Fischbein both used the device of dropping balls down branched channels or into divided receptacles, by which means both symmetrical and skewed distributions could be produced. Subjects were asked to generate, or to predict the shape of, the distributions. Here, perhaps there is a more direct comparison between the two perspectives. Piaget used the experimental tasks to show that younger children did not have notions of random events, etc., while Fischbein used it to show that children could be taught the additive and multiplicative rules of probability with this type of apparatus as a teaching resource (Fischbein *et al.*, 1967).

Piaget's whole notion of the concept of random being dependent on the child first having developed an understanding of predictability and reversibility (not developed until after the age of concrete operations) is not particularly consistent with a view of the child coping well in an unpredictable environment from the time of birth, and for example developing concepts and language from non-deterministic feedback possibly in a hypothetico-deductive, trial-and-error way. For a useful résumé of Piaget's model of intellectual development, readers are referred to Donaldson (1978). We would suggest that the deferment of most of statistical education until the secondary school level was largely the result of a Piagetian, or similar, view of children's difficulties with probabilistic notions, largely based on children's inability to spontaneously develop *formal* probability concepts prior to instruction in them and on observations of *adults'* difficulties with probabilistic reasoning. Current moves to introduce probability and statistics earlier in the curriculum are more in keeping with Fischbein's view that in so doing we may avoid some of the difficulties which our students would otherwise have with probability when they become adults.

Further ideas for research into statistical concepts are to be found in papers by Pollatsek *et al.* (1984), which is concerned with beliefs underlying random sampling, Evans' (1986) paper on intuitive judgements of sample size, and Milsom (1987) who used a meta-estimation process whereby subjects not only gave responses to probability-based questions, but also represented their degree of confidence in their answers on a sliding scale, thereby not having to manipulate figures. Useful references to some of the earlier literature are to be found in Peterson and Beach (1967) and Pollard (1984).

EXTERNALISING SUBJECTIVE SCALES OF PROBABILITY

Readers will realise that in any cognitive research one of the major problems is externalising the thought processes and concepts. Several studies claiming to look at intuitions relating to statistical measures and concepts have been published in experimental psychology journals. In many of these studies subjects were given sets of *stimuli* and were asked to predict the outcome of a random or uncertain event. Such studies relate back to the probability matching experiments originating from Tolman and Brunswick's (1935) work, described in Fischbein (1975). Indeed, generalisations of this kind of stimulus-prediction approach have been one way of attempting to externalise concepts of randomness that run through much of the classic work of Piaget and Inhelder (1951, trans. 1975) and Fischbein *et al.* (1967).

Some of the experimental designs used are quite elaborate, but in many cases the problems being posed are somewhat artificial. General criticisms that could be raised include the small numbers of subjects in studies, and sequential presentation of information which confuses the subjects as to whether they are dealing with *sequences* of events, one-off samples or population estimations. Furthermore, in conducting their studies, some researchers do not give clear definitions of measures, and make little or no attempt to relate their experimental stimuli to real situations. Particularly when younger children are acting as subjects, as in Piagetian-type studies, the influence of experimenter effect cannot be ruled out. Indeed, some of Piaget's 'experiments' required the child overtly to counter the researcher to the extent of accusing him or her of cheating if that child was to be considered to have the concept of chance. It would not therefore be surprising to find that the younger children 'did not display the concept'.

Alternative approaches with young children have been tried. At the First International Conference on Teaching Statistics in 1982, Ruma Falk demonstrated a board game called 'Taking a Chance' which provided children with the opportunity to develop strategies based on their developing concepts of likelihood of events. To play the game each child in turn chose between two different bases on which to spin a roulette-style spinner. The pack of bases consisted of circular discs on which the probabilities that red or blue would come up varied according to the proportion of each colour's shading. Moves in the game were dependent on whether a child successfully predicted the outcome of a spin. Further interest was added because, by virtue of the 'safe' and 'penalty' landing squares, the children sometimes found it beneficial to try to demote their opponents rather than to advance themselves. This game is a fascinating way of developing or consolidating concepts of chance with surprisingly old students. One of the authors has successfully used it with experienced in-service teachers of mathematics on a number of occasions! The way in which it stimulated interactions between the players about uncertain events also made it an ideal research tool for externalising spontaneously emerging concepts.

If we consider that there is an objective probability scale, designated to be from zero to unity, we might wish to establish how a subjective scale of probability relates to this in a manner reminiscent of psychophysical research on the perception, or internal representation, of phenomena such as loudness, heaviness, etc. Lindsay and Norman (1972) or Woodworth and Schlosberg (1966) will provide readers with a basic introduction to the methodologies employed and to the historical developments of ideas about the functional relationships between objective and subjective scales from Weber's (1834) law concerning threshholds and just-noticeable differences, through Fechner's (1860) psychophysical law to Stevens' (1951, 1961) power law.

To do the equivalent kinds of study on subjective probability, it is necessary to externalise the judgements of probability associated with a range of different objective probabilities. Behavioural manifestations based on wagers, observed choices and preferences, or 'button-pressing' registering of predictions in situations of uncertainty have been tried. So too have investigations in which subjects were required to produce their estimates of probability verbally. These are fraught with problems over different understandings of the relevant words like 'possible', 'likely', 'certain', etc. (see also Green, 1982). This incidentally raises some interesting questions concerning cultural variations in the coding of probabilities which might arise from experiences of contexts with inherently different levels of predictability.

Subjects required to use number scales such as 0–100 per cent or 0–1 to express their probability judgements may err or give unreliable responses simply because of their lack of facility with percentages or with decimals, respectively. One way to overcome this is to have subjects mark their estimates on an unnumbered line, and for the researcher later to convert length, or proportionate length, to a number scale. Milsom (1987) tried this in a probability judgement context, as did Harterink (1987a) in research on perception of the average. She also got subjects to estimate cross-modally by tearing paper strips 'to estimate the mean' of a given set of numbers.

For researchers trying to unravel cognitive representations of probability, the problems associated with the manner in which subjects are required to express their perceptions are exacerbated by what appear to be great *within* and *between* subject variations. The former, in particular, makes the notion of a scale of subjective probability, if it exists at all, appear extremely unstable and elusive. Subjects appear to use different strategies, to adopt different biases, and to perceive the 'same' problem differently on different occasions, or in different contexts. In the absence of reliable evidence about the nature of the underlying subjective scale, or scales, however, it is difficult to see how research findings dependent on subjects comparing or expressing probabilities are to be interpreted. The problem is made more complicated by our relative ignorance of the effects of different task requirements on the subjects – for example, those tasks that are *estimation* or *production* tasks as distinct from those in which the subject is essentially expected to *perceive* or to *recognise* different levels of uncertainty.

INTERPRETING PEOPLE'S RESPONSES TO UNCERTAINTY

Probabilistic understanding has typically been assessed by asking 'tricky' probability questions, designed to 'trip up' the respondent in predictable ways (described in detail in Kahneman *et al.*, 1982). One problem with such research, and with much assessment, is that it is geared to looking at what people get wrong, rather than at what they can get right, and, as we suggested earlier, its outcome will always be very much influenced by what the suspected 'errors' might be. There has been some general criticism along these lines, but, in addition, much has been written about the ambiguities introduced into such research by the wording of the questions used. Shaughnessy (1992), Evans (1989) and Pollatsek *et al.* (1987) are particularly useful for their comments on probability questions.

For example, Shaughnessy points out that interpreting research into *representativeness* (whereby an event seems to be more probable the more representative it is of the parent population from which it is drawn) is not as easy as its researchers would sometimes appear to imply. If respondents are faced with a question concerning which birth pattern is more likely, BBBGGG or BBBBGB (B=boy, G=girl) Shaughnessy maintains that they do not know what model is appropriate. The *normative* model says that both patterns are equally likely, but the respondent does not know, for example, whether biologically there is some tendency for families to have offspring of a particular gender (or whether the final ratio of boys to girls should be roughly equivalent). As Shaughnessy says, on assessment items like this it is not possible to determine the *nature* of the 'error' unambiguously on the basis of respondents' responses. For example, it is not clear that *failure to appreciate independence* is really the same 'error' as *using representativeness*.

There are many differences in the way in which people interpret the meanings of terms used in test items or questions. As we saw in Chapter 4, Wagenaar (1988) found such differences concerning the terms 'chance' and 'luck' to be extremely subtle. Green (1982) did attempt to explore some of the semantic difficulties that occur when teaching statistics. However, given the subtleties of interpretation that Wagenaar (1988) has reported, it is unlikely that Green's (1982) test items on the semantics of probability would discriminate finely enough in this respect.

Evans, too, maintains a certain scepticism about the research in this area on the grounds that it is, he feels, very difficult to interpret. For example, Evans (1989) terms 'positivity bias' as 'reflecting the operation of pre-attentive processes which direct attention to positive rather than negative information'. It is relatively simple to demonstrate and replicate examples of this bias, but 'it is most difficult to achieve a consensus on the interpretation of the phenomena observed'. Interpreting assessment outcomes in research contexts cannot be assumed to be unambiguous; nor should it be taken as such in examination contexts. It is difficult to know exactly which processes are being evoked by the questions.

Figure 6.1 shows the different levels at which Evans feels that observed *errors* may occur. Their interpretation, and hence the

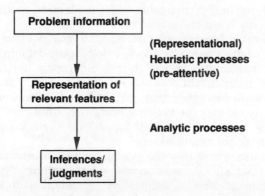

Figure 6.1 **Evans' (1989) view of the many levels at which 'errors' may occur in reasoning (under uncertainty)**

interpretation of the research findings, should take such different *loci* of error into account. According to Evans, *some* research does not evoke any form of reasoning, merely a heuristic approach to judging relevance, which would precede any form of analytic reasoning. At the same time, he feels that 'knowledge can induce biases by pre-empting analytic reasoning by whatever means'. Some knowledge can have a de-biasing effect, e.g. expert reasoning, but it is not clear exactly how the knowledge actually operates.

When confronted with a stochastic problem, students' pre-attentive or pre-conscious heuristics determine what they deem to be relevant features of the problem. Thus research that attempts to attribute errors at pre-attentive representational levels as errors resulting from subsequent analytic processing levels will be misleading.

According to Evans (1989); 'the major cause of bias in human reasoning and judgment [of all kinds] lies in factors which induce people to process the problem information in a *selective* manner'. This may arise because people use a selective mental representation of the information available, or because they selectively process it. Information selection may lead to the omission of relevant aspects *or* to the inclusion of irrelevant aspects. While 'selection is fundamental to intelligence' (Evans, 1989) we must still identify the conditions under which the selective mechanisms will lead to errors and biases.

Research has shown that people appear to have a fundamental tendency to seek information that is consistent with their current beliefs, theories or hypotheses and to avoid the collection of potentially falsifying evidence. This is known as 'confirmation bias'. Garfield and Ahlgren (1988) point out related examples of the 'interference' with 'sound' reasoning that can be caused by belief systems which run counter to orthodox science education. It would be foolish to ignore such tendencies in interpreting responses to research questions.

On the other hand, much research into *recency* effects (e.g. the Gambler's fallacy whereby people bring sequential information to bear on judgements which should objectively relate only to single, or independent, events) says that people *believe* this or that, when in fact, they may merely be adopting some sort of working hypothesis *for the time being*, i.e. until they formulate something better (which will depend on their expecting and getting more information).

Explanations based on the availability of information can also be too simplistic because *available* information depends on: (1) retrieval as well as availability; (2) whether it is seen as relevant or ignored; and (3) its apparent vividness (emotional interest, concreteness and imageability, temporal and spatial proximity/recency). As Bertrand Russell proposed in 1927, 'popular induction depends on the emotional interest of the instances, not upon their number'.

Characteristics of problems such as complexity, linguistic factors, perceptual salience, and the presence of competing features all seem able to trigger Evans' (1989) selective processing mechanisms. For example, people may have difficulty with the *syntax* of conditional probability statements so that performance depends on the details of the wording (see Chapter 4). A second possible source of error is interference from *causal reasoning*, especially since statements about both conditional probability and causality employ key words like 'if' or 'given that'. Errors may also occur because of the belief that causal relationships should be stronger than diagnostic ones [i.e. P(effect|cause) > P(cause|effect), which is not necessarily true, e.g. bacteria and disease].

Assessments of understanding which rule out causal reasoning on the basis that the questions are supposed to preclude it are not necessarily convincing. People tend to assume that causality, about which they feel that they ought to know, must exist, simply because the questions are asked at all. Pollatsek *et al.* (1987) suggest that the factors that can interfere with subjects' basic ability to deal with conditionality

include the wording used to express attributes, the difficulty of making the necessary probability estimates on the basis of real-world knowledge, and perhaps confusion between the notions of 'independent events' and 'equally probable events'.

Pollatsek *et al.* (1987) go on to consider the role of the word 'if' in actually influencing subjects to interpret probability questions as *requiring* a judgement about causality:

Difficulties with conditional probabilities are often due to translation errors . . . we should be cautious about making strong conclusions about flaws in reasoning or underlying concepts until we have determined how sensitive patterns of errors are to details of the wording . . .

A major translation error may be a confusion between P(A|B) and P(A and B) . . . Instead of separate, differentiated concepts of joint and conditional probability, some subjects may have available a concept that is some amalgam of the two.

Shaughnessy (1992) criticises the forced-choice methodology of Kahneman *et al.* (1982), and Pollatsek *et al.* (1987), preferring Konold's (1989b) clinical methodology for investigating students' cognitive and affective processes. He also feels that the questions used are generally too context-specific, making it impossible to deduce what thoughts are *really* going on in the subject's processing. Shaughnessy also claims that, in this type of research, merely reporting the percentages of subjects giving particular responses does not give enough information.

He proposes that subjects should be asked to give ranges, creating a greater impression of repeatability, rather than single values, when they are being tested for their understanding of probability or of sample statistics. This raises an interesting point concerning what might be the influence of *experience* on subjective estimates of probability, which by analogy may be thought of as equivalent to increasing the sample size in statistical estimation. This latter process has the effect of improving the precision of estimation (see Chapter 5) but not necessarily the 'accuracy' in the sense of 'correctness' if the method starts with an in-built bias. Since research suggests that subjective probability estimates often do have such an in-built bias, it would be interesting to find out in what ways their 'accuracy' and their 'precision' are affected by repeated opportunities to estimate probabilities.

The posing of questions which require more than the limited working memory capacity of the respondent has also been a problem area in research studies. When several inferences are required in sequence or at the same time, respondents may make errors even when they would have the competence to make correct inferences if the task requirements were kept within their working memory capacity. The taxi-cab problem, Exhibit 6.1, is a good example of an assessment item which overloads processing power or capacity.

Exhibit 6.1 **The taxi-cab problem** *(Tversky and Kahneman, 1982)*

A cab was involved in a hit-and-run accident at night. Two cab companies, the Green and the Blue, operate in the city. You are given the following data:

(a) 85% of the cabs in the city are Green and 15% are Blue.
(b) A witness identified the cab as Blue. The court tested the reliability of the witness under the same circumstances that existed on the night of the accident and concluded that the witness correctly identified each of the two colors 80% of the time and failed 20% of the time.

What is the probability that the cab involved in the accident was Blue rather than Green?

Tversky and Kahneman (1982) demonstrate that the hit-and-run cab is objectively more likely to be green than blue, despite the witness's report, because the base rate is more extreme than the witness is credible, concluding that because their respondents typically give estimates in the order of 0.8, which coincides with the witness's reliability, the respondents are ignoring the base rate information about the cab colours.

With problems of this complexity, however, it is not unreasonable to suppose that some subjects might recognise that 'they cannot "do" it' at a pre-processing level (see Evans, 1989), and re-route to 'gut' response, whether this is partly propped up with pseudo-normative strategies and heuristics or not. Ignoring the existence of such alternative explanations can mislead researchers, and assessors, as to the extent of a person's understanding.

RESEARCH ON GRAPHICAL METHODS AND PRESENTATION

In the early days of statistics, graphical methods played a prominent part in presenting data and exploring relationships. Later, the use of graphics declined, but the 'pendulum' has now swung back again, partly because of the move to 'look' at data before (or even instead of) using analytical techniques, as advocated by proponents of EDA. Useful histories and accounts of graphical methods in statistics are given by Fienberg (1979), Beniger and Robyn (1978) and Wainer and Thissen (1981).

As early as 1911 Karl Pearson proposed that a Professorship of Graphics should be established at University College London, arguing that 'the subject is quite big enough for this and there is plenty of work to be done in it' (letter dated 16 November 1911, quoted in Bibby, 1986). Also convinced of the value of statistical graphics, a mistress at Roedean wrote in the following year:

Graphical illustration of statistics, . . . the ideas of variation, are all extraordinarily interesting to the average girl, simply because she thinks them practical and useful for the affairs of everyday life. (Ford, 1912)

It is perhaps interesting to muse on the influence of her context, namely a highly selective girls' school, on Ford's understanding of 'average'. We shall learn more about the perception of the mean in the next section.

There has in fact been some research into statistical graphics, tabular formats and the presentation of results. Chapman's (1986) recommendations on how to present data, in many ways similar to those proposed by Ehrenberg (1975, 1982), are based on research evidence which she summarises and references in her Appendix 3. One of her sources, Macdonald-Ross (1977a,b), reviews research on the perception of both pictorial and tabular methods, criticising some studies for having poor stimulus material or inadequate experimental designs. Conclusions are presented in the context of educational research, focusing on the implications for the production of instructional materials. Another of Chapman's sources, Wright (1977), also refers to research findings in discussing the presentation of information in publications. Wright's paper covers topics such as headings in text and the use of illustrations as well as the presentation of numerical information.

More recent research work is reported in a series of papers by Cleveland *et al.*, some of which is reviewed in Cleveland (1987). For example, in Cleveland and McGill (1986) the researchers defined different aspects of visual presentation, position along a common scale, position along identical but non-aligned scales, length, angle, slope and area, any of which might influence the perception of statistical graphs. They then carried out a psychophysical experiment in which each subject made a very large number of judgements between a standard and comparative stimuli, to investigate which aspects were most influential and in what ways, also comparing subgroups of subjects who were assumed to have different levels of statistical experience or competence. They may be criticised for the artificiality of the presentation stimuli. However, their study constitutes a rare example of the use of an *efficient* experimental desion (in the sense that writers such as Cox (1958), Cochran and Cox (1957), or John and Quenouille (1977) would use the term), controlling the design of presentation material and the presentation schedules. Thus their study would be more the sort that might take place in an experimental psychology laboratory than in a classroom, but nevertheless its results could have relevance for education and for the development of graphical techniques.

Much of the published research uses adult subjects, but Wainer (1980) describes an experiment, with 360 children in grades three, four and five, which was concerned with the ability to extract information from bar charts and similar displays. This research was more about stages of a student's development than about how effective are different forms of display.

Pereira-Mendoza and Mellor (1991) also have researched children's understanding of the information conveyed by bar graphs, working with a sample of 121 grade-four and 127 grade-six students. Each student was administered a written test consisting of four bar graphs with three questions per graph. On the basis of their written responses, 35 students from grade four and 37 students from grade six were given audio-taped interviews to obtain additional information. The students' major errors were discussed in terms of the frame theory model developed by Davis (1984). This model defines a *frame* as a knowledge representation structure stored in memory. In processing information people are thought to select a cue from the information which results in the selection of a frame from memory. Data from the frame is then mapped to the variables in the frame, and the 'instantiated' frame is then used as a database for decision making.

Pereira-Mendoza is of the opinion that in graphical perception there is a fundamental flaw in the frame, namely that part of a student's graph frame is that patterns *must* exist in graphical data. This flaw could result from the general stress placed on patterns in teaching *all* aspects of mathematics, as well as from specific experience with graphs (which always do have patterns! or at least do in the teaching context or when encountered in media examples). Overall, Pereira-Mendoza and Mellor's (1991) findings were that students at both grade levels had little difficulty reading bar graphs, more difficulty interpreting them, and had major problems knowing when prediction from bar graphs was possible. The frequency of reading-language, computation, and particularly scale errors was higher at the grade-four level than at the grade-six level. However, errors involving pattern arrangements of the data occurred in similar frequencies for both grades and it was concluded that both grade-four and grade-six students have similar but flawed graph frames.

Abele (1983) discussed the usefulness of getting children to use their own forms of graphical presentation before teaching them the more conventional formats. This may also be a useful way of externalising children's ideas about data, so providing more relevant starting points for teaching statistics. The Comprehensive School Mathematics Program, a CEMREL[3] project, included the use of some innovatory graphical methods, in particular the 'profit-o-meter' in *Shunda's News Stand* (Papy, 1978) which allowed the concept of expected outcome, traditionally considered to be too difficult for young children, to be developed well in advance of the acquisition of the relevant formal statistical techniques. Materials from the Schools Council Project on Statistical Education (Holmes, 1991) also contain some excellent empirical approaches to statistical concepts, supported by a range of visual representation techniques: for example, the representation of probability and expected outcome by simple area comparisons, and the use of the Stirling Recording Sheet (Giles, 1979) for exploring relative frequency of occurrence in biased and unbiased experiments.

Among the newer methods of graphical representation are Andrews plots (Andrews, 1972) and Chernoff faces (Chernoff, 1973), both of which are methods for displaying multi-variate data. The former uses a trigonometric function:

$$f_x(t) = x_1/\sqrt{2} + x_2 \sin t + x_3 \cos t + x_4 \sin 2t + x_5 \cos 2t + \ldots$$

plotted over the range $-\pi \leq t \leq \pi$ to represent each p-dimensional point $X = (x_1, x_2, \ldots, x_p)$. The Chernoff faces, on the other hand, rely on different facial features to represent different values of variables, e.g. upper hair, eye slant, face size. Although people are used to comparing facial expressions it is not clear to what extent they can appreciate and interpret multi-variate data displayed as faces. The Andrews approach relies on perception of line, clustering and density which may or may not be easier for people to appreciate.

Interesting though such approaches are, and undoubtedly offering some promise as teaching aids, there still remains a dearth of research into the relevant pedagogy, let alone into the robustness of such graphical innovations as statistical presentation methods, notwithstanding the fact that 'innovations' dating from the 1970s cannot really be termed 'innovatory'.

The present writers would agree with Fienberg (1979) that:

Before we can arrive at a theory for statistical graphs, we need more attempts at synthesis; but before we can expect effective synthesis, we need considerable experimentation. For a profession that gave rise to the design and analysis of experiments, we have done surprisingly little to foster careful, controlled experimentation with graphical forms to aid us in arriving at an informed judgement on what constitutes good graphical presentation.

However, the solution to the problem is not as simple as Fienberg seems to be suggesting. As Cleveland (1987) points out:

Inventing a graphical method is easy. Inventing one that works is difficult. Figuring out if a particular invention works is more difficult. Evaluation of graphical methods is difficult because, unlike numerical statistical procedures, there is no well-developed theory that gives us criteria for evaluation.

Cleveland's proposed solution is field-testing, that is, using the method to analyse a large number of data sets, and comparing the insights gained by subjects who are confronted with the data presented in the new format with those gained by subjects when the data are presented in other formats. This view of validating a form of data presentation reflects Tukey's (1982) thoughts on the subject. It does not, however, provide would-be researchers with clear guidelines on how to design appropriate research studies.

THE CONCEPT OF THE MEAN

There have been some interesting studies of understanding of the mean, and Mitchem's (1989) paper on paradoxes in averages may provoke some further thoughts on possible research priorities.

Mevarech (1983) reports on two experiments. The first, based on an analysis of the test responses of 103 non-mathematical college students, was designed to identify their misconceptions. Exposure to a further statistics course did not seem to be sufficient to overcome these students' errors, and so a second experiment was conducted to investigate the use of a learning strategy aimed at overcoming the misconceptions found in the first experiment. The subjects were 139 education freshmen, assigned randomly to an experimental and a control group. The 64 students in the control group received conventional instruction via lectures and discussion, while those in the experimental group received feedback and 'corrective activities'. These consisted of statistical problems plus solutions (some incorrect) in which the students had to identify the errors (misconceptions) and suggest how to correct them. By this means their own misconceptions were highlighted. They were then asked to solve problems designed to help them to overcome their misconceptions. At the end of the courses students who were exposed to this diagnostic procedure were found to achieve significantly higher scores than those in the control group.

Experiments done with children in Israel by Strauss and Bichler (1988) were repeated, with modifications, by Leon and Zawojewski (1991) in the USA. Seven properties of the mean were identified, and children's understanding of these was specifically investigated:

- The average is located between the extreme values.
- The sum of the deviations is zero.
- The average is influenced by values other than the average.
- The average does not necessarily equal one of the values that was summed.
- The average can be a fraction with no counterpart in reality.
- The average value is representative of the values that were averaged.
- When one calculates the average, a value of zero, if it appears, must be taken into account.

Whereas in the original study the investigation was by in-depth interviews with children aged 8 to 14, Leon and Zawojewski developed items that could be administered via pencil and paper to slightly older age-groups (grade four, grade eight, and college students). Many of the questions were presented as stories and no technical knowledge was required to answer them. For example, for the property 'The sum of the deviations is zero', the test item was:

Everyone brought cookies to the class party. So everyone would have the same number of cookies, some children gave away cookies and some children received cookies. The total number of cookies given away was more than the total number of cookies received. Could this be? Yes–No. (Leon and Zawojewski, 1991)

In some cases, however, Leon and Zawojewski reported experiencing great difficulty in devising appropriate anecdotal wording for their test items. Some questions therefore involved numbers with no attempt to put the problem in a realistic setting.

Unlike the original research, Leon and Zawojewski's study did not use concrete objects such as pieces of Lego in any of the presentations.

There is still much scope for research into the concept of the mean, but perhaps more pressing is the need to investigate how to research such a concept. The comparison of Strauss and Bichler's (1988) study with that of Leon and Zawojewski (1991), as well as with all the other empirical approaches, is beginning to provide a framework within which to advance our research-based knowledge.

As has been said, in order to find out what thought processes are taking place, it is necessary to externalise them. Harterink (1987) used psychophysical methodology to expose her students' ideas of 'average'. Her study provides an interesting insight into the different kinds of concepts held by her students, as well as a good discussion about the methodology of investigating 'average', including the choice of range and distribution characteristics of the data to be 'averaged', the manner in which data to be averaged are presented, for example in an array or sequentially, etc. Her experimental methods may usefully be compared and contrasted with those of researchers such as Hendrick and Constanini (1970) and Anderson (1964).

In more of a Piagetian style, Goodchild (1988) carried out in-depth interviews with students aged 13 and 14 years, asking them to work out, and explain, their estimates of 'average' in a variety of different contexts, including the average contents of a box of matches as distinct from a packet of crisps. He identified three types of meaning for the arithmetic average: measure of location, representative number, and expected value. His students seemed to experience more difficulties with these last two aspects than they did with the average as a measure of location. Goodchild encountered some problems in maintaining a standard approach to interviewing his students, despite having a schedule of questions as his starting point. Of course, one of the advantages of such case-study approaches is the possibility they afford for obtaining more detail, but as in all research designs, a price must be paid for the advantages gained.

As described earlier, Pollatsek *et al.* (1981) asked their subjects (17 volunteers) to think out loud and also interviewed them to try to find out about their reasoning processes while they solved statistical problems involving the arithmetic mean. Pollatsek *et al.* inferred that the arithmetic mean was generally understood and used in a *simplistic* way which did not always accord with the complex requirements of the data, such as the need to consider weightings for subgroups. They concluded that students' concept of the mean was usually impoverished and limited to knowledge of a formula rather than of its representational functions.

These interview and 'thinking aloud' techniques can be useful for revealing misunderstanding, and thereby lead the way to pedagogical improvements. The study reported in Hardiman *et al.* (1984), however, is a step forward in the sense that it addresses the pedagogical process more directly. In their study they found that students given training in the use of a balance beam could transfer this knowledge to weighted means problems *provided that they recognised its relevance*. In fact, the balance beam analogy presented as a teaching aid in some texts is not well understood, and may even lead to incorrect reasoning as regards arithmetic means. Perhaps the most important conclusion that Hardiman *et al.* present is the fact that educators should be wary of using models or analogies, the implications of which are not completely familiar to the students. Yet ironically this may seem so obvious that it should not need researching!

PERCEPTION OF CORRELATION

There are a number of empirical studies dealing with the counter-intuitive aspects of correlation and its interpretation. These generally involve manipulations of the amount of causal evidence or belief available to the person evaluating the degree of relationship. With a view to evaluating the research methodology as much as the particular substantive findings, examples of relevant studies in this area may be found in Part 5, 'Covariation and Control', (Kahneman *et al.*, 1982), and Cleveland (1987) provides a bibliography which includes some studies on the perception of correlation.

One interesting example is to be found in the paper by Jennings *et al.* (1982) in which a series of experiments is described on the perception of correlation and association between variables. The researchers' concern was with the way in which preconceptions influence the perception of associations in contingency tables and bivariate tables and scattergrams. They found that discrepancies between subjective impressions and calculated coefficients can occur for a variety of theory- and data-based reasons. For example, belief that a causation exists between two variables can lead to the over-estimation of their correlation, and vice versa where people do not believe that causation is present. The relationship between data-based and theory-based judgements was explored empirically and the conclusion drawn that people need theories to guide them or they are unlikely even to detect covariations that are not close to unity. Certainly, it appeared that if there was such a thing as a subjective scale related to the perceived sizes of correlations, then it was far from being a linear one.

In general, Well *et al.* (1988) feel that people seem to be better at using perceived relationships to predict the degree of correlation than they are at providing numerical judgements. This has important implications for the design and interpretation of research studies, because expecting subjects to give conventional numerical correlation coefficient types of response (i.e. between 0 and 1, positive or negative) may be neither a reliable nor a valid research strategy. In some of the work reported by Jennings *et al.* (1982) an alternative method was tried, whereby their subjects used a rating scale to describe their subjective impression of the direction and strength of relationships between pairs of variables.

Cleveland *et al.* (1982) describe a study in which subjects made judgements based on their perceptions of the degree of association between two sets of values plotted on scatterplots. The researchers concluded that increasing the scale of a scatterplot resulted in people perceiving higher degrees of association for the same data set. In the light of what Jennings *et al.* (1982) found, such studies of covariation must be made in somewhat abstract terms, or within carefully controlled contexts, if the theory-based biases are not to interfere with the current objective of the research. Such studies may therefore attract similar criticisms about their artificiality, and about the experimental tasks being removed from reality, as those levelled at the even more extreme example of controlled experimentation reported by Cleveland and McGill (1986). Such criticisms, although to some extent factually justified, should not lead to the research paradigm being abandoned. Rather, the results should be critically evaluated in the light of findings from other studies, and vice versa, whether these employ essentially educational or psychological research methodologies. As we indicated in Chapter 3, we are somewhat perturbed by the general rejection of the *experimental* approach to aspects of statistical education.

Strahan and Hansen (1978) explored the tendency to underestimate correlations from 13 bivariate normal scatterplots of 200 points each. This last type of research, which on the face of it seems quite straightforward, has already been shown to be prey to problems of variable labels and to scale differences. Furthermore, one might conjecture that number and configuration of points, etc., would be a further source of confounding, making such research far more difficult to design and control than at first was thought. Above all, there will be individual differences between subjects in the kind of strategies they bring to the task which, so far, have largely eluded, or been avoided by, the researchers.

Kunda and Nisbett (1986) studied lay persons' ability to assess everyday life correlations. One of their concerns was with the *aggregation principle*, a derivation of the Law of Large Numbers, which suggests that the perceived magnitude of a correlation increases with the number of units on which observations are based. Item–item correlations – for example, degree of agreement between two students – are at a low level of aggregation while total–total correlations – for example, degree of agreement between two student classes – are at a high level of aggregation. By using the relationship between the coefficients of correlation known as Kendall's *tau* and Spearman's *rho* it was possible to ask subjects questions according to the format 'Suppose X thought that A was greater than B. What do you suppose is the probability that Y would also think that A was greater than B?' and report results in terms of perceived correlations.

In one study, students were asked to estimate the likelihood that they would agree with a particular student on the ranking of two courses (based on course ratings) or the likelihood that the rankings of two courses in one year would agree with their previous year's rankings. In another study, students were asked similar questions about ratings of personal characteristics of members of a group to which they belonged. Kunda and Nisbett found substantial accuracy in correlation estimates *if subjects were very familiar with the data* involved and if such data could be scored by the subjects, but inaccuracy otherwise. They found only limited appreciation of the aggregation principle.

Although an interesting study, it is still perhaps as far removed from reality as some of the other studies on correlation, in spite of its commendable attempt to use real-life situations. Its findings are therefore possibly of more use to the psychometrician than they are to the teacher of statistics. Indeed, it is this kind of division – between findings that have some relevance to statistical education and those that have direct applicability to classroom practice – which remains a problem in many areas of research.

NOTES

1. Published by the Centre for Statistical Education, Department of Probability and Statistics, University of Sheffield, Sheffield, S3 7RH
2. Publication details available from the Centre for Statistical Education, University of Sheffield, Sheffield S3 7RH.
3. CEMREL-CSMP, 3120 59th Street, St Louis, Missouri 63139, USA.

CHAPTER 7

Statistics practicals and projects

DOING STATISTICS

If students are to learn to do statistics, then they need to learn to do 'real' statistics. Firstly, we want to make it clear that doing 'real' statistics is not represented by the sort of 'Have data, will analyse' approach common among students in the late 1970s and early 1980s, and outlined in Figure 7.1.

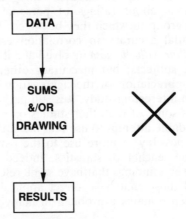

Figure 7.1 **How not to do statistics**

In contrast, Figure 7.2 shows more closely what is entailed in doing 'real' statistics. Students must be taught, and be given the opportunity to learn, how to digress from the unthinking 'straight down the middle' route, and how to embark on the highly iterative subroutes, some of which are suggested in the diagram. Figure 7.2 may give the impression that, iterations apart, the process is fairly clear-cut and organised. In reality, much of the background thinking done by the students is more characteristically of the *'fumbling in the dark'* kind, often with too many possible ideas circulating, and students may have great difficulty homing in on definite strategies.

There is no one 'right' answer, and it takes a great deal of experience to acquire the speed of attack which Braithwaite (1976) sees as the hallmark of the good statistician, whereby an incisive approach can quickly be brought to bear on a problem, whatever its context, generating hypotheses, asking useful questions about the context, eliminating unreasonable proposals, determining preferences between alternatives, and finally selecting one and operationalising it. Braithwaite would not see such skills as necessarily correlating with mathematical ability, and the present authors would be firmly of the opinion that they are skills which, to some extent, need to be taught.

The following three activities must feature in students' statistical education. None can really be properly executed unless the student knows how to take account of the special circumstances and context in which the activity takes place. Hence there must be adequate practical experience of how to carry out the following tasks *within applied contexts*:

1. *Represent, or model, data* (whether with a table, a diagram, a derived statistic, a regression model, etc.).
2. Look for *differences between* (groups of) observations.
3. Look for *relationships, or similarities, between* (groups of) observations.

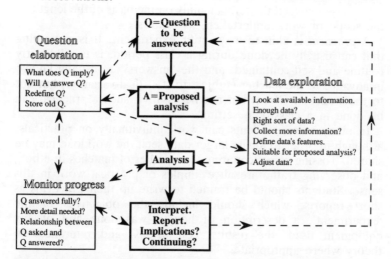

Figure 7.2 **Doing 'real' statistics involves iteration upon iteration**

DIFFERENT KINDS OF PRACTICAL WORK

Gilchrist (1980, see also 1982) identified a number of different ways of distinguishing between the types of practical activities that have a place in the teaching of statistics.

- Simple experiments, for example coin-tossing and dice throwing. (In fact, he finds 'success' and 'failure' cards more flexible because the probabilities of 'success' can more easily be changed.)
- Practicals that can be *passive* – i.e. classroom demonstrations. Practicals that can be *active* – i.e. hands-on experience for students.
- Practicals that can be *closed* – i.e. the 'one right answer' type of investigation. Practicals that can be *open* – i.e. where the answer is not pre-defined.
- Tutorial practicals, which expand the material that has been taught by other means, often being used to give computation practice, and *practical* practicals, in which the student imitates the statistician. It is this last type that we might call a *project*.

There is often confusion over the terms *practical work* and *projects*. Although the majority of projects would include some practical work (that is, some 'doing' of statistics), many projects also involve some theoretical work. A practical session as such would not usually constitute a project, although its purpose may well be to illustrate a piece of theory. We would tend to distinguish between the terms mainly on the basis of the length or the scope of work undertaken, as follows.

A *practical* is akin to a scientific experiment. It is something that can usually be done during a class period, is usually fairly routine and self-contained, and the 'answers' are usually known in advance to the teacher (subject to statistical variation) but not to the students. Often, but not necessarily, such a practical can be done in a classroom setting.

In many cases, students can work individually on practicals, although in order to amass larger data sets, the workload may be shared. Tossing coins, counting the number of matches in a box, and observing traffic are all examples of practical work in this sense. Students should be trained to write up their practicals as short reports, which should include the objectives of the 'experiment', a description of how it was done and of any equipment used, the results, conclusions, and references to theory where appropriate.

Sometimes it will make sense to organise a series of linked practicals over a period of two to three weeks. This would permit a progression in the level of abstraction in the concepts encountered, for example, starting with real-world observations yielding distributed data, followed by practical coin or dice simulations of the real-world distribution, and finally possibly encountering the same concept in a computer-modelling context. Even if such a series of linked practicals is not used, good practical work, carefully scheduled, can help the student to understand concepts and can provide appropriate bases from which students can move confidently to larger, more complex, investigations.

Although we would not necessarily agree with Reynolds and Walkey's (1990) proposals for a practical examination which would, we feel, suffer from all the faults generally inherent in timed examinations (see Chapter 10), the specimen paper that they give is not out of line with the description of a practical given here. The suggestions by Davies, H. (1970) and Jowett and Davies (1960) are also written with the timed practical in mind, and offer a great deal of helpful advice on what types of practical lend themselves to such an assessment or teaching approach, even to the extent of discussing the effect the time of year has on the availability of possible experimental materials such as leaves, peas in pods, etc.

A *project*, on the other hand, is usually understood to be a piece of work of an investigative nature, done over a period of several weeks, where even the teacher does not always know exactly what the findings will be. Several students might work simultaneously on the same project, either independently or as a group, but with the minimum of direction from the teacher whose role is mainly to give advice and encouragement. Important elements of a statistics project are designing the study, collecting and analysing the data, interpreting the results, and presenting a report. A project might also involve some background research of existing literature or data sources, and incorporation of the information thus obtained.

The analysis stage could require the application of known techniques in new situations, or the application of new techniques in familiar situations, and would possibly involve the use of a computer. It is in this part of the project that students learn about the use of statistical models to describe the real world and about the choice of appropriate techniques. It is here that they have the opportunity to demonstrate their understanding of statistics as a whole as opposed merely to showing that they can apply one of a range of techniques in isolation. A project should give students the training, ability, motivation and confidence to tackle statistical problems outside the school environment, which will help them later in the world of employment.

ADVANTAGES AND DISADVANTAGES OF PRACTICAL WORK

It may be argued that, without practical experience, students will fail to grasp the essential nature of statistics. This begs the question of whether doing statistics *necessarily* endows students with practical skills. However, when statistics is taught in an applied way, students are likely to be able to see the relevance of statistics over and above its being merely a branch of mathematics. There may also be motivational gains, especially when the students choose their own areas of research. Furthermore, students should learn more about the accuracy, variability and reliability of data when they have had close involvement in the design and data-collection stages, and when they encounter issues of measurability at first hand.

As a counter to these perceived advantages, the following drawbacks of teaching statistics through practical projects should be borne in mind:

1. They focus on research-oriented procedures rather than dealing with day-to-day teaching of concepts.
2. They tend to teach global procedures (and/or statistical 'half-stories').
3. They can be very demanding for the teacher, especially if individual students engage in different individual projects on subjects of their own choosing.
4. Unless the need for particular concepts arises in the chosen contexts, these must be taught by some alternative means.

The Schools Council Project on Statistical Education, known as POSE (Holmes, *et al.*, 1981; Holmes, 1991) attempted to overcome such difficulties by starting with carefully selected themes from a range of application areas, within which the relevant concepts and techniques could be developed in a practical way. Part of the POSE philosophy is that a full theoretical justification of all the topics is neither necessary nor desirable. Also, techniques might not necessarily be completely developed until students have had several encounters with them.

The materials produced by the POSE project provide a full statistics curriculum for students aged 11–16 years old, and demonstrate that there are many different sorts of practicals available to teachers of statistics, striking a good balance between, and progression through, traditional classroom experiments (dice throwing, coin tossing, and the like) and more lengthy projects. Braithwaite (1976) cautioned against the trend away from traditional classroom experiments if it meant 'throwing the baby out with the bath-water'. As he rightly points out, the real failure of dice throwing, etc., is that often the teacher is left unable to relate the results of such experiments to the overall schemata of statistics. The argument against class experiments based on the fact that they can become 'unmanageable' is not a sufficient reason for replacing them with projects, for obviously these too can become unmanageable. What is required is the development of a good way of linking the purpose of such experiments to real-life problem solving. This is something which we believe the Schools Council Project materials (Holmes *et al.*, 1981; Holmes, 1991) do very well.

The following list of skills represents a series of objectives for a statistics curriculum, as well as indicating the interdependence of *theoretical* (at least in the sense of underlying principles, but not necessarily of mathematical axioms) and *practical* understanding:

1. Problem identification, and an awareness of its relationship to other studies, whether or not in the immediate area.
2. Consultation.
3. Designing and conducting experiments, surveys and simulations, and being aware that estimators and test statistics are also *designed*.
4. Coping with small and large data collections, not just the pre-digested 'practical'-sized data sets usually found in textbooks and examination papers.
5. Using and evaluating published data.
6. Analysing data, including data verification, oriented nowadays towards the use and evaluation of computer resources.
7. Questioning the validity of research assumptions.
8. Carrying out routine, repetitive analyses, for example in quality control, and being aware that statistical methods applied in an unfamiliar context are different from those used once some preliminary model has been established. For example, initially a regression model might be established on the basis of a few observations made at equal intervals within the independent variable's range. Thereafter, more precise estimates can be obtained by concentrating observations at chosen extremes of the independent variable.
9. Modelling.
10. Interpreting and communicating findings.

SIMULATIONS

Harterink (1987b) found much of the literature on statistical education of the late 1970s and early 1980s to be 'of the "we-must-do-more-practical-work" type, rather than addressing itself to the quality of work that is done'. Starting from the premise that practical work would be done, she was more concerned with finding better ways of incorporating it into teaching programmes. She made the important point that 'a class*room* practical is not the same as a class practical' [the former being restricted by the school or college environment] and therefore looked at ways of 'bringing the practical into the classroom', thus expanding the classroom's and the students' horizons. (See the appendix at the end of this chapter.)

One way of bringing the practical into the classroom is by using simulations. These will vary in their level of abstraction and Harterink would presumably be particularly interested in those which model reality, rather than merely modelling abstract statistical concepts. As Ahlgren (1989) says 'urns and dice are not enough'. A good example of a simulation being used for a real-life purpose is that already mentioned in Chapter 1 in connection with the Schools Council Project on Statistical Education (Holmes *et al.*, 1981; Holmes, 1991) where in the unit entitled *Fair Play* students explore the concept of Expected Outcome of 'Shove ha'penny' or 'Roll a penny' games in both geometric and empirical ways, with the latter allowing for the additional study of the effects of other variables, such as practice, on performance.

Simulation can be used with students of different ages and at different stages of statistical knowledge. The methodology of simulation is very simple and its best use is in solving problems which are difficult to solve by other means. Thus it can be used on problems that have been solved, but where the analytical solution is beyond the students, as well as on problems where the analytical solution is unknown. It can be used as part of a teaching method. Engel *et al.*'s (1976) book has lots of examples of simulations and games, many of which can be used with very young children. Although written in French (and a 1972 version in German) teachers should not be discouraged. The explanations used are not difficult to translate.

Such examples are pre-designed to *use* simulations rather than to expect the student actively to engage in *producing* simulations. They therefore serve a different pedagogic role from that of the latter approach. As Reinhardt and Loftsgaarden (1979) state: 'One of the pedagogical values of simulation is that a student cannot simulate a problem which he doesn't understand.'

It is sometimes worth demonstrating to students that simulation 'works' by using it on problems where they can already follow the analytical solution. Probability problems are particularly suitable for this purpose (see Moore, 1985). However, as Reinhardt and Loftsgaarden (1979) suggest, teachers must expect the unexpected and prepare their students to do the same. After all, this is the nature of uncertainty which we wish to convey.

Experience with simulations . . . where one can compute exact results gives students much confidence in the method. Sometimes, in fact, they have too much confidence; they need to be urged to question the accuracy of their estimates. One way to promote this healthy scepticism is to have each student make a small number of simulations. The laws of chance practically guarantee that at least one student will have a 'bad' result. (Reinhardt and Loftsgaarden, 1979)

Sometimes things go wrong for other reasons, but this can be used to advantage too.

Often a student will get a misleading result because of an incorrect simulation. The instructor, knowing which results are misleading, can identify these incorrect methods. Such monitoring of results provides an excellent example of statistical inference. (Reinhardt and Loftsgaarden, 1979)

In the first instance, a manual, or concrete, stage of simulation should be used, possibly using dice. Such simulations can be undertaken by children of quite young ages. The slowness of such exercises can be a disadvantage, of course, and we would favour more use of experiments and games where the properties of, say, the dice-throwing outcomes are *used* to shed light on a real contextual situation, rather than merely to demonstrate something about dice throwing. In fact, one merit of the boredom which inevitably sets in during tedious dice-throwing interludes, although not a particularly laudable teaching objective, may be that it motivates students towards thinking about 'better' ways of generating the random elements, and provides them with an appreciation of random number tables (themselves often painfully tedious to use) and then of computer simulations. Such progression should not be made, however, without ensuring that the students have at least begun to grasp the real concept of randomness, and to appreciate that some random numbers are in fact only pseudo-random.

Although the evidence is mainly anecdotal, it is thought that proceeding too quickly to computer simulation may be a problem for students, who cannot then relate that level of abstraction to the reality it models. It is our personal experience that even mature students find the manual, concrete, stage illuminating (see, for example, Goodall and Jolliffe, 1988). It is also true that, in the case of some simulation software, the designers have been conscious of the need to incorporate training on how to use the computer. Such software, with its copious instructions on which keys to press in order to record choices, etc., merely serves to come between the student and the simulation.

One approach to teaching students how to *use* rather than merely to derive or demonstrate probabilistic models is being piloted by Simon and Oswald (1989). Based on the Monte Carlo methods advocated in Simon *et al.*'s earlier publications (1969, 1976), they have now developed a dedicated programming language, RESAMPLING STATS, to help students to see how coin, dice, playing card and computer simulations can be turned into powerful empirical tools for solving applied stochastic problems. It is clear that Simon *et al.* see the concrete stage as a crucial intermediary process. Working with students using this software, it has been interesting to observe that students seemed to find the material and the underlying simulation ideas more accessible than did their in-service mathematics teachers. For the latter, the difficulties of acquiring fluency with the language, and/ or with the use of the computer itself, are additional major stumbling blocks to the real process of statistical concept development.

The journals *Teaching Statistics*,[1] *Mathematics Teaching*[2] and *Mathematics in School*[3] sometimes carry short articles with suggestions of simulation exercises that can be done at a relatively early stage in a course or with young students. Selkirk (1983), for example, describes a simulation inspired by an account that Colorado beetles had been found in a cargo of potatoes imported into Gainsborough, Lincolnshire. The aim of the simulation is to investigate how the pest might have spread. It is particularly interesting because of its cross-curricular nature since both geographical and biological factors need to be taken into account. Other, less ambitious, suggestions are made in other parts of this article, and also in Selkirk (1973, 1974). Examples of slightly more challenging simulations which involve some mathematics may be found in Hinders (1981), Travers and Gray (1981) and Onions (1987). Computer simulation exercises based on the Central Limit Theorem are common. There is no shortage of software designed specifically for this purpose (see Chapter 9).

It would be wrong to leave this section without commenting on the fact that many published simulation exercises are related to the teaching of *probability* concepts, although they need not be used exclusively for this purpose. For example, Reinhardt and Loftsgaarden (1979) give examples of simulations at various levels of sophistication on some of the standard probability 'teasers'. As we have already indicated, we believe that where possible, the teaching of statistics and probability concepts can and should go hand in hand, and we are therefore inclined to be more excited by those developments that do this. However, it would be incorrect to give the impression that the alternative simulations are merely those that teach probability. There are in fact a number of examples of simulations which are designed to develop statistical ideas. Again, however, from our perspective as statisticians, it is easy to see the possibilities for using even these to teach *stochastics*.

It is also important to remind ourselves that not all simulations use coins, dice and the like, and their computer equivalents. Szmidt and Bissell (1977), for example, have included a desk-top factory simulation for the investigation of quality control concepts. See also Hawkins (1985) for an example of equipment for teaching concepts of statistical comparison and standardisation to a normal distribution.

SOURCES OF PUBLISHED DATA

It is important to teach students how to handle data, whether it be a raw data set or data that is already in summary form. Carefully constructed data sets in which there are no 'problems' and where answers come out exactly to, at most, two decimal places are useful as a teaching device to illustrate methods and for manual processing that will probably precede calculator and computer work. However, they will not particularly stimulate the students' or, for that matter, the teachers' interest.

Singer and Willett (1990) argue strongly in favour of using *real* data in teaching statistics. To be useful pedagogically they feel that such data should be authentic and should have accompanying background information on the research design, measurement techniques, definitions of variables and so on. Furthermore the data should have some substantive learning content, should (ideally) provide the opportunity for different types of analysis, and must be presented in raw form. It can be advantageous if the case identifiers permit the students to use their own background knowledge of the origin of the data in formulating appropriate analyses and interpreting particular features observed in the data. Realising that it can be difficult to find suitable data, Singer and Willett (1990) have compiled an annotated bibliography of published data sets.

Many US statistics texts now include real data sets of moderate size (about 200 observations and 15 to 20 variables). In some cases, data are published in diskette form, although not always in an appropriate format for the computer systems commonly found in schools in the UK. Often, the data have arisen from a small survey of college students, and they may not therefore be particularly suitable for school students. However, it is worth looking at such sources, if only to gain ideas for the possible construction of similar data sets. Although it refers to American undergraduates, the paper by Loyer (1987) is useful both for suggestions as to how to use class-generated data and also for the details that it gives on how to collect the data.

Demonstration data sets are often included with particular statistical analysis packages. For some time now, however, smaller data sets have been commercially available as separate items for use with UK school computers and certain of the more popular data-processing packages. These contain variables of interest on topics such as birds, countries of the world, meteorological data, early census data, and dietary analysis of foods. The marketing policy has so far tended to promote these as being of interest to primary level and 'user'-discipline teachers, rather than more generally in the areas of mathematics and statistics. This will presumably change as cross-curricular projects become the norm for secondary as well as for primary levels.

Each issue of the journal *Teaching Statistics* now contains a data bank feature which may be copied. Where, as in this case, the data are not already produced in disk format, a *text* scanner (now available as a hand-held OCR, Optical Character Reader, as distinct from a graphical scanner, for a relatively modest price) may seem to be an attractive proposition for capturing the data. However, scanners are not 100 per cent reliable in their interpretation of input data, and although errors of transcription in a prose passage may be relatively easy to spot, typographical errors in a list of numerical data are notoriously difficult to find.

Large sets of real (British) data are held by the ESRC (Economic and Social Research Council) Data Archive at the University of Essex. Many of these are beyond the reach of individual teachers, both from the financial and from the practical point of view. Some very useful data subsets based on the General Household Survey, the National Child Development Survey, and the British Election Studies, however, have been produced for use with higher education students. Although these have been prepared with specific analyses in mind, some secondary level teachers may find that the accompanying information is sufficient to enable them to adapt the materials for use with their students.

The attraction of such data subsets is that they have contextual relevance and give insights into the broader interpretation of the full data set. In addition, the information collected is of wider statistical interest, retaining some of the problems which occur in real data, e.g. missing values, and values out of range. They would perhaps be items which a resource centre in a local educational area might obtain. A number of other countries have similar data banks that can be accessed for educational purposes.

Many teachers will know about the BBC Domesday project

(see Chapter 9), and some will have been involved in surveys of land use, amenities, and so on, in areas local to their schools to provide input to the project. The data collection can briefly be described as an up-to-date version of the Domesday Book. It comes in the form of interactive video disks and includes ordnance survey maps, data, photographs, moving film and text. Clearly it contains a wealth of material suitable for studies across the curriculum, although it and its sequel, the Countryside disk, are expensive.

An interesting development in Canada is the exchange of data sets through a remote bulletin board system. This is known as the Nightingale Network and access to it is via microcomputers and modems. Schools can download datafiles only if they in turn contribute data to the bulletin board. The idea, which has proved to be very successful, is to form a collection of data sets found to appeal to students. The principle is that data collected by students, possibly about themselves, is likely to be of interest to other students.

A similar initiative in the UK, organised from the Centre for Educational Studies, King's College London, is called the National Environmental Database (NED). At present the system only serves BBC-B, BBC Master and Nimbus machines although there are plans to develop an Archimedes and IBM version. It is also restricted to the data-handling packages *Key* [4] and *Grass*.[5] Students perform common data-collection activities and feed the data into their own data-handling package in their local computer. NED software encodes the data into a common format which is then sent electronically to be stored within Campus (which used to be called The Times Network for Schools, TTNS) from where it can be downloaded and decoded by other schools, along with other national data files.

Published tables, such as those produced by the Central Statistical Office, are very useful as examples of data in summary form from which further information can be extracted. In fact, the first stage in a research study is often to do desk research, part of which involves looking at published sources of data. Published tables are also useful as a kind of benchmark against which one can compare the results of one's own study. In some cases figures relate to a population, e.g. the Population Census. In many cases they are derived from a sample. Topics are diverse and include demographic data, housing, health, education, employment, production, and incomes and expenditure. *Social Trends*, an annual HMSO[6] publication, contains statistics from many other HMSO publications and also some comments and articles. It is therefore useful as an introduction to the wealth of material that is available. Other useful, and regular, HMSO sources include the *Annual Abstract of Statistics*, *Key Data*, *The*

General Household Survey and *Regional Trends*. There are also 'specials' which HMSO publishes on an occasional basis. The annual publications clearly provide scope for comparisons over time and explorations of trends, with all that this implies about the need to consider whether the data have always been collected and recorded in the same way, whether or not definitions have changed over time, and so on.

HMSO publications relate to information collected by and for the government about us and the way we live. As such, they are of general interest. Other countries have government statistical services also, and it is possible to obtain similar publications for the purpose of drawing comparisons. An example of appropriate and interesting material on gender differences in Sweden, relative socio-economic status of men and women, and so on, is published in English in an inexpensive pamphlet form (Statistics Sweden, 1990).

Useful comparisons can be made between sets of local and national data, depending on the availability of information in appropriate formats. Sometimes the local data can be collected by the students themselves, thereby giving them experience of both primary and secondary data, but existing data sets like parish records can also be used. Such records of births and deaths over substantial periods of time provide interesting comparisons of trends in family life, or changes possibly associated with periods of local, national or international 'emergencies'.

Tables published in newspapers are probably worth collecting. The background information about the exact origin of such data is not always clear, however, and the data sets are not necessarily complete, possibly having political or journalistic biases. If so, this fact in itself provides an important debating point and a learning experience for the students, around which a course might be based. Definitions of the terms used are often not clear, and sometimes they do not correspond exactly with the user's needs, nor do they strictly correspond, for comparison or amalgamation purposes, with the classifications, collection methods, etc., of variables recorded in other related tables.

Tables relating to specialist interests, for example psychology, can be found in research journals pertaining to those subjects. A journal which concerns itself with perception or learning research will probably contain examples of relatively small-scale studies, often well enough described for the students to try a replication in the classroom, and with some of the data from the original study for comparison. Such research reports also provide useful material for training students in the critical evaluation of research, and can disabuse students of the assumption that just because a study has been published it is necessarily an example of good methodology.

USING PUBLISHED DATA

Often published figures have already been rounded, for example, to the nearest thousand, or to the nearest percentage, making it impossible to derive exact frequencies, and thereby limiting what can be done with the data second-hand. For example, suppose that the total frequency is 21,437 and 27 per cent are in a particular group. Although 27 per cent of 21,437 is 5787.99, we cannot assume from this that the number in the group is 5788. Here students could be introduced to the ideas of projection based on upper and lower limits. In other words, it is possible for them to make separate estimates at the extremities of the 'rounding' factor. It also obliges them to consider what is *likely*, and how useful their estimation is if it is not very precisely defined.

In the given example, the exact percentage in the group might be anything from 26.5 to 27.5, so that the range of possible frequencies is 5681 to 5895. If the total frequency is quoted to the nearest thousand, we are even less sure as to how many 27 per cent is. In some cases, of course, the difference in the results of such computations may not be particularly great. It is worth while spending time discussing this with students, and encouraging them to explore the notion that there may be circumstances when the use of *exact* frequencies is not worth the additional expenditure of research effort.

Groupings adopted in published tables can cause difficulties. It is by no means unusual to find open-ended groups, or differing class widths in the remaining groups. See, for example Exhibit 7.1 on length of residency, which is derived from the *General Household Survey 1980* (Office of Public Censuses and Surveys).

Exhibit 7.1 **Length of residency at current address (in years)**

Under 1
1–5
6–10
11–20
21 or more

Few school textbooks give full discussions of how to represent such distributions diagrammatically, or how to obtain summary measures from them. Sometimes the examination boards have (more or less) hidden conventions, but it must be said that these are *conventions* and students need to be aware that not all data summaries will have used the same conventions that they themselves have been taught.

Take, for example, a value of a continuous variable given as '5'. The exact meaning of such a measurement always needs careful consideration. It is commonly interpreted as '5 to the nearest integer', i.e. covering the range 4.5 to 5.4999, recurring. However, in real life, when measuring, for example, time in years, 5 years usually means '5 but under 6', i.e. covers the range from 5 to very nearly 6. Thus the class boundaries of the class 1–5 in Exhibit 7.1 are 1 and 6 and the class mark or mid-point is 3.5. The majority of texts ignore this contextual dependency when discussing class boundaries, as do examiners when setting questions where they expect students to follow *conventional* rather than *contextual* dictates.

Sometimes considerable time is needed to find out the meanings and significance of terms and variable labels used in tables. An example of this, which might be discussed in class, is how to count the number of rooms in a dwelling. The 1991 UK Census encountered some problems over this very question. Should kitchens and bathrooms be included? How should we count two rooms that have been knocked into one, or one which has been subdivided into two? Just as important, but often not easy to discover, is knowing how the data were obtained. How were the questions asked? Were the respondents aware of the definitions used, or the purpose of the survey? If the table is based on a sample, what was the sample design?

As well as being sources of data, government publications provide plenty of opportunities for teaching about the practical aspects of statistical research. For example, the questionnaires, sampling design, and other aspects of the *General Household Survey* (a large-scale continuing survey) are well documented. The collection of data needed to compile the *Index of Retail Prices* (the 'cost of living' index) can be used to illustrate many definition and measurement problems. How should a *typical* 'basket of goods' be defined? How is the price of bread obtained? This can lead into a small project to obtain a 'cost of living' index for the members of the class. Lay-persons' guides to the *Index of Retail Prices* and associated topics are occasionally published by HMSO in the *Department of Employment Gazette*. Further help and ideas may also be obtained from the book by Anderson (1989), and Vännman (1990) gives more suggestions about teaching centred on the presentation of 'cost of living' data in a Swedish newspaper.

Students should also be given the opportunity to experiment with the construction of tables and diagrams. This could possibly be based on published data sets, or selections from them. A useful project could be developed whereby the students use different ways of highlighting relevant comparisons and features of the data, for example different colours, emphases, fonts, horizontal/vertical presentations, and juxtaposition, etc. They can then explore experimentally the effect such changes have on people's perceptions of the tables or diagrams. (See Chapter 6 for further ideas on how to research into statistical graphics.)

PRELIMINARIES TO RESEARCH

Students should be made aware of the fact that their own work does not constitute the one and only study in the area; nor is it, or anyone else's work, usually the definitive study. Most research is part of the on-going process of learning more in that field of enquiry. As such, any particular study should take account of other researchers' methods and findings. A popular subject for students' projects entered for the Annual Applied Statistics Competition has been left- and right-handedness. Because it has also been a popular research topic in the field of psychology, the methods for investigating handedness have been refined. *Before* starting their own work, therefore, students should be encouraged to do some literature research to get ideas on the context of study, its terminology and the better methodologies that they themselves should adopt. It is not good enough merely to ask subjects whether they are left- or right-handed, for example. The research literature contains examples of behavioural observations which are more reliable indicators of the type of laterality of the person concerned, for example how people would fold their arms, or how they would hold a broom or a racquet, etc.

To look at other studies, however, students need to be helped to develop their skills of critical evaluation. In general, it is easy to find fault with even the best research studies. The statistics teacher should teach students that a superficial approach to criticism is not the end of the story. There are further points for the students to consider:

1. Do the methodological weaknesses invalidate the results and inferences, or will some or all of these still stand?
2. In what ways could the study's methodology have been improved, and how practical would these changes have been?

Students will undoubtedly find it easier to answer some of these questions if they have the opportunity of trying out a similar study, or of piloting some of their proposed modifications.

Of course, the importance of preliminary pilot work cannot be over-emphasised. In already over-crowded syllabuses, however, it is difficult to arrange for students to do both pilot and subsequent main studies. In a sense, all the studies that students carry out will tend to be 'pilot' studies. It is, however, important to convey the ideas about the continuing research process based on earlier findings, e.g. the influence of observed variability and presence of subgroupings on subsequent sample design, field-testing measurement and observation instruments, etc. Literature research can be an important way of developing understanding about such issues, and we would advocate that all students gain at least some limited experience of piloting questionnaire items prior to any survey that they conduct, as well as going on to plan a subsequent 'main' study which could be carried out based on the findings of one of their pieces of project work.

MANAGING STUDENTS' PROJECTS

With the introduction of the UK National Curriculum (Department of Education and Science, 1989a,b), coursework will now be formally assessed *from primary level upwards*. Furthermore, GCSE examinations, at the age of 16, have recently increased the weighting for coursework assessment (e.g. 20 per cent min., 50 per cent max. for mathematics). Experience with entries to the Annual UK Applied Statistics Competition suggests that many teachers and their students will find it difficult to cope with these changes. Certainly, relatively few teachers have had experience of conducting practical statistical projects themselves, let alone of supervising those of others.

Usually the syllabus suggests that some kind of (questionnaire) survey would be an appropriate project, thereby tending to convey the erroneous impression that statistics is only made up of social surveys. Faced with a class of thirty students, all of whom are to be individually assessed, a teacher may well resort to encouraging each of the students to adopt an apparently 'prescribed' project format, by providing all the technique teaching in a (theoretical) class lecture for the students to mimic in practice.

The result tends to be projects undertaken 'for the sake of doing projects'. A class of thirty students produces thirty project reports based on thirty essentially identical studies, with identical styles of questionnaire, the same sampling design (almost invariably accessibility, but sometimes thirty class censuses), finished off with the same (obligatory) pictures, tables, graphs, and computations of the same derived statistics. Only the specific topic differs from project to project, e.g. preferences for 'pop' records rather than for videos, etc. Discriminating between them is almost a case of deciding which student draws the prettier pie chart. (Hawkins, 1991a)

Since the objective is seen to be that of producing something tangible to be assessed, the data presentation and analysis stages come to be perceived as the most important stages of the process, rather than the reasoning behind them. Hawkins (1991a) cites the following example of the sort of mindless rote activity that may then result. A group of geography students, having been 'taught to take three measures of a river's depth 'in order to eliminate error', blindly follow this rule, apparently unaware that the arithmetic mean of measures such as 24 cm, 28 cm and 77 cm is *never* going to eliminate the obvious error of a ruler held upside down'.

Saving time can often be a major preoccupation for the teacher and one which arises whenever practical project work is considered. Collecting data of an experimental kind – say, for example, on reaction times – can pose some unexpected problems for teachers. In order to make the data collection relatively quick for the students, and yet to amass enough values for study, it is often the case that the students each collect a limited number of observations in different contexts, from an ill-controlled non-representative sample, and in ways which may differ (subtley) from those decided upon in the classroom. The data are then not suitable for amalgamation although this was the original intention.

Much careful thought needs to go into ways of overcoming this problem, and it should be shared with the students during the design stage of their project. It is, of course, analogous to the sort of arrangements that must be built into large-scale social survey work where many different interviewers may be respon-sible for obtaining responses to a schedule. Training those interviewers to ask only the questions provided, and only in the ways specified, is a major problem since it may run counter to human nature, it being difficult for people not to 'help' respondents to interpret the question as it was intended. Such issues are a legitimate part of an applied statistics course, and students should be given practical experience of trying to find solutions to the problems and of evaluating the effectiveness of these 'solutions'.

One way of saving time when dealing with questionnaire surveys is to eliminate the really lengthy process of actually obtaining most of the data. In other words, the students might go through the process of designing a questionnaire on a topic for which the teacher already has a supply of data. The students then pilot it in a limited way in order to gain some experience of the data-collection process, and of the usefulness of pilot studies. This may well be most successful if some poorly constructed questions can be left in so that the student can find out, at first hand, something about the ways in which things might go wrong.

After appropriate modification of the questionnaire has taken place, the teacher then provides students with the 'responses' to the final version from the already established database, and the students continue with the data exploration, analysis, inference and report stages. Ideally, of course, the data should be real, and, because they must be collected in advance, they need to be wide-ranging if the teacher is to avoid having to over-manipulate the students' questionnaire content. At its worst, this 'short-cut' method may be strictly analogous to cookery programmes on the television with the teacher announcing, 'Here is one [question-naire] "we" prepared earlier!' However, this apart, it can be a useful strategy for managing survey work while still having time to complete coverage of the syllabus.

In fact, a school might well develop an interesting cross-curricular database over a period of time. Each year, students could research a different aspect of their locality, collecting more information to contribute to the school database. In addition to their own practical research (which might then be on a quite modest scale), they can also spend time interrogating the database information collected in previous years by their predecessors. This has distinct advantages for the teacher. It can take a great deal of time to get to know the detailed characteristics of data. In successive years, however, the teacher's knowledge and understanding of the interesting aspects contained within the data set builds up. It also gradually becomes clear as to what would be important additions to the database, potentially fruitful areas of enquiry that would fill in missing information about the school's environment, and so on, extending the original limited objectives of the database.

Of course, a proper consideration of how to conduct *efficient* research is one way of 'saving time'. Students should be taught to put into practice what they learn about piloting research instruments, and how to design an efficient, representative sample of an appropriate size for a given level of precision, rather than letting them automatically conduct a census (or an unplanned accessibility sample). This will result in better research and a better understanding of research design and efficiency, together with less wasted time than when the students are collecting and analysing unnecessary masses of inappropriate or useless data. What students need is to experience a wide variety of research tasks, not merely to carry out many time-consuming repetitions of a small minority of them.

Just because it is 'only students' projects' that are being considered, it is wrong to fall into the trap of thinking that they are merely an exercise for the students to learn about how to do research, with its corollary that any topic will do, provided it interests the students to some degree and is manageable. It is perfectly possible for students to do good-quality research which produces worthwhile results of interest to other researchers in the field. This will not happen, however, unless the work is not only well conducted but also takes account of the current state of knowledge or tried and tested methodologies. If the findings are to be made available to a wider audience, then the students should also learn about and observe certain conventions concerning the style of report writing. In recent years the journal *Teaching Statistics* has provided an important opportunity for students to publish their own research, particularly in the regular Project Parade feature, which in turn acts as a stimulus to other teachers and students to raise the standards of the practical work they undertake.

Hawkins (1991a) describes two alternative approaches to project work which may convey more sense of purpose to the students. The first is to have all the students carry out a variety of investigations under one general 'umbrella' heading, for example 'Fashion'. Individual students could choose to investigate one of many different aspects: sales, marketing, clothes design, standardisation, production, attitudes and preferences, etc. Meanwhile many different statistical concepts and approaches to data gathering and processing will be encountered, both directly and through comparisons with other students' work. The teacher-centred approach gives way to a more student-centred one. It relies on the group collaborating to identify useful and interesting aspects to investigate, and to plan how to obtain information that can sensibly and fairly be pooled, compared or contrasted. Students are encouraged to describe what they are doing and why, to talk about its relationship to other students' investigations, and to contribute to debates about which approaches are better, which evidence is stronger, and what has been discovered overall.

Not only is the statistical teaching/learning process more efficient, but it may also give important vocational insights into the 'umbrella' subject itself. Furthermore, in describing and evaluating their investigations within the group, students exercise the important skills of statistical communication, providing more meaningful possibilities for *oral* assessment. In contrast, the more traditional approach whereby all the students do essentially the same projects tends merely to test the student's ability to give a résumé of the teacher's notes. Students' critical evaluation skills are not invited because the teacher's directives pre-empt them.

The second approach described in Hawkins (1991a) is that in which a team of students carry out a *single* project, dividing up the relevant research and statistical work between them, each taking responsibility for different aspects, be it data collection, analysis, art-work, typing, coordination, etc. Although not necessarily better than the 'umbrella' approach, it does reflect the style of much of the real-life statistical work, and in the Statistics Prize, which requires *group* work, it has generally produced more evidence of real teamwork and synthesis of effort.

If this last approach is adopted, the teacher must rely heavily on the opportunity to assess on-going oral contributions to see that no student's acquisition of statistical knowledge and skills is impoverished as a result, since not all students will have equivalent or direct experience of all the research processes. This second alternative approach is generally unacceptable to school level examiners, for whose benefit an individual's particular contribution must be identifiable and separately assessed. It is not certain that this should necessarily be so. Is it more important to assess the *doing*, or the *understanding*, of the research processes? If we assess only the doing, especially when the student is essentially following the teacher's instructions, we learn little about the student's understanding. It may be that students can gain, in ways which are just as important statistically, by taking part in, and contributing to, group project work, even though they do not directly execute each single statistical process themselves. See Chapter 10 for further discussion on the assessment of project work.

LEVELS OF SUPERVISION

The whole question of how much 'control' should be exercised by the teacher, and how free the students should be to carry out their own research projects, is a difficult one to resolve. There can be no doubt that research skills, in particular the skills of operationally defining an appropriate research strategy, can be very difficult for beginners. Also, it is not too infrequent for project 'mortality' to occur for a variety of (non-statistical) reasons. For example, one team of students entering the Annual UK Applied Statistics Competition submitted a part project, because their collaboration with a local firm terminated suddenly when the relevant employee, who was providing the data, resigned unexpectedly.

When left entirely to their own devices, students can often embark on projects that are either too ambitious, or trivial in the extreme. This is especially the case for students in the pre-GCSE age-group, whose youthful enthusiasm and wish for independence often wrongly convey the impression that they know what they are doing! Primary school children tend to be more used to project work than secondary school students at present, and as they also attract more teacher involvement students in this age-group do not pose such a problem. Post-GCSE students may also be more focused in their work, and their added maturity may make team cooperation more viable. Experience with the Annual Applied Statistics Competition suggests that it is students in the 13- to 16-year-old age-group who particularly need more guidance than might be expected. The emphasis is on 'guidance', however, rather than 'control', and it is a matter of professional judgement as to how this can be achieved. Possibly the difficulty will become less of a problem as project work becomes more the norm for this age-group.

Assuming that, for whatever reason, project 'mortality' does occur, the teacher needs to be ready to step in and salvage a useful learning experience for the students. This implies that there is a need for the teacher to keep at least a watching brief throughout all stages of all students' practical work, and to have a clearly defined knowledge of what statistical concepts and experiences should arise from any given piece of research. It is good practice to make the students give a succinct statement of their intentions and expected statistical methodology, etc., soon after they start planning. Thereafter, regular short reports from the students as the projects are progressing are a good way for different groups to learn from others' experiences, while the students consolidate their own ideas and practise their communication skills.

CROSS-CURRICULAR CONSIDERATIONS

Teachers are now under pressure to collaborate across the curriculum, partly for academic reasons, and partly to rationalise the otherwise burdensome coursework requirements in each separate subject area. Statistics, and more particularly data handling, can provide a bridge, enabling one project to serve several subject areas. Hawkins (1991a) describes an example of an attempt to initiate a cross-curriculum project involving science, English and mathematics, which went sadly wrong in statistical education terms.

Broadly speaking, the science teachers wanted the students to collect data relating to an ecological issue; the mathematics teachers wished to use it to teach data handling; and the English teachers wished to teach communication skills relating to technical report writing. The project proceeded to the general satisfaction of most of the teachers and students. Data were collected, analysed and talked and written about. However, the coordinator was aware of major problems which seemed to occur at the project-planning and data-collection stages, which were the responsibility of the scientists. Their priority seemed to have been to obtain data, surprisingly with no real consideration of sampling or controlled experimental design. The resultant data were therefore inappropriate for teaching the required statistical inference processes, even to the extent that one group had not even managed to collect data from both of the designated comparison areas. To that particular science teacher, it was more important that her students learned to collect data 'in a scientific way', which in fact turned out to mean using a particular measuring instrument, and for them to be taught to graph the data (by the mathematicians) than to see an investigational purpose to the exercise.

It would, of course, have been better to have the students plan the study, generating their own research questions and working out how to find answers and how to ensure that the answers they obtained would be reliable and helpful. This would also have given the English teachers the chance to develop the students' discussion skills. Furthermore, team teaching would have been a more satisfactory approach here because:

(a) *all areas* have important perspectives/contributions to make at *all stages* of the teaching/learning process; it is not particularly useful to say that the project is to be cross-curricular if it is still partitioned by discipline boundaries;

(b) such an approach provides an important in-service training function and yields real cross-curricular work, not merely one-off liaisons;

(c) it allows students to see statistics in action, as it often is in vocational settings, as a collaboration and interaction between specialists with different skills and perspectives working on a common task.

From the point of view of statistical education, however, it seems as if the teacher of each discipline must first find his or her own discipline's relationship to statistics before statistics can provide the anticipated common 'language' with other disciplines. This kind of cross-curriculum project is usually handled more effectively in primary schools, where the teachers already have an eclectic view of research activities, and where one teacher generally teaches a wide (possibly full) range of subjects to a class. At secondary level, however, teachers may be too over-specialised at present to give their students a taste of *real* cross-curricular work. Moreover, it is still unclear whether the designers of the National Curriculum really intended 'cross-curricular' work to be truly integrating, or merely a convenient means for separate disciplines to teach their usual substantive content and methods, while sharing a common theme with other disciplines.

OBJECTIVES FOR TEACHING PRACTICAL RESEARCH METHODS

Practical statistics teaching should start from the principle of finding out how to do *efficient* research. This is such a simple and yet flexible concept. Efficiency, being defined as the *most* or the *best output* for the *least* or for a *given amount of effort*, can be interpreted in so many different ways that the elements of choice and decision making are immediately introduced. For example, *most* may be measured in terms of many different quantitative and qualitative aspects of the information gained, while *amount of effort* may be evaluated in terms of cost, convenience or time, etc. In designing research, all such considerations must be carefully weighed and gains of one kind must be balanced against losses of another kind. This is usually an important new experience for students and their teachers, who are not used to being given such 'power'. As a theme for research, efficiency has an obvious appeal. It is hard to see how practical research can be efficient if the resulting message is wrong, so it fixes the most crucial research objective, that of finding the truth, from the very outset. Students are obliged to consider alternative strategies, however, and to find criteria, probably the more common-sense and intuitively based the better, for critically evaluating different ways of *investigating* and *describing* that *truth*. Such a guiding theme has utility for all ages and at all levels of statistical sophistication.

Research is still needed to discover what are the *necessary*, and *sufficient*, conditions for developing *(practical) statistical under-standing*. Statistics Prize entries certainly indicate large gaps in students' understanding which the present approaches to project work do not solve. Students do not acquire the ability to apply statistics merely by being told about how to do projects, nor apparently by doing practical work. Relevant *perceptual and cognitive skills* must first be *identified*, after which an appropriate pedagogy must be researched so that students can be *specifically trained* and *exercised* in these skills, and appropriately *assessed* in their execution of them.

APPENDIX: FURTHER SOURCES AND IDEAS FOR PRACTICALS[7]

Many practicals are duplicated within the following references. Where reasonable, the suggestions have been classified as PO (Problem-oriented practicals) and SO (Syllabus-oriented practicals). Other descriptive terminology is derived from Gilchrist's (1980) distinctions. Further discussion about practicals tending to be of an SO kind, derived from published software (simulations), may be found in Chapter 8 on statistical computing.

Anderson, C.W. and Loynes, R.M.L. (1987) *The Teaching of Practical Statistics*. Wiley. University level, but some useful ideas on general principles and scope for adapting examples to school level.

Andrews, D.F. and Herzberg, A.M. (1985) *Data: a collection of problems from many fields for the student and research worker*. Springer-Verlag, New York. 71 sets of raw data with the emphasis generally on the physical and natural sciences.

Carlson Roger (1973) Random digits and some of their uses. In Mosteller Frederick *et al.* (eds) *Statistics by Example – Weighing Chances*. Addison-Wesley. Uses coins to simulate a marksman. Directed (SO).

Centre for Statistical Education, University of Sheffield (1979) *Statistical Education and Training for 16–19 Year Olds*. Somewhat dated in its description of syllabuses, etc., but contains some useful suggestions for projects derived from an A-level syllabus (pp.164–5) and further ideas can be obtained from an examination of the range of 'user'-disciplines described in the report.

Centre for Statistical Education, University of Sheffield (1984). Useful booklets: *Games, Fair or Foul*, containing suggestions for simple probability games, the fairness of which students are encouraged to discuss before playing them; simulating tennis using a coin and tree diagrams; also *Larger or Smaller* and *Experiments in Probability*.

Centre for Statistical Education, University of Sheffield (1985) *Practical and Project Work in A-level Statistics*: pp.11–12 give suggestions for projects (PO); pp.16–20 give ideas for practicals, both closed and open, individual and class (PO and SO).

Centre for Statistical Education, University of Sheffield (1986) *Statistics Topics in the Classroom: Classroom Practicals*. General ideas for a variety of ages. All are open and active for small groups or classes (PO and SO) including: rolling marbles towards a matchbox target; measuring reaction times; simulating packaging and studying variability; estimating the (given) length of a strip of paper without a ruler; breath-holding experiment.

Centre for Statistical Education, University of Sheffield (1984, 1991) *Understanding Statistics*, originally marketed by BBC *Soft as Advanced Level Statistics*. Computer software that includes, for example, the basic ideas for a practical simulating queueing theory.

Continuing Mathematics Project; CET/Schools Council (1976) *Descriptive Statistics, 4. Some Experiments in Statistics*. Longman. Instructions for experiments such as dart throwing, investigating ESP, time perception. Active, for small groups. Could be a useful start for teachers who want to encourage the class to be less directed and to design their own investigations. Openness depends on the extent to which the teacher divulges the instructions to the students. (Mainly PO.)

Davidson, R. and Swift, J. (eds) (1988) *Proceedings of the Second International Conference on Teaching Statistics*. University of Victoria, Canada. Many ideas.

Davies, Hilda (1964) Practical experimentation in the teaching of basic statistics. *Mathematical Gazette* **48**: 271–80. Describes experiments suitable for illustrating various topics. Includes such details as how long it takes the instructor to prepare the material.

Davies, Hilda (1970) The role of practical experimentation in the teaching of probability and statistics. In Råde, L. (ed.) *The Teaching of Probability and Statistics*. Wiley, pp.69–77. One practical discussed in detail – copying lines of different lengths (PO or SO). Two appendices with further ideas.

Dear, Russell (1989) *Modelling Activities for the Classroom*. New Zealand Mathematics Association. Available from the Mathematics and Statistics Department at Massey University, Palmerston North, New Zealand. Contains a wide range of simulations, including those related to standard statistical models. It also includes a number of tests for randomness, other statistical experiments, and chapters on descriptive and exact modelling and modelling with recurrence relations. The level is pitched at final-year secondary to first-year tertiary.

Engel, A., Varga, T. and Walser, W. (1976) *Hasard ou Stratégie*. OCDL. Lots of ideas for games that can be used to teach or investigate students' probabilistic ideas and understanding. Although written in French (a German version also exists, *Zufall oder Strategie*, 1972), potential users should not be deterred. The explanations used are not difficult to translate.

Graham, Alan (1987) *Statistical Investigations in Secondary Schools*, with accompanying software. Cambridge University Press.

Graham, Alan (1990) *Investigating Statistics*. Hodder & Stoughton.

Grey, D.R. *et al.* (1983) *Proceedings of the First International Conference on Teaching Statistics*, ICOTS-1 (1982) Session 3, Workshop – *Ideas for Teaching Statistics to 16–18 year olds* – consisting of a variety of ideas from different contributors. Individual and class practicals (PO and SO). For example: height and handspan (males, females, and both together); pebble sampling, comparing estimating characteristics of different sampling strategies; searching the telephone directory for special sequences; guess the height of a student, knowing the mean of the parents' height; and Do you smoke pot? using the randomised response method.

Gubbins, S., Rhoades, D.A. and Vere-Jones, D. (1982) *Statistics at Work. A handbook of statistical studies for the use of teachers and students.* New Zealand Statistical Association. Eleven (real) case studies followed by suggestions of further similar exercises. Some ideas could be adapted for use in the UK.

Harrison, R.D. (1966) An activity approach to the teaching of statistics and probability. *Mathematics Teaching* **34**: 31–8, **35**: 52–61, **36**: 57–65. Some non-standard ideas, e.g. dropping grains of rice to generate normal and other distributions.

Harterink, Joy (1987) Classroom practicals in A-level statistics. Unpublished MSc report, available from the Regional Centre for Statistical Education, Institute of Education, University of London. Evaluation of classroom practicals such as: awareness of flavour differences in brands of crisps; subjective estimates of 'average'; quality control and the weights of commercially available chocolate bars; evidence of 'guessing' in a multiple choice test (use of binomial and normal approximations); relationship between length and breadth of leaves taken from different parts of a tree.

Hawkins, Anne (1985) Stretching the imagination. *Teaching Statistics* **7**(1): 6–11 (PO and SO).

Hawkins, Anne (1986) Practical sports judgments. *Teaching Statistics* **8**(1): 2–6 (PO).

Hawkins, Anne (1989) The Annual United Kingdom Statistics Prize. In Morris, Robert (ed.) *Studies in Mathematics Education*, Vol. 7, *Teaching Statistics in Schools*. UNESCO, chapter 17, pp.217–27. Contains outline of the range of topics and evaluations of many of the entries.

Hawkins, Anne (ed.) (1990) *Training Teachers to Teach Statistics. Proceedings of the International Statistical Institute's Roundtable Conference*, Budapest 1988, particularly the contributions on Exploratory Data Analysis in the classroom by A. Dunkels (1990) and K. Vännman (1990). See Bibliography.

Holmes, Peter (1991) *Statistics in Your World: Laying the foundation* and *Statistics in your world: Solving real problems.* Foulsham Press. New edition of the 1982 materials produced by the Schools Council Project on Statistical Education for 11–16 year olds. Based on practical project work throughout. (Mostly PO.)

Holmes, Peter, and Rouncefield, Mary (1990) *From Cooperation to Coordination*, particularly section 6, pp.75–94, where cross-curricular examples and fieldwork organisation are discussed. Centre for Statistical Education, University of Sheffield.

Holmes, Peter and Worsnop, Robert (1986) *Statistics Education Project, 16–19* (Leverhulme Project). Centre for Statistical Education, University of Sheffield. Complete booklets on single topics (PO): What goes fastest?; Canteen choice; Limb dominance; Learning new skills, etc. Uses practical work as a basis for part of a course. Students are taken through an analysis of given data and then encouraged to do the experiment and analyse their own data in a similar way. A lot of reading, directed, partly open. Some practicals could be done by individuals. Some need small groups.

Jowett, G.H. and Davies, Hilda M. (1960) Practical experimentation as a teaching method in statistics. *Journal of the Royal Statistical Society, Series A* **123**: 10–35. Suggestions for practical work in an introductory statistics course at Sheffield University. Some of the practicals need a fair amount of preparation by the teacher, but useful details are given, including notes on their appropriateness for examination purposes.

Malpas, A.J. (1969) *Experiments in Statistics*. Oliver & Boyd. Detailed instructions for many experiments (PO and SO), for small groups or classes, including: cards and drawing-pin experiments; Müller–Lyer illusion; comparing sentence lengths from two authors.

Mathematics Association (1975) *An Approach to A-level Probability and Statistics*. Suggestions for two probability experiments – using marbles and simulating a cigarette card problem using digits from a telephone directory. Closed. Individual rather than group (SO).

Mosteller, F., Kruskal, W.H., Link, R.F., Peiters, R.S. and Rising, G.R. (eds) (1973) *Statistics by example – Series*. Addison-Wesley: *Weighing Chances. Exploring Data. Detecting Patterns. Finding Models.*

Murdoch, J. and Barnes, J.A. (1974) *Basic Statistics*. Laboratory Instruction Manual. Macmillan Press Ltd. Detailed instructions for statistical experiments, many of which use special equipment (e.g. populations of rods). An artificial laboratory situation rather than an everyday practical (SO). Data often amalgamated from small groups. Emphasis on the way results are recorded. Closed.

Owen, D.B. and Mann, N.R. (ed.) *Popular Statistics Series*. Marcel Dekker, New York. Although not written as books on practical statistics, some ideas contained in the books in this series may be adapted.

1. Hooke, R. (1983) *How to Tell the Liars from the Statisticians*.
2. Katz, S. and Stroup, D.F. (1983) *Educated Guessing; How to cope in an uncertain world*.
3. Hollander, M. and Proschan, F. (eds) (1984) *The Statistical Exorcist; Dispelling Statistics Anxiety*.
4. Brook, R.J., Arnold, G.C., Hassard, T.H. and Pringle, R.M. (eds) (1986) *The Fascination of Statistics*.
5. Jaffe, A.J. and Spirer, H.F. (1987) *Misused Statistics: Straight Talk for Twisted Numbers*.

Rouncefield, Mary and Holmes, Peter (1989) *Practical Statistics*. Macmillan. Suitable for A- and AS-level students.

Russell, S.J. and Friel, S.N. (1989) Collecting and analysing real data in the elementary classroom. Ch.11 of the 1989 NCTM Yearbook, National Council of Teachers of Mathematics.

Simon, Julian (1989) *Resampling Stats – A wholly new way to do probability and statistics.* Practical problem solving using Monte Carlo methods and BOOTSTRAP computer language (PO).

Spicer, Douglas H. (1973) Organising and reading population data. In Mosteller, F. *et al* . (eds) *Statistics by Example – Exploring Data.* Addison-Wesley. Uses the class, their parents and siblings as a population to study. Could pose problems for students without a traditional two-parent family.

Szmidt, T. and Bissell, A.F. (eds) (1977) *Statistical Teaching Aids.* Institute of Statisticians. Many different examples of practicals and experiments for classes or small groups. Some complicated, others very simple. (Mostly SO; a few PO.) For example: using punch cards to generate a normal distribution; counting number of particular species of weed in an overgrown garden; quality control with an 'artificial' production line setting; variability of a piece of string of estimated length; myth of the 100 per cent inspection.

Tanur, J. *et al.* (eds) (1978) *Statistics: A Guide to the Unknown.* 2nd edition. Holden-Day.

Teaching Statistics. Contains many useful ideas, both SO and PO. *N.B.* This journal now has a regular 'Project Parade' feature for articles on real projects undertaken by students and written up by teachers and/or their students. It also publishes reports of the Annual UK Applied Statistics Competition entries with short evaluations. Publication details available from The Centre for Statistical Education, Department of Probability and Statistics, The University of Sheffield, Sheffield, S3 7RH.

Vere-Jones, David *et al.* (eds) (1991) (in print) *Proceedings of the Third International Conference on Teaching Statistics.* International Statistical Institute, Voorburg. Many ideas.

NOTES

1. Publication details available from The Centre for Statistical Education, Department of Probability and Statistics, University of Sheffield, Sheffield, S3 7RH.
2. Edited by Lawrinda and Tony Brown, 7 Shaftesbury St., Derby, OE3 8YB.
3. Publication details available from Education Department, City of Birmingham Polytechnic, Westbourne Road, Birmingham, B15 3TM.

4. Published by ITVA Ltd, 6 Paul Street, London EC2A 4JH.
5. Published by Newman College Computer Centre, Bartley Green, Birmingham B32 3NT.
6. Her Majesty's Stationery Office publishes materials produced by government departments such as those indicated above from the Central Statistical Office and the Office of Public Censuses and Surveys.
7. The authors would like to thank Joy Harterink for her contributions to this appendix.

CHAPTER 8

Statistical computing

One of the biggest influences on the subject of statistics in the last few years has been the development of all aspects of computing. The evolution of more powerful computers has resulted in the development of new methods of statistical analysis, and made the implementation of some previously suggested techniques a reality, particularly in the realms of graphical displays and multivariate analysis. Computing has also led to the saving of hours of computation time, enabling the study of larger data sets than previously.

Both these changes have had an impact on statistics syllabuses. New topics have been added and some techniques, which were mainly ways of coping with awkward or time-consuming computations, have been dropped. Gradually all these changes and developments are beginning to affect the teaching of statistics. The emphasis on teaching can now be on understanding rather than on computation. Statistical software can be used as part of the teaching method, and students can be asked to explore and study real data sets. Figure 8.1 shows all this in schematic form, and suggests that the links between some of the activities in the boxes should be two-way. The process is, of course, on-going through time. Statistics is a living subject.

The statistics teacher should bear in mind that as computers have become smaller and cheaper they have become part of everyday living. Many families own a home computer, and in the workplace computers are used increasingly for record keeping, assembly, design and training, and for mathematical, statistical and scientific work.

In this chapter we discuss the types of software available for use in the statistics classroom, giving some very general guidelines as to what is available and how to evaluate it. We were mindful of Taylor's (1980) distinctions between the computer as a *tutor*, *tool* or *tutee*, in our descriptions of the use that is, and can be, made of computers in statistics instruction. The choice and management of *equipment* is considered in Chapter 9. We have purposely avoided detailed reference to, or recommendations of, particular software products, other than citing occasional examples in order to identify the type of software being discussed. Clearly, the rate of software publication is increasing very rapidly and

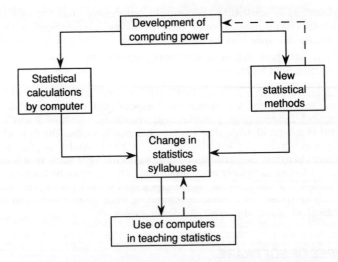

Figure 8.1 **The role of computing in the development of statistics**

existing packages may well soon become redundant or obsolete. We therefore considered it to be more important to try to identify useful characteristics and facilities which software (and hardware in Chapter 9) might have and leave the specific choice to the reader, from whatever may be available when the choice is being made.

Before looking at the different types of software, however, we believe that readers should take the following words of warning to heart:

There are indications that time released from possible tedious calculation [by increased use of computers] is in some places being used for students to 'try out' a whole host of packages whose merits or failings they are not yet competent to assess . . . The teaching must focus instead on critical consideration of issues relevant to the fruitful application of statistical techniques. (Preece, 1986)

Whatever software we choose to use in our teaching, we must beware of giving the impression that statistics is little more than the use of packages, or we shall risk turning our students into 'package addicts'.

It can also be very tempting to turn the statistics course into a course instructing students in the use of commands to obtain output from computer packages. This would be a form of the 'pluginski syndrome' (Freedman *et al.*, 1978a) consisting of blindly 'plugging' numbers into a computer command, and it must be avoided. An admirable way of teaching commands is to use them to build up routines to teach concepts. This should be seen as a supplement to software designed for teaching concepts and not as a substitute. We would emphasise that the ability to execute commands is only part of using a statistical package. Selecting an appropriate analysis and being able to interpret the output are just as, or even more, important. As Searle (1989) says:

It seems to me that in one's first years the important thing is to know 'what to compute' and 'when to compute' before learning 'how to compute'. Learning *how* provides little knowledge about *what* and *when*. Yet it is *what* and *when* that a researcher needs so that the *how* will be truly appropriate to whatever data are at hand. And since the *how* is forever changing, as software and hardware change, I think that learning *what* and *when* is initially more important. The *how* can be learned when needed. If learned early on, at the expense of statistics itself, the student can easily spend more time on computing than on statistics, and so be deficient in some important statistical topics.

TYPES OF SOFTWARE

There are basically three types of computer software available for use in statistics teaching: (1) software for teaching and simulating concepts, that is, Taylor's (1980) *tutor* software for *showing* statistics, (2) statistics/graphics packages for *doing* statistics, Taylor's *tool* software; and (3) programming languages and software which allow the student to learn about statistics by 'instructing' a computer, Taylor's *tutee* software. To these, we could add more recent developments in the area of expert system software, although it may be reasonable to think of these as subsumed under the *tutor* type of software, depending on how much the intention is one of teaching statistical processing (including decision-making and consultancy skills) as distinct from automating these processes by more user-friendly front-ends to processing packages.

There is already a wide choice of software available, expert-system software being the exception as yet, both in price and in quality. In secondary education, microcomputers (either free-standing or networked) are more common than mainframe computers and it is for this former market that most of the educational software has been developed.

Teachers should ideally be looking for software that provides an *integrated environment* for statistical computing, giving the student access to:

- word-processing facilities for report writing;
- graphical tools for generating pictorial and tabular presentations;
- an editor with which to correct errors, and to amend data and other files;

- a library of statistical computational procedures;
- communication or translation facilities enabling files to be imported and exported between different, otherwise incompatible, systems.

By allowing easy access to a variety of tools, the student will be encouraged to present statistical reports and relevant diagrams in a professional and sophisticated style.

Catalogues of microcomputer software have been produced by the Centre for Statistical Education (1986) at the University of Sheffield, and by the Advisory Unit for Microtechnology in Education (1988) at Hatfield Polytechnic, and by the British Computer Society (1990) among others. Reviews of software are already an established feature of many journals. *The Professional Statistician*,[1] for example, devotes one issue annually to statistical computing with detailed reviews of software. Microcomputer magazines give non-specialist reviews of all types of software and sometimes give tips as to the best buys. However, as with all fast-growing fields, prices go down and the facilities available increase each year so that catalogues and reviews quickly become out of date.

The updates on software that are available through an increasing number of newsletters and (electronic) networks should mean that this will be less of a problem in the future. Particularly useful in this respect may be the activities of the Computers in Teaching Initiative (CTI) Centres for Mathematics[2] and Statistics[3] (at Birmingham and Glasgow Universities, respectively) providing their level of funding allows them to continue to develop as intended. Although particularly aimed at the higher education reader, useful information can also be found in *The Academic Advisor*, the computer products directory for the education sector, produced in association with CHEST (the Combined Higher Education Software Team) by Academic Advice Ltd.[4]

SOFTWARE FOR 'SHOWING STATISTICS'

All demonstrations, even of an apparently static situation such as a pie chart representation of a frequency table, tend to be more dramatic and interesting when done by a computer than by a chalk-and-talk method. If the students' interest is aroused they should be more eager, and more likely, to learn. Some of the software for teaching concepts consists of what might almost be described as games – using pictorial devices and sounds to illustrate situations, and to develop students' probabilistic strategies. Exploring patterns of randomness, detecting trends, and prediction are obvious topics for this kind of treatment. The user can control such things as the speed of the presentation, the parameters, and the sample size. Examples of what is available as areas of application include the distribution of raisins in cakes, traffic flow along a road, crops growing under various weather conditions, the growth of queues in a doctor's surgery, light bulbs failing and stock control.

Students can simply be encouraged to play with such routines and discover things for themselves, but will probably benefit more if given some teacher guidance. In fact, many of the programs come with teachers' and students' notes, and it is important to examine these as part of the software evaluation as they sometimes indicate the scope and objectives of the programs, and report on experiences of their use in the classroom.

The games-like software that is available tends to be particularly suitable for younger age-groups (say up to age 16) although there are examples, such as queuing programs, which are intended for sixth-form statistics students. Often at pre-sixth-form level the availability of hardware is so limited, and the class sizes so large, that optimal use of such games is not possible. It is probably easier at primary school level where groups and timetables can be more flexibly organised. Biehler *et al.* (1988) have written a wide-ranging paper on the use of computers in probability education in which they address both hardware and software characteristics, and classroom strategies for their use.

There is a large choice of software available for demonstrating probability and sampling distributions. Indeed, a noticeable feature of the Second International Conference on Teaching Statistics in 1986 was the enthusiasm of many delegates in demonstrating newly developed examples of Central Limit Theorem software. The contributions to statistical computing sessions at the Third International Conference on Teaching Statistics in 1990 were far more varied in their content, indicating considerable progress in this area. However, software to simulate statistical distribution theory is still a popular teaching resource, and may be the *only* reason for *some* teachers using the computer in their statistics teaching. Some basic knowledge of probability and random variables is needed to understand many of the demonstrations, which are partly under the control of the user, so that this type of software is of most use with older students.

Although such software undoubtedly has its uses in allowing the concepts to be explored quickly and efficiently under a variety of conditions, it is not safe to assume that students will grasp all the important ideas of sampling, variability and sampling distributions and so on unless they also have some experience of the 'concrete' versions of the experiments symbolised by the software. There simply has not been enough cognitive research in this area to offer clear guidelines as to when a computer simulation can stand in for 'reality'.

One of the few research studies in this area, but one which highlights the difficulties in evaluating software, is that by Green (1990). This reports on a small research investigation into classroom experiences of using Microcosm Software (Green *et al.*, 1986). As the published software required several hours of pupil computer time, and as it was not feasible to devote this amount of time to the investigation,

two specific closely focused programs were specially written which introduced the essential concepts of the published software in a more immediate fashion, using a game format to concentrate attention. Special pupil worksheets were prepared to guide the pupils in recording their results. . . . It is clear that testing investigational or experiential software is a major problem if what is often claimed for it is to be verified. . . . Certainly the misconceptions which are common in the field of probability (and about computers) must give cause for doubt as to whether the pupils get from computer simulations what the teachers or software writers assume. There seems to be a built-in assumption that the basis of the simulation is understood and accepted and the role of the computer (especially the random number generator) is appreciated. (Green, 1990)

Questions to bear in mind when choosing software of this simulation kind would include the range of probability distributions available, the statistics that can be found, the sizes of samples allowed, and the form of presentation of the results. Graphical displays, as well as summary statistics, should be available. Some form of demonstration of the Central Limit Theorem is essential. Since students are often confused about the distinction between original and sampling distributions, between standard deviations and standard errors, the software should emphasise such comparisons and distinctions, using juxtaposing, superimposing or split-screen techniques as appropriate, taking advantage of colour or shading distinctions where possible.

Probably the one characteristic which marks out 'better' from 'worse' or 'merely adequate' software of this kind is the speed at which the distributions can be generated. Some examples, particularly those developed before 1984 or thereabouts, can be painfully slow and boring. Unlike later versions, earlier software often relied on the students recording successive sample statistics and then generating their own sampling distribution manually, the software merely acting as a sampling device.

Ironically, however, this 'intermediate level of technology' might have provided an important half-way house between the hours spent tossing coins and dice in pre-computer days, and the all too remote and automatic derivation of sampling distributions now available. Perhaps, as well as experience of the 'concrete' experiments, students also need experience of the processes the microcomputer is going through in arriving at its final display. Once this is grasped, the student should then be ready to use the resources of the software for generating the outcome of similar experiments repeatedly under a wide range of different conditions. Repeated generation of confidence intervals is one such experiment. The 'best' software, then, might well be that which took account of, and varied with, the particular stage of the student's learning, as does *SIMPAC* by Perry *et al.* (1989).

Some software is available which allows students to experiment and to find concepts empirically through optimising some specified criterion. Some of the available software on the least squares regression line is an example of this. The 'best' type of software in this respect is that which allows the students some choice in, or control over, the criterion to be optimised. There are programs which enable the user to add and delete values to a data set and to *see* on screen with dynamic graphics how such changes affect summary measures such as goodness of fit measures, the mean, median, and standard deviation. Many students find demonstrations such as these more convincing than an algebraic argument presented without reference to data. Teachers might consider adapting packages to do these things if specific software is not available, or such adaptations might serve as interesting projects for students following computer studies courses.

SOFTWARE FOR 'DOING STATISTICS'

Many statistics packages – that is, software containing routines for working things out from data – are available. Some of these also have graphics facilities. The balance between statistics and graphics emphases varies considerably. So too do the emphases on 'traditional' statistical techniques and tests as opposed to Exploratory Data Analysis approaches. As many spreadsheets now have statistical functions as part of their 'chest of tools' they can often be considered to be statistics packages. *StatView*[5] and *EXCEL*[6] are examples of such software, which is increasingly finding its way into UK schools.

MINITAB[7] is a general-purpose statistical package popular at higher education level. Originally designed for mainframe computers, it is now also available for microcomputers. It is fairly user-friendly and has a wide range of statistical procedures. It is essentially a teaching package and as such its graphical and tabular output, and its data management facilities, are as yet relatively unsophisticated.

An alternative kind of software, touched on in Chapter 7, which may be of use for 'doing statistics' is that designed for solving real-life statistical problems by simulation methods. One example of this kind of software is *RESAMPLING STATISTICS* (Simon, 1990, first developed as bootstrap statistics for a non-computer environment by Simon and Holmes, 1969) which provides a purpose-written programming language for using Monte Carlo methods to solve statistical and probability problems.

Criteria to be considered when selecting statistics packages include the functions available, the size of data set that can be accommodated, and whether students can input their own data, the quality and characteristics of any data sets supplied, the speed of execution, the ease of editing, transforming or manipulating individual or subgroups of the data, and of obtaining good hard copy of the results, possibly exported to a word-processor context. The facility to transfer from one statistical representation to another, and back again, is important. Preferably, this should also allow for concurrent viewing. For example, it is very useful to be able to see a regression line resulting from the whole set of data, at the same time as one where outlier(s) are omitted.

The ability to select data points from a screen diagram directly without having to return to the original database is extremely useful, and is sometimes available with mouse-driven, as distinct from keyboard-driven, systems. Ideally, it should be possible to include or exclude selected points at will, identified by whatever variable label is desired, and to find and display the new values of derived statistics, all without having to redraw the diagram. All of this really adds up to evaluating the software in terms of how *interactive* the system is.

Very little software currently available in schools has any, let alone all, of these kinds of characteristics. At present they are the domain of professional software packs, selling at prices beyond most schools' resources, and aimed at machines more often found in offices than in classrooms. Such is the rate of technological development, however, that they or something like them will probably be available at an acceptably low price within a relatively short space of time. This applies particularly to graphics facilities. Some packages written originally for use by researchers are now available on microcomputers at competitive prices with academic discounts. Their background is their recommendation. It is fair to say, though, that in general schools' hardware resources are also a limiting factor, and until advances are made in the kinds of machines available in schools, the better kinds of statistics packages cannot be handled.

Some of the packages written specifically for the school market will cope only with relatively small data sets and have few functions. Not all of them are completely reliable, either in computational terms or in being 'crash-resistant'. It is worth investing in a package that goes beyond the syllabus and can cope with moderately large data sets in a 'user-friendly' way. On the other hand, it should be remembered that if a package is more general than the user requires then input might be unnecessarily complicated, the method of calculation used by the package might not be the best for the simpler situation, and the output might contain details beyond the user's state of knowledge. All of this can be confusing to students.

Much care is needed in using the graphics facilities of some packages and in interpreting the output. For example, a histogram produced by a package might consist of rows of stars and look similar to a bar chart. Sometimes the same command is used for both types of diagram, which does not help learners who are already confused by superficial similarities between histograms and bar charts and by the wrong terminology used in some textbooks. Labelling on diagrams produced by computers tends to be minimal, and there are obviously inaccuracies in diagrams such as scatter diagrams where points are plotted as symbols. There are good graphics packages available which produce professional and accurate diagrams, but these are relatively expensive, and as the diagrams produced look so good there is a risk that the novice may be deluded into thinking that they must be correct even when they are inappropriate for the data under consideration. Most packages, of course, will do what is requested regardless of whether it makes sense. Only the best packages can even pretend to think!

Some of the available software has been written as a companion to a text, sometimes designed for self-study. In a few such cases, the software is somewhat of a pretence in that it is little more than a small statistics package and in no way essential to the understanding of the text. In other cases, neither text nor software stands alone. There are some excellent products of this kind, for example, the Computer Illustrated Texts of Robinson and Bowman (1986) and Bowman and Robinson (1987, 1990), but using them requires a very different approach to teaching from that traditionally adopted. The cost and availability of multiple copies of the text and/or software need careful investigation if many students are to gain 'hands-on' use of such materials, and it may well be that teachers find the ideas incorporated useful, but would not wish, or do not have the hardware resources, to adopt the intended teaching methodology.

MENUS AND MICE

A general aspect that needs consideration when choosing computer software is its mode of operation. Is the program controlled by a menu system, possibly with a mouse, or does the user have to input commands in a specified form in order to access particular routines? Novice users tend to find menu systems easier to operate than those requiring commands. In command-driven systems, learning the language syntax, as well as acquiring the necessary typing skills, can get in the way of the real purpose of the software. Much of the software for teaching concepts is menu-driven. More experienced users can, however, find a menu system slow and limited in scope, especially those earlier forms which rely on a lot of screen-clearing and 'to-ing and fro-ing' between main and sub-menus.

Of those statistics packages using commands, some use 'ordinary' language, e.g. 'mean of c1' would be a request for the arithmetic mean of the data stored in column 1. Others use 'computer-style' language, e.g. 'c1 (5)' relies on the user knowing that '5' stands for the routine deriving the arithmetic mean of the specified column. The former type of command is easier for the beginner, and easier too for the teacher when checking what students have done!

Packages that require data to be entered afresh for every new command should be avoided. Packages really need to be simple enough for new and occasional users to use easily, but at the same time to be suitable for use by experienced users who might require more advanced techniques. The types of command should be essentially the same both for the simplest and more complex analyses. Progress in statistics should not of necessity have to entail learning a different method of computing, although there may be good reasons why pupils should be introduced to a different type of statistics package at a later stage.

TO PROGRAM OR NOT TO PROGRAM

Some packages enable users to store a sequence of commands as a routine. This is useful not only in saving time, but also in training students in the rudiments of statistical programming. This raises the question of whether there is in fact anything to be gained in statistical education terms in teaching students to program in, say, BASIC, and then getting them to write their own programs for deriving various statistical concepts like the mean and the variance. A similar question can be asked concerning spreadsheet manipulations.

The argument would be that if a student can make a machine do the computation, then that student should have gained insight into the nature of the concept. To us, this smacks of re-inventing the wheel, and we do not think that it is a very efficient way of using students' time. It is possible that some students might benefit, but probably not as much as they would, for example, by experimenting with deriving the mean from a variety of different distribution shapes, using software that is already available. In this way, they can explore the *functional* characteristics of the mean as a *representative* value, discovering, for example, the influence of distributional characteristics on its robustness and usefulness.

Software in which the users effectively 'write' their own program raises the general issue of 'home-grown' versus commercial software. In the main, 'home-grown' programs are extremely inefficient in terms of development time. Given the competitive market in commercial software for 'doing statistics', and the ever-increasing sophistication at lower costs, it is rare that 'home-grown' programs can really be efficient in cost terms either. Even where commercially available programs do not meet the exact needs of teachers and students, it may well be better to make do, or at most to construct a short 'home-grown' routine as a supplement to purchased software. We see this as a relatively short-term problem, since commercial software which *does* meet their exact needs is not likely to remain prohibitively expensive for long if current trends continue.

For 'showing statistics', it may be worthwhile constructing some software. Available concept-teaching packages are by no means all of a good standard, and there are many areas of statistics that are not covered adequately, or at all. Although the writers would prefer to see commercial outlets developing such software, leaving teachers of statistics free to teach, it is probable that the shortfall in software to 'show statistics' will take longer to be made up than that in the area of 'doing statistics'.

One other area of weakness where 'home-grown' efforts might be appropriate is in the development of expert-system software, designed to *train* students to 'be statisticians' and to 'do statistics'. In fact, the general intention of expert-system software is to simulate the processes that a consultant statistician might go through in interacting with a client. This is an area that is often very much underplayed in statistical education, but one that has serious vocational implications.

GENERAL-PURPOSE SOFTWARE

As well as software specific to statistics, some other types of package also have a place within practical statistics work. These include word-processing, database management and artwork packages. It would seem from entries to the Annual UK Applied Statistics Prize that many schools which make use of the computer do so first and foremost as a wordprocessor, and the second most popular use seems to be for data processing. Since 1986 a special prize has been offered for 'the best use of a computer in an applied statistics project'. So far, the entries have tended to reflect the use of word-processing and standard, relatively modest, statistics/graphics packages. Indeed, some of the 1990/91 entries were impoverished by their over-reliance on standard screen-dumped output of graphical displays. Statistically superior and more appropriate presentations can often be produced where displays are first 'tidied up' within an artwork or drawing package, allowing the quality of labelling, etc., to be improved before incorporating the display into a word-processed research report.

In future it is hoped that much more wide-ranging use will be made of the technical resources available. For example, if as a result of their research, students generate a set of recommendations for change, that change could be simulated and subjected to examination, rather than merely leaving the recommendations untried. The computer could also be used in experimental situations, providing appropriate visual stimuli, for example, and/or monitoring reactions or performance on learning tasks.

ON CHOOSING SOFTWARE

When purchasing software it is important to check whether documentation, including both a novice's section and more technical details, is supplied. Documentation needs to be clearly written and presented and preferably should include worked examples where relevant, showing both input and output. Most importantly it should tell the user how to run the software. A menu system is of no use at all if we are unable to access it. You have been warned! This is an obvious point, but one sometimes overlooked by producers of software, especially the kind which is available to teachers on adoption of a text. In addition to documentation, on-line help facilities within the software are useful.

A potential purchaser of software needs assurance that the program is not going to crash or get into a loop too often. Even the most renowned and expensive packages occasionally suffer from these faults, or 'bugs' as they are known. In testing a program be sure to make incorrect responses. Do not be shy about this. Students are bound to make silly responses, either accidentally or wilfully, and the aim is to get student-proof software. Put in nonsense values such as a negative variance or a probability larger than one. Try to input a larger data set than is allowed. The better programs will flash up a message describing the error and how to rectify it. The worst programs will crash or carry on regardless (but it may not be obvious how they have proceeded). Between these two extremes are programs which give terse error warnings. To interpret these, reference to the manual is needed, but make sure that the manual explains the error in everyday language and not in 'computer speak'. Check what appears on the screen for the different routines. Are the instructions clear? Is output labelled so that we know what has been found? Is output well-spaced or does it look cramped or otherwise distorted?

Test the full software if possible. Demonstration versions may work differently and probably will not cover all the options available in the real thing. One of the authors was recently very irritated to discover that the demonstration disk for a non-parametric statistics package only allowed a total of fifteen observations overall to be distributed in a single contingency table. This made it impossible to ascertain what algorithms were being used, and how robust they might be, for computing so-called 'exact' confidence limits for odds ratios (for which the research literature shows that different 'exact' methods produce different 'exact' results!). It also precluded the software's operation being checked with larger as opposed to small expected cell frequencies. Needless to say, the photocopied extracts, supplied by the producers of the software, from two chapters of the manual did nothing to clarify the situation.

We tend to take a rather 'robust' line on software which its manufacturers and retailers might like to consider. We believe that if the product is worth having, it is worth its producers showing it off adequately. One company, Odesta Corporation[8] which produce *Data Desk* and *Double Helix* also produced 'test-flight' software, providing not only a comprehensive 'hands-on' working version of the software, but also a detailed users' manual, specifically to accompany the demonstration version, thereby showing also the quality that can be expected of their documentation. A company adopting this approach may safe-guard itself from commercial loss by limiting the storing of data-sets and results, rather than by limiting the processing capabilities of the software, which we believe to be an appropriate way for producers of *statistical* software to display their wares.

Some companies produce *demonstrations* of software which are just that, i.e. they are not 'hands-on' working versions. Instead, the prospective purchaser receives a disk which when run 'shows' how the software works. Some of these can be quite attractive presentations. Aldus[9] who produce *Pagemaker* and *Persuasion* have made considerable efforts in this respect. Others, however, can be extremely boring and frustrating for the prospective purchaser who is prevented from finding out exactly what he or she really wants to know about the software, but who nevertheless must keep pressing 'Return' to drive the demonstration!

Teachers should not overlook the evaluation of the *classroom* use of the software. It may be appropriate to choose software which students can use without teacher assistance, but on the other hand it may also be desirable to ensure that the software is compatible with any presentation that the teacher will give, or with that in recommended texts. Software which enables the higher ability students to circumnavigate some stages can be useful. It is also important to consider the exact nature of the output of results and the ease of obtaining output in a classroom context. This is discussed further in Chapter 9.

Teachers and others who may have responsibility for computer policies in schools should be aware of the rapid developments in statistical graphics and of the dominant role that graphics will play in the statistics of the future. The American Statistical Association now has a special section devoted to research and developments in statistical graphics. It is important that schools making software and hardware purchases choose items that will allow them to respond quickly to new developments in this area.

ON USING SOFTWARE

The great advantages of computers are their dynamic nature and their speed. In data analysis computer programs enable us to explore the data quickly, both before and after analysis, to get a 'feel' for it and for how things would change if values of some of the observations were different. When considering theoretical concepts such as sampling distributions the computer enables us to see changes over time as the generating process progresses. There are many examples of relevant software available, for example *StatLab* by Stirling (1987), *SIMPAC* by Perry *et al.* (1989), *Understanding Statistics* (originally called *Advanced Level Statistics* and marketed by BBC Soft) now available from the Centre for Statistical Education, University of Sheffield, and MEI[10] Mathematics Programs (Mathematics in Education and Industry Project).

Graphical representations are particularly important in checking whether models are appropriate and as an aid to understanding, but it is also important to look at alternative representations, for example, frequency distributions and summary statistics, and to appreciate the links between them.

The computer makes it easy to see more representations than would be possible in an ordinary classroom. For teachers with

relevant experience, LOGO programming might offer an interesting approach for students learning about variability, (un)-
predictability, random influences and bias, etc. LOGO provides
the opportunity for very quick, almost on-the-spot interactive
programming with immediate graphic feedback. Students can
learn a great deal about modelling when trying to explain failures
of the 'turtle', the robot or screen equivalent under their control,
to do what is expected. Butt (1986) describes an innovatory way
of teaching the concept of random variation based on this idea.
The students essentially have to discover a *black-box* algorithm
by alternate prediction and experimentation. Unknown to them
the *rule* controlling the spatial movement of the 'turtle' contains a
random element. Gradually, in their efforts to discover the *rule*
that will enable them to complete a geometrical figure, the
students come to appreciate the distinction between the deterministic models they try to apply and the probabilistic model that
would be more appropriate.

Simulation is an important method of solving problems that are
difficult to solve analytically. Many probability problems lend
themselves to solution by this means, for example, random walk
problems *(SIMPAC)* and queuing theory problems (included as
part of the BBC Advanced Statistics software) which would
otherwise be beyond the majority of school students. Another
interesting use of simulation is for the instructor to get the
computer to produce a random sample from a specified
distribution and then to ask the students to try to discover the
characteristics of the original parent distribution.

THE WAY FORWARD

In teaching statistics it is no longer necessary to spend time on
ways to make manual computations easier or on practising such
computations. This does not mean formulae can be ignored
completely, but sometimes algebra can be avoided, and sometimes analogy can be used to suggest generalisations. We think
that some small hand computations are still useful as an aid to
understanding. Arithmetic can be kept simple here using suitable
small sets of integers leading to integer answers (e.g. see Posten,
1982; Read and Riley, 1983). The same quantities should be
found with a computer as a two-way check, thereby helping to
remove the *black box* aspect of the computer. Discussion of the
fact that computer calculations sometimes use different methods
from 'hand' calculations to avoid rounding errors can also be
illuminating.

Use of a computer enables us to look at real data sets having
many observations on several variables. Mostly in school level

statistics we consider one variable at a time, and sometimes two, but with the computer we can begin to think about extensions to more than two variables. Developments in graphical methods and software will have an important role to play here (Chambers *et al.*, 1983; and see also Chapter 1, Figure 1.3). Use of real data sets means that students can investigate real questions of interest. Often these will be ill-defined and open-ended. Redefining the problem into one that can be tackled, sorting out the relevant data, and noting the limitations of the data (and sometimes the unrealistic aspects of the problem) are important steps in becoming an applied statistician. Realising that there is no unique right answer is another one. This would be a good time to give a warning about two of the bad habits that computers have encouraged: the collection of too much data with little thought as to why it has been collected, and the production of vast numbers of meaningless analyses.

Spreadsheets have an important role to play in the teaching of statistics in that we can use the spreadsheet's facilities for quick calculations over rows and/or columns to demonstrate certain statistical algorithms (Soper and Lee, 1985). For example, Lee and Soper (1987) describe the way in which the value of a chi-square statistic can be calculated for an $r \times c$ contingency table, where r is the number of rows and c is the number of columns in the table. Neuwirth (1990) demonstrates the use of a spreadsheet in teaching correlation. In his view, 'spreadsheets not only can be used to analyse existing data but also to create data illustrating important statistical concepts'. The row and column format of a spreadsheet is ideally suited to a data matrix in which the rows normally represent the cases such as respondents to a survey and the columns represent the observations on the cases over a set of variables, so that in using spreadsheets students stay closer to the data. In this respect it is easy to change the values of one or more entries in the data set and obtain recalculated values of statistics of interest. However, an undesirable side effect of using spreadsheets might be that computational aspects of statistics are emphasised rather than functional aspects.

Database construction and management are important statistical activities which should feature in students' statistical education. They should be given experience of working with pre-formed, possibly 'messy' datasets as well as those which they produce themselves. The processes will include data preparation (for example, coding verbal responses to a questionnaire, or defining 'missing' as distinct from 'not-applicable' codes), designing the structure of the database (for example, whether it will be a simple matrix format or a more complex relational database, and whether it will be freefield or fixed format entry, etc.), data input to the computer (by keyboard entry, electronic scanning or importing from other computer-readable formats, in which case an appreciation of the merits of ASCII files will be important), data checking (for example, whether the input is correct and whether the data satisfy various constraints such as values in allowed ranges, possibly establishing in-built routines to sense this on data entry), data editing (for example re-coding and transformation by computer) and data correction.

All data sets will require some form of data verification before any analysis stages can proceed, and the skills exercised during the checking and editing stages can be considered to have some affinity to those employed during Exploratory Data Analysis. For the purposes of teaching such skills, it may well be that a data set that has had all the problems removed is less useful than one that still has at least some of its 'warts' present!

NOTES

1. Published by the Institute of Statisticians, 43 St Peter's Square, Preston, Lancs., PR1 7BX
2. CTI Centre for Mathematics, Dr M.H. Beilby, Faculty of Education, University of Birmingham, Birmingham, B15 2TT. (e-mail: ctimath@bham)
3. CTI Centre for Statistics, Dr A. Bowman, Department of Statistics, University of Glasgow, University Gardens, Glasgow, G12 8QW. (e-mail: ctistat@glasgow.vme)
4. Academic Advice Ltd, 3 The Parade, Mulfords Hill, Tadley, Hampshire, RG26 6BR.
5. Abacus Concepts, Inc., Published by BrainPower Inc., 24009 Ventura Boulevard, Suite 250, Calabasas, CA 91302, USA.
6. Microsoft Corporation, One Microsoft Way, Redmond, Washington 98052-6399, USA.
7. UK suppliers, Clecom, The Research Park, Vincent Drive, Edgbaston, Birmingham, B15 2SQ.
8. Odesta Corporation, 4084 Commercial Avenue, Northbrook, Illinois 60062, USA
9. Aldus UK Ltd, 39 Palmerston Place, Edinburgh, Scotland, UK, EH12 5AU.
10. MEI Office, Monkton Combe, Bath, Avon, BA2 7HG. Eastmond Publishing Ltd., 33 West Street, Oundle, Peterborough, PE8 4EJ.

CHAPTER 9

Multimedia for teaching statistics

Chapter 8 was concerned with various aspects of computer software and its use in statistical instruction. In this chapter, we discuss recent developments in pocket calculators, computer hardware and peripherals, and suggest some ways in which these might be used in teaching. Ideally, students need to become familiar with both calculators and computers, and to learn how to choose the most appropriate tool (which *could* simply be pencil and paper!) for their data processing. Consideration is also given to the management and evaluation of other educational media, both technical and non-technical. Textbooks, the traditional teaching resource, are considered from the point of view of their content, their presentation style, and the design of their exercise material.

MICROCOMPUTERS OR A MAINFRAME?

Few teachers are in a position to choose the type of computing facility to use in statistics teaching, and, in general, the provision that exists at school level is of the microcomputer variety. Nevertheless, we feel it is worth making some comments on the use of networked or time-share terminal access to a central, possibly remote, mainframe computer resource. Often this facility has a less advanced graphics capability and less 'pretty' output than do microcomputers. Its operation will generally be via batch-mode processing and so there is a considerable delay between time of input and receipt of output. Errors in setting up batch processing jobs can, if undetected, cause considerable frustration and waste of time since they may not be flagged until the work has been passed through the queue for the central processor, failed to run, and then passed back through the output queue. In contrast, one of the chief advantages of microcomputer support is its relatively high level of interactive access.

The advantages of a mainframe system may seem few, but, particularly in the early days of microcomputer development, they may have included access to greater computing power with the possibility of handling larger data sets. Generally, mainframe access is likely to be less appropriate for demonstrating statistical concepts *per se*, but may have advantages for showing and doing *real* statistics. Given the advances in microcomputers, resulting in their ever-increasing storage and processing capacities, probably the greatest remaining advantage of having terminal links to a mainframe is that this may also yield communication and information transfer possibilities through widespread networks of users, and give access to public domain software and data sets.

The organisation of the computer access and its integration into the overall statistical education process will, of course, have to take account of the particular type of provision that is available. There is little research to offer guidelines. As usual, trial-and-error and common sense seem to be the most valuable assets that a teacher can call upon at present. In general terms, for those who are in a position to select or upgrade existing facilities, the provision of interactive microcomputers with networking possibilities is probably optimal. In addition, a modem to an external central facility would then be a way of obtaining the best of all worlds.

OUTPUT FROM COMPUTER SOFTWARE

As mentioned in Chapter 8, it is important to consider the exact nature of the output of results from computer software and the ease of obtaining it. Hard-copy printouts may or may not be necessary, and may or may not be wanted during a particular session. Noisy, slow printers can seriously disrupt the real classroom purpose of statistical education. Sometimes it is possible, and preferable, therefore, to delay printing the results until after the session, letting the students rely in the meantime on their on-screen observations. Some of the software designed for *teaching concepts* does not provide the opportunity for printing copies of the results of simulation experiments. Even where printout possibilities exist, however, it may still be more useful to have a computer connected to a monitor or an overhead projector so that the teacher can show routines in action and discuss the results with the class.

It is also possible, with appropriate software, to generate computer-drawn overhead transparencies and 35 mm slides, but the cost of the necessary peripherals makes this more of a facility for the future than one widely available in schools at present. As (colour) ink-jet printers come down in price, undercutting the more sophisticated laser printers and plotters, and improving in print quality, the situation will change. For the time being, most teachers who want this sort of presentation material are relying on black-and-white printouts which may then be photocopied on to transparencies. Whatever the precise hardware provision for the output, statistics teachers will inevitably need access to at least one printer which is capable of producing high-quality, including graphical, output.

It is, of course, essential to be able to obtain a printout from a statistics package. A few packages allow the user only to send the contents of a screen to a printer by means of a 'screen dump'. This can impose severe constraints on the quality and readability of the hard-copy output. In most packages, however, results can be stored in a file, which might need to be created before the session begins, or which might be there by default. It is usually then possible selectively to incorporate the results thus saved into a word-processing package, if required, before printing out a fuller report. As has been said, it is often best to edit graphical output first in a general-purpose drawing package.

When purchasing a statistics package it is worthwhile checking that the printed output is as good as that obtained on the screen, and that files can be edited on screen before re-use. A further consideration is the ease with which the results from a first analysis can be accessed for further study. In the main, it is important, for pragmatic as well as academic reasons, to encourage students to restrict their taking of hard copies. The facility to select easily and print only the most relevant parts of the results is therefore a valuable asset, as is flexibility of *export* and *import* of information between the packages to which the teacher and students already have access.

THE COMPUTER LABORATORY

To a certain extent events have overtaken Kerridge's (1973) visionary view of a class of tertiary-level students, each having a computer terminal to work at. We are now moving towards a position where *all* educational establishments, not only at the higher education level, have access to a computer laboratory. Ideally there should be enough microcomputers or terminals for every student in a class to have exclusive use of one if required. In some cases, though, it is beneficial for a small group of students to share a computer, particularly when engaged in a problem-solving context, when the interaction between students can provide an important source of momentum. It may be, however, that sharing a computer can lead to a tendency either for the dominant member to take over the machine or for students to take turns rather than work jointly, neither of which is very satisfactory. As yet, there is little research initiative in *statistical* education to enable more than speculation concerning the way in which computers should be used.

As a general rule, the equipment should be the most powerful that the institution can afford. (Money in educational establishments does not flow so freely that this will ever be likely to result in the institution having excessively more computing power than is needed!) The requirements made on computing resources continue to increase as software and the whole computing environment are made more user-friendly. In addition, the more advanced packages need more than a minimum computing capacity, as does the processing of data sets of non-trivial size.

As common sense will indicate, an institution spending 'all the money it can afford' on *any* resource does need to be very clear that it is spending the money on the appropriate products. Much market research in advance of such an acquisition is crucial, as well as the in-service training of potential users who at the outset may not be particularly computer literate. A *shared* resource, such as computer provision, must be chosen to support not only the perceived needs of the *enthusiast* in the school or college but also those of other teachers whose students may benefit. The sort of hardware, and software, requirements of teachers of statistics in the 'user'-disciplines may well be rather different from those in the mathematics department. Moreover, such needs may easily be overlooked when the money is being spent, when the scope and potential for these former areas may not have been fully recognised by the relevant teachers.

In choosing equipment, the role of the computer as a manager of the learning experience may also feature. Clearly some computers may be used to good effect for organisational purposes, record-keeping and the analysis of student progress, and for storage and generation of examples designed for each individual student. However, faced with the need to teach very large numbers of students at tertiary level, some institutes have resorted to the computer as manager–teacher–assessor, etc., all rolled into one in order to resolve staffing problems. We would not want to endorse the extreme version of this approach, where students self-pace themselves, unaccompanied by a teacher, through a statistics course, experiencing much isolated programmed learning, with mainly repetitive number-crunching exercises on artificial, and unrealistic, data sets, gaining little or no insight into different types of data drawn from different contexts, and having no experience of project planning or execution.

When buying equipment, it may be helpful for those with little experience to choose items that are already in use locally. There are great advantages in having access to friendly advice from someone who has already experienced the teething problems that are bound to occur. The speed of technological development inevitably means, however, that the later purchases will be more advanced and that what was a good buy last term is now 'old stock', or discontinued altogether! A consideration of whether the hardware manufacturers have maintained a reputation for compatibility with their own, and others', earlier models and with the available software is important if the useful life of the equipment is to be extended for as long as possible.

It may also be sensible to buy from a local supplier as it should then be possible to obtain maintenance and other support relatively quickly and cheaply. A common mistake is to forget the running and maintenance costs when budgeting for new hardware. In the initial stages, this may not be a problem, but as microcomputers and peripherals spring into being overnight in different departments within a school or college, such *extras* can become a major problem, especially when there is no on-site computer technician.

The BBC microcomputer was once very popular in UK schools, largely because of concessionary purchase schemes. Some schools have 'migrated' from this to its successor, the Archimedes, with its quicker and more powerful processing capabilities. This is essentially an entry-level machine into the world of workstations, offering relatively high-speed, high-resolution graphics facilities. In fact, with the demise of Acorn's BBC-B machine and its contemporary, the Research Machine 380-Z, and the subsequent development of relatively expensive models by these two companies, educationalists have started looking towards the many other machines on the market.

The two major types of computer system in use outside schools are those of the Apple Macintosh family of machines and those of the IBM, and IBM clone, family. Originally, these two developments were distinguished by the former's emphasis on graphics, and its in-built flexibility of font and style selection and its icon-driven, very user-friendly pull-down menu and window systems, common to almost every piece of software developed for the Macintosh. IBM machines had much more emphasis on colour and have only recently begun to adopt the 'windows' and 'icons' approach of the Macintosh family. IBM machines were, however, probably more established as data-processing machines than were Macintoshes. At the time of writing, these two strands are converging to some extent. Many of the software packages that were originally Macintosh- or IBM-specific have now been produced in a form which may be used on the other system. This does not mean that a user familiar with the Macintosh version of 'Wordperfect', for example, will necessarily be immediately comfortable when using its equivalent on an IBM. The differences are not insignificant, although the principles are the same.

The recent introduction of low-cost *colour* Macintosh machines will probably have a significant market impact by the time this book reaches publication. For prospective purchasers choosing between Macintosh- and IBM-based systems, however, perhaps the most important developments are software and hardware solutions which can make possible the transfer of data and text files between the two. Document translation, for example by means of MacLink Plus/PC software[1] (which, in its latest version, can transport graphics as well as text), and the possibility of using compatible, usually high-density, 3.5 inch disks is an important step forward.

It is rare for a school or college to install identical machines *at a stroke*. More often than not, the different requirements of, and the sponsorship possibilities for, different disciplines have yielded a hotch-potch legacy of hardware, each item having different, but mostly long-since passed, 'sell-by' dates. In planning for future purchases, there are many important lessons to be learned from the purchases of the past. We feel that there is still sufficient difference between the two major systems for there to be requirements for both within a particular school or college, and statistics teachers, in particular, may well wish to capitalise on the strong points of each system. For them, questions of compatibility and transferability must be very high on the list of priorities.

It must be said that not all IBM clones are as clone-like as one might expect. There appears to be compatibility and compatibility! Caution should be exercised and information sought from the producers of both software and hardware in advance. We feel that if an IBM clone is to be purchased, it *must* be 'fully IBM compatible' if future problems and disappointments are to be avoided. It is clear that, in UK schools at least, many so-called IBM-compatible machines fall short of this requirement, as is witnessed by their failure to run software designed for IBM machines.

It is true that *some* software will not run on machines that lack a mathematics co-processor. This is true whether the system is Macintosh or IBM. In the absence of such a co-processor, care must obviously be taken in the choice of software because the subsequent purchase of a co-processor, assuming that one is available for the given hardware, may be a very expensive additional cost.

If schools and colleges adopt an approach where the computer is brought to the students rather than the students going to the computer, as a means of mobilising limited computer resources,

the *portable* computer may well become a significant consideration for future purchases. At present, considerations of cost and
freedom of choice would probably dictate an IBM, or IBM clone,
machine. Lagging a little behind the sophistication available at
equivalent prices in a non-portable version, and generally with
non-standard keyboard layouts, there are nevertheless portable
machines which have large working memories and hard-disk
storage. Advantages for fieldwork are obvious, provided the
portable computer really is portable, and not merely 'luggable'
(in excess of 7 to 10 kilogram bags of sugar in weight), and that it
does indeed have an independent and adequate power supply.
(Some are mains-only!) Coupled with large, colour VGA
monitors for demonstration purposes it may well be that schools
will begin to venture into this area of the market in the not too
distant future. Again, caution must be observed, because the
cheapest high-street bargains are often old stock, which on closer
inspection display a variety of tiresome shortcomings associated
with old technology.

CALCULATORS

Much has already been written on the use of calculators in
mathematics and other fields. In statistical education, the
arguments in favour of their use would be much the same as
those rehearsed elsewhere. The gap between very sophisticated
programmable calculators with graphics facilities and portable
computers is narrowing as we move towards 'pocket-sized'
computers. We are generally of the opinion that such computers
are more 'user'-friendly than those calculators which are capable
of performing similar statistical tasks, but as yet their size and
cost do not make them direct competitors in the high-street
shops.

The published account of the international inquiry organised
by the International Statistical Institute on the design of statistical
functions for calculators (Råde, 1985) makes interesting reading,
although it has in many respects been overtaken by the pace of
technological development. In that report, the main disadvantage
of calculators was seen to be their small screen and their main
advantages over computers were their availability. Three hypothetical calculators were considered, a programmable calculator
especially designed for statistical calculations, a programmable
calculator of a more general nature, and a low cost non-
programmable calculator. Respondents were asked what basic
statistical functions should be pre-programmed on the three types
of calculator. For the most basic statistical calculator the
functions selected were:

- Calculation of mean, variance and standard deviation for ungrouped data.
- Calculation of median, quartiles, and extremes for drawing of box plots.
- Calculation of $F(x)$ for given x for the normal distribution.
- Calculation of x for given $F(x)$ for the normal distribution.
- Calculation of random numbers between 0 and 1.
- Calculation of quantities for one variable linear regression (to include an estimate of sigma squared, standard errors of estimates and residuals).

A similar, slightly longer set of functions was thought to be appropriate for the cheaper programmable calculator, and the list for the sophisticated calculator predictably resembles the facilities of a statistics package. We would feel that a computer would be preferable to such a calculator because the former is more likely to have the additional advantages of facilities for storage and editing of data sets, for results being held in accessible files, and the possibility of obtaining hard copy of data and results. At the time of writing, there is at least one *calculator system* on sale for which the software, and the peripheral hardware, including storage, communication and printing facilities, may be bought much as one would buy them for a computer. The range of applications for it is quite impressive, but the cost of any reasonable selection from the system components begins to come close to that of a portable computer without having the advantages of a larger screen size and the variety of applications that the latter would provide. The potential purchaser should evaluate this and similar developments by taking account of whether or not they have immediate compatibility with desktop computers. The manufacturers of the particular system currently available have made provision for transfer to an appropriate desktop machine either directly by cable or indirectly by portable modem connection.

One of the most recent developments in calculators, the full impact of which has yet to be realised, is the introduction of small, and relatively cheap, *graphical* calculators. (As has been indicated, it is arguable whether these should be classed as *calculators* or pocket-sized *computers*.) The market is highly competitive, and to some extent it is true that 'the more you pay, the more you get'. However, there are differences between the facilities available on various models and it might be a case of opting for a smaller screen size in order to have more built-in functions or more programming storage, for example.

Some of the newer calculators have *statistical* graphs as a built-in feature and some do enable the storage of data sets, including the storage of the results of simulation experiments performed on the calculator. Some allow the display of algebraic symbols and/

or the display of a sequence of algebraic expressions in addition to more conventional graphs. Those calculators which can display and do operations on (small) matrices may be particularly useful for teaching introductory multivariate work. In general, calculators with a reasonable selection of statistical facilities also tend to have extensive mathematical and scientific functions. Their 'user'-friendliness for the beginner statistician may therefore be limited, and problems of acquiring calculator literacy may well stand in the way of their use for acquiring statistical literacy in a way that a good 'user'-friendly piece of computer software would not.

In many cases graphical calculators can be made to do the same things as computers. For example, with some it is possible to 'draw' lines of best fit on to scatter diagrams and to see the way in which the least squares line changes when points are added or deleted. In evaluating such calculators, the same considerations that would be used for computer equivalents are relevant, one of which would be the degree of dynamic interaction that is possible with the data. The present authors always favour a visual display system that does not have to be cleared as modifications are made to the underlying data or computations, a facility which is relatively rarely available.

One of the main advantages of graphical calculators over small computers is their price. In particular, the disks for the *very* small computers are relatively expensive. Maintenance costs of calculators are almost non-existent, which is certainly not the case with computers. It is possibly true to say too that calculators need fewer repairs than computers, although the other side of this argument is that a calculator which is not functioning as intended might not be worth repairing, whereas computers can usually be repaired on a number of occasions, should the need arise.

From the point of view of the teacher there are obvious advantages in every student having access to his or her own individual computing power in the form of a graphical calculator if the alternative is sharing a single microcomputer or terminal. In fact, many students do acquire their own graphical calculators and may even learn how to use them ahead of their teachers. Another point in favour of calculators, where equipment is provided by an institution, is that it is much easier to lock up calculators securely at the end of the day, although a counter-argument here is that calculators are more easily stolen before the end of that day!

We note that unless a fairly large amount is paid for a *calculator system*, probably with the intention of its being used to supplement existing desktop facilities while the user is, for example, working in the field, the calculator system at present is often second best compared to the portable computer by being more application-specific. That is, there is a tendency for the manufacturers of such systems to produce either a text-oriented *or* a number-oriented resource, but not both at the same time. Furthermore, although data, or text, files may be transferred to a desktop machine, the *calculator system software* may well be rather machine-specific. This will inevitably influence its cost since the market forces on such specific software are less competitive. Another consideration with this kind of provision is that software will have to be purchased to provide for the *calculator system* as well as for the desktop computer, rather than the user making a single software purchase for use on both, which would be possible if an appropriate portable computer were to be chosen.

USING CALCULATORS

At the simplest level, calculators and computers can reduce the drudgery of arithmetic, thus opening up the possibility of using real and realistic values in problems instead of artificially contrived examples in which answers are nice exact numbers. In addition, calculators can remove some of the fear of computation which prevents some pupils from learning probability and statistics. We would make a similar point about calculators to the one that we made about computers in Chapter 8, and that is that there has to be a 'hand' pre-calculator stage, as well as an appropriate 'concrete' experience stage, with easy numbers, where pupils can concentrate on the concepts involved and on *understanding* the formulae. This is especially true in the case of pre-programmed calculators where intermediate calculations are hidden. As usual, the writers must emphasise that there is insufficient research specifically aimed at exploring the role and efficacy of calculators and computers within a stochastics curriculum.

Mosteller (1965) produced a useful set of games and experiments which lend themselves well to a teaching approach and which use the calculator to demonstrate and explore statistical concepts. Råde (1977) and Råde and Kaufman (1980) also provide relevant 'fun' calculator exercises. Depending on the quality of calculator, and the functions available, these can be quite sophisticated. What may be lacking is the convenience of use when compared with some microcomputer equivalents.

It is important that users of calculators have some feeling for orders of magnitude, both as a check that they have not inadvertently pressed a wrong key and as a check that the calculator has not introduced unacceptable rounding errors. A mental arithmetic check, or sometimes a 'hand' check, that the answer is 'about right' is always sensible. This is in line with some of the targets in the National (Mathematics) Curriculum (Department of Education and Science, 1989a,b). In statistical calculations, simple checks such as estimating the arithmetic mean by eye and checking that the standard deviation is not more than half the range should be used routinely. Realising that the answer can be affected by the order in which intermediate steps of a calculation are performed is also important. For example, the answer obtained by performing a calculation as $(a/m) \times (b/n) \times (c/p) \times (d/q)$ might be more accurate than if found as $(a \times b \times c \times d)/(m \times n \times p \times q)$. Demonstrating how things can go wrong in calculator calculations emphasises the need for calculator *know-how*.

Caution is needed with respect to some of the calculators which rely on inadequate algorithms or have limited accuracy (see Hill, 1979). For example, some of the earlier calculators relied unnecessarily on so-called 'computational formulae' that were originally more easy for those statisticians relying on manual computation methods. For such users, closely in touch with their data, the effects of *rounding* or *overflow* errors should have remained obvious. The same might not be true when the computation is handed over to a *black box*. Of course, with the increased power of calculators, the use of such approximate formulae should be unnecessary. However, the point remains that students should be encouraged to explore the limitations of their software and hardware, and to appreciate the type of data that may be particularly susceptible to yielding statistical errors when analysed using the more modest types of technology available. It may, for example, be necessary in appropriate circumstances to make an adjustment to the observations by subtracting a constant to prevent calculator overflow when computing a standard deviation. Confirming the result by such an approach will also serve as a protection against input errors.

Hill also expressed concern about the shortcomings of calculators and computers with respect to their random number generators. An interesting teaching example is to be found in the MacSpin[2] software (1989). This features a nice 3-dimensional demonstration and discussion of the non-randomness of numbers generated by RANDU, a random number generator (of the linear congruential type, see Knuth, 1969) originally used on IBM mainframe computers, but since incorporated on a variety of systems including the Digital Equipment Corporation's VAX computers. Points which initially appear to be uniformly distributed in a unit cube, as would be expected if the coordinates were randomly generated, are found to lie in planes when the scatterplot is rotated and selectively viewed. (This non-random phenomenon was first described in Marsaglia, 1968.)

In fact, it can be a very useful project for students to explore the characteristics of their calculators' random number generators, for it provides important insights into the nature of randomness and into the basis of inference, that is, into how to test whether an outcome is within the bounds of reasonable expectation given certain initial premises. Another experiment might be to compute the variance or standard deviation of a set of figures and to repeat the exercise with the same figures raised to several powers of 10, and then again with them divided by several powers of 10, testing their calculators' reliability *to destruction*, as it were. There are also important lessons to be learned in this way about absolute as opposed to relative measures of spread, precision and accuracy, and the shortcomings of software and hardware when dealing with data located about extremely large or extremely small values.

THE AVAILABILITY OF COMPUTERS AND CALCULATORS

The 1989 survey of teachers of statistics (Hawkins, 1989a), described more fully in Chapter 2, looked at what students appeared to be experiencing with respect to the availability and use of computer hardware. Approximately 41 per cent of respondents reported *using* some kind of software, and approximately 50 per cent reported *using* one microcomputer or computer terminal (approximately 20 per cent *using* more than one in a classroom) in their teaching. The discrepancy between the first two percentages is interesting. One might suggest that the former is a more reliable estimate of computer *use*, on the grounds that teachers will not use software for which they have no hardware, and conversely teachers with hardware will also need to use software. In any event, the availability of at least some computing facilities for these teachers of statistics is presumably in the order of slightly less than half. The greatest computer users would appear to be teachers of 'user'-disciplines at both lower and upper secondary levels, and statistics teachers at upper secondary level.

The *use* made of hardware, however, is not necessarily synonymous with its *availability*. Much can depend on individual teachers' perspectives and confidence, as well as on apparent syllabus requirements. Resource availability to particular teachers may also depend on things like their background level of training and their position of seniority, sometimes reflected in their years of teaching experience. It should be noted here, perhaps, that 46 per cent of the respondents said they would welcome in-service training on how to handle technical resources.

Only one in three of the respondents expected students to have access to *statistical* calculators, whereas approximately three-quarters of the respondents overall, and a much higher proportion in the case of the mathematics and statistics teachers among them, expected their students to use *mathematical* or *scientific* calculators. These figures actually conceal the distinctions between the teaching contexts. At least 60 per cent of the students specialising in statistics used *statistical* calculators, but fewer of those who were taking statistics within mathematics, and only a very small proportion of those studying 'user'-disciplines did so. Apart from those teaching specialist statistics courses, a higher proportion of respondents had relied on using a micro-computer or a computer terminal in their teaching than on a *statistical* calculator.

Assuming that, overall, approximately 50 per cent of the respondents regularly use a single microcomputer or terminal, and only one in four or five use several with their students, a relatively small number of students are actually getting 'hands-on' experience. At upper secondary level, nearly 70 per cent of specialist statistics teachers use a single computer and nearly 40 per cent give their students 'hands-on' experience using a number of computers in the classroom. The use made of *any* computer resources by upper secondary *mathematics* teachers, however, is relatively low, and only one in four of the mathematics teachers reported using several computers with their students. At upper secondary level it is possible that some teaching groups might be small enough for students to gain 'hands-on' experience when only one computer is available. In fact, however, the survey data suggest that in contrast to statistics and 'user'-discipline specialists, *mathematics* students are still more likely to *observe* their teacher operating a single computer than to gain any '*hands-on*' experience themselves.

Our belief that the provision of computing resources is generally inadequate is reinforced by the results of a March 1990 survey of information technology in schools (Department of Education and Science, 1991). Responses to the survey were obtained from 718 primary and 399 secondary schools. In the primary schools, the average number of students per micro-computer was 40, with the student-to-micro ratio ranging from $5 : 1$ to $211 : 1$. In the secondary schools, the average was 18 students per microcomputer, and the student-to-micro ratio ranged from $3 : 1$ to $57 : 1$.

The average number of microcomputers per primary school was 4.3 and the average number of printers was 3.2, whereas there were on average 41.1 microcomputers per secondary school and 13.7 printers. Clearly, these figures conceal variation between schools, and also the extent to which schools might have a number of microcomputers networked to a single printer. Nearly all students in primary schools, and 84 per cent of students in secondary schools, had had 'hands-on' experience of microcomputers.

STUDENTS' EXPERIENCES OF HOW CALCULATORS AND COMPUTERS MAY BE USED

The Department of Education and Science survey (1991) asked about the use made of software during the previous school week. In all age groups (apart from 5 year olds, whose main use of packages was 'for practice exercises and puzzles') the greatest use was for word processing, which for example accounted for about 30 per cent of the use made of microcomputers by secondary school students aged 11 or more. Data handling accounted for 15 per cent of the use of technology by younger secondary school students, and 19 per cent of the use by students aged 17 and over. In secondary school Mathematics departments, 31 per cent of staff used microcomputers at least twice a week on average, but the survey also found that 10 per cent of Mathematics departments in secondary schools used no information technology at all in their teaching.

Obviously the type of use to which the hardware is put will differ according to the exact nature of the hardware available. Table 9.1 gives some indication, based on the 1989 survey (Hawkins, 1989a) of the kinds of experiences that students are having with calculators and computers, bearing in mind that it will not all be of a 'hands-on' type. There is considerable

Table 9.1 **Different uses of hardware in teaching statistics**

Hardware use	Respondents' Teaching level and its context (%)							
	Primary	Lower secondary			Upper secondary			
		Stats	Maths	User	Stats	Maths	User	Overall
Collection	**77.6**	37.9	38.5	**43.5**	33.9	18.2	**44.0**	44.4
Storage	**51.7**	**41.4**	25.0	**43.5**	37.3	18.2	38.1	37.0
Processing	**60.3**	**75.9**	**63.5**	**78.3**	**74.6**	**65.9**	**73.8**	**70.4**
Display	**60.3**	**48.3**	40.4	47.8	**54.2**	**43.2**	**56.0**	**52.8**
Simulations	6.9	0	23.1	26.1	**54.2**	**40.9**	36.9	29.8
Experiments	12.1	13.8	28.8	13.0	**44.1**	15.9	20.2	23.0
Computation practice	34.5	**48.3**	38.5	8.7	**50.8**	29.5	17.9	33.3
Per cent (Total)	100 (58)	100 (29)	100 (52)	100 (23)	100 (59)	100 (44)	100 (84)	100 (349)

Table entries show numbers of respondents expressed as percentages of *column* totals, with large or otherwise noteworthy entries highlighted in bold typeface. 'Primary' level means teaching students aged 11 and under. 'Lower secondary' means teaching students in the 11–16 years age-group. 'Upper secondary' means teaching students in the 16–19 years age group.

differentiation in the use made of technical resources according to teaching level. Primary schools seem to use computers more extensively for the functions at the top of the list, as do the 'user'-discipline specialists at both secondary levels. This is predictable since the application-, project-oriented approach may be similar in these cases. There is a wider range of uses at upper secondary level. Only at this level, for example, do experimentation and simulations really begin to feature.

The extensive use of technical resources to provide *computational practice* is a little worrying, especially if it refers to algorithm training. It seems to be particularly popular with teachers of specialist statistics courses at both secondary levels, however, which may imply repetition with similar analytical exercises designed to train students in statistical processing with the particular software and hardware available. Further research is needed to elucidate exactly what teachers mean when they say they use resources for this purpose, especially in the light of the present move to switch the emphasis of statistical education from computation to application. Another area that needs clarification is evidenced by the unexpectedly high percentages of teachers claiming to use computers for data *collection*. These may be indicative of some confusion among respondents between what is strictly the *collection* and what is the *compilation* of data.

Data processing uses are common, but slightly less so in the context of mathematics. Simulations are more prevalent at the upper secondary level, mainly in statistics and mathematics contexts, and surprisingly do not feature at all at the lower secondary statistics course level. In general, data storage is the province of the lower levels of teaching, while experimentation is almost exclusively an activity for upper secondary statisticians. Concept simulations are surprisingly little used, even though recent years have seen the proliferation of software for this purpose. Simulations or models of *real-life* applications are not mentioned at all, and this must surely be an area of statistical work that needs to be developed at school level This is especially pertinent when teachers find it difficult to teach their students to link theory to practice. (See Chapter 2.)

THE STATISTICAL LABORATORY

It is useful if a room can be provided for statistical work in which equipment for experiments and relevant publications can be stored. Equipment might range from the (almost) costless variety through scientific apparatus to specially designed kits. The more comprehensive commercial statistical kits will probably contain six-sided and twenty-sided dice, shakers, a roulette wheel, populations of rods, and a binomial sampling box. It is important for students to experience the relative frequency characteristics of the outcomes from *biased* dice as well, and the Schools Council Project on Statistical Education booklets (Holmes, 1991) provide instructions for making and using biased dice, as well as giving many other ideas for practicals which require only very modest items of equipment.

In fact, teachers should easily be able to put together their own teaching kit and there seems to be little to recommend the purchase of a pre-packaged kit. Some useful items to have are boxes of matches, bottles of marbles or beads, a good supply of stiff paper, and maps. Apparatus should include scissors, geometry implements, calculators, rulers, statistics templates such as the one produced by the Centre for Statistical Education at the University of Sheffield (1988), and weighing scales. Statistical tables and graph paper, including normal probability and other specialised statistics paper, should be available. It is also useful to have large sheets of lined paper with some column rulings for recording results. The Schools Council Project on Statistical Education booklets (Holmes, 1991) have provided further copyright-free tables and charts for the recording of results, including the Stirling Recording Sheet mentioned in Chapter 6 (see also Giles, 1979) for use in investigating the *settling down* of the relative frequency diagram.

Publications kept in the room could include published data, statistical case studies, and possibly some statistical journals and publications such as *Teaching Statistics*,[3] *Statistics in Society* (the Series A Journal of the Royal Statistical Society),[4] and *The Statistician*,[5] in addition to a selection of statistics texts and reference books. Journals such as the *American Statistician*[6] may be beyond a school's budget, but it is important that students should be encouraged to use local library resources to gain access to such statistical publications. Unfortunately it is probably the case that higher education institutions will have a more useful stock of relevant journals than local authority libraries, in which case students will probably only benefit if their teachers are prepared to consult such resources.

Visual aids in the form of charts and models, for example of probability distributions, could be on display in the statistical laboratory. One advantage to the teacher of having all these resources for statistics teaching in the statistical laboratory is that they are then readily to hand for illustrating points as they arise during practical and project work. Some computing facilities must be available in the statistics room, but it should not be thought of as a computer laboratory to the exclusion of its primary purpose, namely that of affording opportunities for *statistical* activities.

AUDIO-VISUAL AIDS

Technical resources aimed specifically at helping the teacher to teach, and which are not unique to statistics, should not be forgotten. These include films, programmed learning aids, assessment materials, and overhead transparencies. The variety of resources available can be seen by looking at the listings that are produced by the American Statistical Association Committee on audio-visual instructional materials and published in the *American Statistician*. Although only USA sources are listed there, some of the items would also be of value to UK users, although care must be taken with respect to compatibility with UK technical requirements. This is particularly important for those who wish to purchase video-cassettes from the US. The American format is not the same as the PAL format used in the UK and conversion is expensive.

Masters for overhead transparencies can be bought as separate packs or, sometimes, form part of teachers' handbooks. Those showing diagrams, for example, of probability distributions, are particularly useful, as producing one's own is time-consuming, although statistical templates such as the one mentioned earlier, produced by Centre for Statistical Education at the University of Sheffield, are a help.

The use of films to bring experiences into the classroom can be important for statistics, which has applications in such a wide range of contexts. They may, for example, be used to prepare students with relevant context-specific knowledge prior to their embarking on designing a practical project. Alternatively, they might provide a source of national data or information that can encourage students to conduct their own local investigation for comparison purposes.

Films and video-tapes showing the *use* of statistics can provide important material for critical discussion about the reliability and validity of the methods adopted and the conclusions based on them. Films about the work of different kinds of statisticians can also demonstrate the power and scope of the subject, suggest areas for project work, and sometimes stimulate contacts with local commerce and industry.

An exciting way in which video films have been used to bring experiences into the classroom is described by Rubin *et al*. (1990). Based on an 'interactive video' set-up using cassette recordings as opposed to disks, students capture relevant data on film themselves and then use a Macintosh computer and a software package called *TAPEMEASURE* to take their required measurements off-screen. The particular example described relates to a student investigation of the characteristics that enable some people to run faster than others. The software provides the opportunity to measure distance, angle and time elapsed. Designing an appropriate study, calibrating field and on-screen measurements, deciding on relevant variables such as stride length, angle of knee bend, etc., all provide challenging problems for the students. The software also has statistical and graphical capabilities built into it to cater for the subsequent analysis stages.

Films can be used to demonstrate some of the routines found in software for teaching concepts. In general, films can quickly show how things change over time, for example they can illustrate how queues form in supermarkets or in traffic, or can show crops growing and the kinds of changes in growth rate that occur. In other words, they illustrate the processes we model or simulate with the help of statistical theory. The British Broadcasting Corporation's programmes for pre-16-year-old students (1982) and Advanced level students (1984) are particularly good examples although, as with all broadcasts made with content of topical interest, their dating eventually renders them unacceptable to the broadcasters. One can only hope that they will be replaced by other materials at least as useful. The Open University television programmes on probability and statistics, each course being intended to have a five-year lifetime before modification, also contain excellent teaching resources. Some of the material is appropriate for school level because it provides introductory tuition for non-specialist students, often with the emphasis on dynamic graphical presentations and contextual applications rather than on pure theoretical statistics. The mathematics courses often include statistical material, but teachers should also look at other discipline areas in the Open University programmes.

After researching the availability and quality of existing video training courses on statistics, the International Statistical Institute and UNICEF designed a video training package aimed at improving teaching effectiveness in developing countries. The pilot video-cassette was chosen to be *Assessing the Nutritional Status of Young Children*. This package is now being produced by UNICEF together with the British Broadcasting Corporation and the Open University. Although tentative drafts for other video training packages have been produced, they are being held back through lack of funding.

Audio-cassettes and video-tapes of eminent statisticians reminiscing and talking about their work could be good general interest resources. The Royal Statistical Society keeps a number of video-tapes, featuring such personalities as Barnard, Lindley, Boreham, Moser, Bartlett, Kendall, Finney, Yates and Cox, which are available for purchase or hire.[7] The Centre for Statistical Education at the University of Sheffield produced an audio-tape called *The Statistician at Work* (Barnett, 1987), again featuring eminent statisticians. Such recordings might provide important insights into statistics as a career.

While it has been suggested that audio-tapes could be useful as revision aids (see Green, 1989, for a review of such materials for GCSE level students) some of the audio-tapes which claim to give instruction in statistical methods are not worth consideration, especially if there are no accompanying notes. One particularly *un*-forgettable example was the use of an audio-cassette to teach data presentation. The 'dit-dit-dit-dit-da' sound effects taking the student through the process of producing a tally chart had to be heard to be believed!

On the other hand, one advantage of audio-tapes over texts is that a more informal manner can be used in the former. It is also perhaps a little easier to indicate the relative importance of different aspects by moderations in the presentation tone. The Open University uses tapes to talk students through problems. There are accompanying texts and the tapes are designed to be switched off while the listener performs a prompted 'activity'. Many foreign language courses use similar techniques, and indeed, a number of the Open University *televised* programmes insert still frames for the same purpose, anticipating the use of home video-recorders to record off-air for later study.

The need for a variety of modes of instruction and learning is particularly marked among younger students whose concentration span can be relatively short. Some teachers feel that even a 20-minute video containing both sound and visual stimuli can be too long. The BBC films mentioned earlier were designed for the teacher to show a section at a time with activities and discussions taking place in the interludes. Given this problem of concentration lapse, audio-tapes would have to be even more outstanding in some way if they were to have any chance of success with the younger students.

Both audio-cassettes and video-tapes can make statistics real and can supplement teachers and other resources where these are in short supply, although it goes without saying that if the latter is the case then technical provision is also likely to be limited. Replay and review possibilities can help provide for students who come from a variety of backgrounds with widely differing skills and competence levels, something which can be a particular problem in the teaching of statistics where students are often neither specialists nor particularly numerate.

A slightly different use of videos is in providing feedback to the students when they have been involved in a role play situation, for example acting as a statistical consultant or giving a statistical presentation. Videos of statistics teachers in action might also have their uses in pre- and in-service education, in the event of such education in the area of statistics being recognised as important, and its being provided at all!

PROGRAMMED LEARNING AND INTERACTIVE VIDEO

Programmed learning aids in statistics are not a major resource in schools and programmed learning is not likely to become a main method of instruction at school level in the foreseeable future. In fact, the available software tends to be inflexible, and is generally of a very poor standard, being geared towards 'fact' and definition teaching, or, worse still, the rote practice of arithmetic computations. This is not in keeping with the general principles of statistical education which emphasise skills development and understanding. Programmed learning might occasionally be used to supplement the usual teaching methods for remediation or revision, and it is sometimes thought to be useful for stretching more able students, but we would suggest that there is already plenty to stretch this group in the realms of applied statistics.

There are some developments in programmed learning, however, which might be worth watching for in the future. These are mostly in the contexts of higher education and in distance learning, and they are not particularly directed to the area of statistical education at present. The move is away from the traditional programmed textbook approach of sequenced questions, towards more imaginative uses of computer software and interactive videos. As yet, it is too early to say how successful these approaches will be, or indeed whether their development will be accompanied by the necessary research into their design and use to secure that success. In the main, the prototype developments of interactive video-disk systems in the area of skills training at school level, for example, have generally not proved to be cost-effective. The production cost and time are excessive and the results are as yet decidedly crude.

One related development, namely the interactive video-disk as a data source, however, has some potential prospects for statistical education. The UK Domesday Project materials, described in Chapter 7, comprise a vast amount of data contained on two video-disks which can be accessed interactively. There are also floppy disks and resource books to help the teacher and student make good use of the material.

A number of general issues relating to databases and the implications of different ways of obtaining, inputting, storing and accessing data have already been discussed in Chapters 7 and 8. However, it is worth pointing out that the use of compact disks as storage devices will greatly increase the scope of on-site database sizes in the future. Cost considerations at present mean that the impact of such a storage medium has yet to be felt in schools. Nevertheless, this is a development that will undoubtedly eventually have significance for the teaching of statistics.

TEXTBOOKS AND THE TEACHING OF STATISTICS

The growth in importance, influence and popularity of probability and statistics in the curriculum is reflected in the flooding of the market with new textbooks. These texts come in many 'flavours', presenting a variety of 'philosophies', structures and content. We have indicated in the previous chapters that the teaching of statistics requires special care and attention. These warnings apply not only to the preparation of a lecture to be delivered verbally in front of a 'live' audience, but also to the written literature that will accompany and guide our students on a statistics course.

It goes without saying that the textbook is an indispensable part of teaching statistics. The text and the syllabus together provide course cohesion. Both must be considered with the greatest of care. The choice, therefore, of a suitable textbook for a particular course must be guided by some basic and carefully thought-out criteria.

How does the teacher relate to the textbook in the classroom? In *College Mathematics: Suggestions on How to Teach It* (Mathematical Association of America, 1979), some attitudes of teachers to mathematics texts are described. They apply to teachers of statistics as well. A teacher may feel obliged to bypass a textbook (suggested or imposed by an examination board, say) and to provide alternative material by handing out lecture notes and guides. The teacher may even criticise the text in front of the class of students. This is clearly an undesirable state of affairs. It undermines the students' confidence in the particular text (and perhaps in textbooks in general) and may adversely affect morale. It is simply a reflection of a mismatch between the course content and the textbook. Where they have the appropriate freedom, teachers can avoid such a mismatch by paying attention to guidelines suggested below for choosing sound reading material.

Teachers sometimes have to correct specific errors and misconceptions in textbooks. Indeed, in the light of our earlier discussions about the difficulties of teaching statistics and probability we should be on our guard, expecting statistics texts to be more prone to misconceptions than texts in other subject areas. Brewer (1985) discusses the myths and misconceptions that are prevalent in statistics texts for the behavioural sciences and a number of these common misconceptions have been discussed in more detail in Chapters 3, 4 and 5. Again, as we emphasised before, the teacher must be aware of such sources of conceptual difficulties so as to pinpoint them more easily in textbooks and bring them to the attention of students.

There is, of course, the other side of the coin. A textbook may be so well written that it can relieve the teacher from explaining the basics. In this case we recommend that the teacher clarify and augment the text with additional examples and applications. Hopefully the text itself will contain complementary and supplementary materials and exercises that will encourage this. If the text is well written, then it is no bad thing to read salient extracts from it in class, discuss important ideas that will inevitably emerge from such extracts, and thus clarify the more elusive statistical concepts. An important additional advantage of having a good text is that the teacher can devote more attention to a student's individual needs, while being reasonably secure in the knowledge that, meanwhile, material gleaned by the other students from the texts should be soundly based.

The textbook must act as support and background material for a course in statistics. It is, therefore, not too surprising that teachers choose texts whose contents are structured in a manner similar to the course syllabus. We have indicated in Chapter 1 that the traditional statistics syllabus displays the following structure:

descriptive statistics – probability – inferential statistics

But the syllabus can be structured in other ways. Exhibit 9.1 lists some possibilities.

Exhibit 9.1 **Structures for syllabuses**

Structure	Description
1	descriptive statistics – probability – inferential statistics
2	probability – descriptive statistics – inferential statistics
3	probability – inferential statistics
4	descriptive statistics – inferential statistics
5	exploratory statistics – confirmatory statistics

Most standard textbooks follow the pattern of Structure 1 with the emphasis being placed on descriptive statistics for introductory students, and on the inferential section for students who are more advanced.

A change in order in Structure 1 produces Structure 2. Structure 3 omits descriptive statistics or mentions it only in passing. Textbooks adopting Structures 2 and 3 tend to emphasise the mathematical and/or theoretical approach and to treat probability, random variables and probability distributions in more depth.

In a textbook based on Structure 4 some probability is clearly necessary for the section on statistical inference, but only the barest minimum is presented with the emphasis on an empirical and intuitive approach (see Hodges *et al.*, 1975).

Since Tukey's pioneering work (1977) on Exploratory Data Analysis, there are an increasing number of texts adopting Structure 5 with a heavy bias towards exploratory analysis. Some texts have taken on board only the basic techniques of EDA and ignored the more exotic ideas proposed by Tukey. These basic techniques have been combined with some of the standard topics to produce a balance of what is good in both traditional and current statistical practice (see Koopmans, 1981).

There are of course textbooks which follow structures not mentioned above, but these appear less frequently as essential reading material. Indeed, one of the present authors was recently disturbed to find the chapter concerned with data collection positioned several chapters *after* the one on hypothesis testing in an introductory statistics text intended for use by students of psychology and education. Such misleading representations of priorities can be very dangerous.

Having decided that the structure of the textbook matches that of the required syllabus, the teacher should assess the text according to the following additional criteria proposed by Graham (1976):

(a) The discursive nature of the content – that is, how much prose or 'chat' there is and how it will contribute to the transmission of statistical concepts to students. Hansen *et al.* (1985), Myers (1983) and Myers *et al.* (1983) have attempted to research and contrast the effects of high-explanatory texts and low-explanatory texts on the acquisition of basic probability concepts. There is the suggestion that students given the high-explanatory content were subsequently more adept at handling 'story' type problems. Since a major function of the statistician involves the unravelling of a natural language representation ('story') of a problem, high-explanatory texts would then be preferred to low-explanatory texts where the emphasis tends to be on providing ready 'recipes' (formulae) and on encouraging rote-learning.

(b) The theoretical approach: Is there too much or too little emphasis on mathematical notation and explanation?

(c) The development of technical and applied skills: How much concentration is there on worked examples and exercises?

(d) The scope of the text: How many and what topics are covered?

(e) The level of the contents – as assessed by the teacher intending to use the text.

Graham went on to suggest some further, possibly more pragmatic but nevertheless important, criteria:

(f)   Last date of publication: While a textbook published 10 or even 20 years ago might still be regarded as sound and still retain its popularity, teachers should check whether a new edition is available. They should ensure that the material has been updated and that examples and exercises reflect the trend towards realism and relevance. Often new editions of standard textbooks will revise their examples and exercises for implementation in a statistical computing environment.

(g)   Publisher: A number of publishers produce texts as part of a series devoted to various areas of statistics (from the introductory to the advanced). Such series will have respected academic and practising statisticians as part of an advisory editorial board and teachers will be able to rely on such collections of texts for source material.

(h)   Price: If a textbook is recommended for purchase, then in addition to academic criteria for choosing it, the text must be priced within the means of students on limited budgets.

(i)   Number of pages: A textbook consisting of more than say, 500 pages might prove attractive in that it suggests thorough coverage of all standard topics. However, the teacher should check whether all the material in the text is relevant to the syllabus and whether it can be dealt with in sufficient depth in the time available. A textbook should match the requirements of a course and both should be modest in size.

With the expansion of statistics in the curriculum teachers may be attracted by the large and 'all-embracing' textbook (assuming a reasonable price). From his personal experience of teaching statistics in the USA, Anderson (1989) relates that textbooks (especially those for introductory business statistics) often consist of 700 or 800 pages and are supposed to be covered in a single semester (15 weeks). Clearly the most that students can hope to achieve on such a programme is to absorb some recipes without the underlying conceptual understanding.

For evaluating textbooks Cobb (1987) puts forward criteria similar to those indicated above. He concentrates, however, on the quality of the exercises provided by the text and regards this aspect as perhaps the most important:

Judge a book by its exercises and you cannot go far wrong.

In the past (especially before the availability of high-speed computing facilities) data sets used in statistical exercises were usually fictitious or obtained from real-life sources but 'massaged'

Exhibit 9.2 **A framework for evaluating textbooks** (Cobb, 1987)

Question	Justification
Are the data sets real or fake?	Real statisticians don't analyse fake data.
Does completing the exercise answer an interesting question, or is the number-pushing a dead end in itself?	Real statisticians don't stop with the arithmetic.
What is the ratio of thinking to mere grinding?	Real statisticians think.

beyond recognition in order to accommodate the 'recipes' propounded in the text. If we are to impress upon our students the wide-ranging applications and the importance of statistics, then we need to feed them *realistic* data sets as exercises and ask questions with interesting and relevant answers.

When evaluating exercises for their realism and relevance, Cobb encourages teachers to ask the three questions shown in Exhibit 9.2. He also points out the justification for these questions.

While endorsing the ideal of using real data, the present authors would not wish to go as far as advocating the use of nothing but real data. There is a sense in which *realism* may be more important for some teaching purposes than *reality*.

To enhance the realism of statistical exercises, wherever possible data sets should be accompanied by background information, as they should be in the case of real data. Application area(s), source(s) of data, purpose(s) for which data were collected, clear descriptions of cases and variates associated with the data, and any other relevant facts should be provided (see also Chapter 7). Many textbooks are now accompanied with the data in machine-readable form (floppy disks, etc.) thus allowing the exercises to be performed in a computing environment. By doing so, the exercises in textbooks can encourage statistical thinking and reasoning and avoid blind number crunching.

Unfortunately, but not surprisingly, we do not find uniformity of symbolic notation and of terminology from one textbook to another. When evaluating a text for a statistics course, teachers must pay close attention to the author's use of notation and check whether this matches the notation with which the teachers (and students) are familiar, and which is expected by any relevant examination boards. At this point it is also worthwhile asking whether the author of the text gives crystal clear definitions in those instances where there is a strong possibility of confusion with their common usage in natural language or with definitions in other sciences (Mainland, 1983).

As has been raised, for example, in Chapters 4 and 5, confusion can arise with definitions of terms such as chance, error, random sampling, bias, normal, etc. In the case of 'normal' there are so many meanings attached to it both in natural language and in other scientific areas (especially medicine) that the term 'Gaussian distribution' seems to be an increasingly popular alternative to 'normal distribution'. Velleman and Hoaglin (1981) claim that, after exploring data, statisticians realise that 'normal' shapes are, in fact, rare. They therefore prefer the name 'Gaussian' and employ it in their text.

In summing up the desirable characteristics of textbooks, Anderson (1989) has this to say:

Textbooks should be dense in ideas, but short in length, and modest in coverage. The aim should be to cover selected material briefly and well – the selection consisting of core concepts, filled out and reinforced by examples of their application.

Note that an interesting statistics text as opposed to a boring one is an important consideration, especially for students whose main areas of study are not in the contexts of specialist mathematics/ statistics.

It must also be remembered that, for some non-specialist students, the 'best' textbook is likely to be the one they can pick up and read immediately, without assistance, subject to its not having technical inaccuracies, rather than one that might be chosen for them by a specialist in mathematical statistics. Once embarked on reading statistical material, such students can be encouraged to move on, but for many the size of the hurdle associated with using their *first statistics textbook* may prove so daunting that it also becomes their *last hurdle in statistical education*! Certainly with mature students from widely differing backgrounds, and with different precursor mathematical experience, a useful starting point is to encourage each to brouse in the hopefully well-stocked local library or bookshop. The students' expressed views of which book each would choose as their 'first reader' can provide important insights for the teacher as to 'where the students are at'.

NOTES

1. Manufactured by Data Viz, UK distribution Principal N&C.
2. Abacus Concepts, MacSpin. Copyright 1985–89. Abacus Concepts, Inc., Berkeley, California, USA.
3. Publication details available from The Centre for Statistical

Education, Department of Probability and Statistics, The
University of Sheffield, Sheffield, S3 7RH.
4. Available through the Royal Statistical Society, 25 Enford
Street, London, W1H 2BH.
5. Available through the Institute of Statisticians, 43, St Peter's
Square, Preston, PR1 7BX.
6. Available through the American Statistical Association, 1429
Duke Street, Alexandria, VA 22314-3402, USA.
7. Royal Statistical Society, 25 Enford Street, London, W1H
2BH.

Assessing statistical knowledge, understanding and skills

Possibly the only arguments in favour of assessing statistical understanding by traditional written examinations may be that this is one of the very few forms of assessment where we can be sure that the work is the candidate's own, and that, as they are used extensively in higher education and by professional bodies, similar examinations at school level can be seen to be preparation for post-school examinations. Arguments that are often made against this form of assessment, however, stress its artificial nature and the unfairness that the time constraint may cause for some candidates. Examinations usually test only the relatively short-term memory and there is no guarantee that facts learned for the test will be retained.

Certainly, by its nature, statistics does not lend itself to assessment based solely on the students' ability to produce answers to written questions in a timed examination. In statistics, in addition to testing factual knowledge and mere rote computation, we need to assess understanding and the practical skills of doing and communicating statistics. These last two skills involve interaction with other persons and the activities associated with them give rise to measurable output. They are skills that are seen to be important by employers of statisticians. See, for example, the Centre for Statistical Education report (1985).

Figure 10.1 indicates that understanding comes through doing and communicating, but that understanding needs to be present before the doing and communicating can be really successful. One conclusion that might be drawn is that the assessment of understanding may take care of itself if we concentrate on reliably and validly assessing the doing and communicating. At present, however, this is not a true reflection of the currently used approaches to assessing statistics. Indeed, there are those who may consider it to be more of an ideal than a practical and attainable reality.

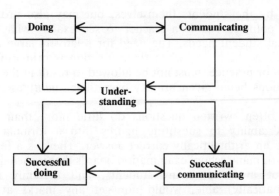

Figure. 10.1 **Successful doing and communicating of statistics implies its understanding**

Some of the problems associated with obtaining valid research items were highlighted in Chapter 6, and test items criticised in a research context are not likely to be any more appropriate than the same kind of items used in an assessment context. The moves in education towards more coursework and projects assessed by teachers, both within the aims of the National Curriculum and at GCSE and 'A' levels, are bringing the assessment of statistics more in line with what is required for evaluating students' practical expertise. It is to be hoped that similar reforms in assessment will become more widespread at higher, college and professional, levels. Skills must be taught before they can be considered to be available for assessment, however. It is not sufficient to move towards the more appropriate assessment techniques without first developing an appropriate pedagogy for teaching the skills to be assessed. Indeed, it is first necessary to develop a consensus of what those skills will be. In the UK it is not clear at present that those who set statistics examinations always share the same views in this respect as those statistical educationalists who write about the objectives of teaching statistics and its assessment.

'TRADITIONAL' WRITTEN FORMS OF ASSESSMENT

Written questions, whether done for unseen or 'open-book' examinations, or with no time constraint and with access to assistance from teachers and other resources, will undoubtedly be used for many years. If well designed they may serve a useful purpose. Written questions, even those of a relatively repetitive nature, can assist students in learning by practice. They can be marked by the students themselves, but may also provide the starting point to enable a teacher to see exactly what help an individual student needs. The need for relatively large numbers of questions, however, when their function is primarily one of *rehearsal* or practice, must not be allowed to result in the *quantity* of questions being given priority over their *quality* as statistical exercises.

Very often, written questions do little more than test the students' ability to substitute figures into a formula and to compute an arithmetically correct answer. There is a feeling on the part of many school examination boards that if such questions were not available, many students, and certainly the less (mathematically) able, would not get any marks at all. In response, of course, most teachers will train their students to be successful in tackling such questions, with the result that statistics stagnates into a computational, rather than an interpretive, discipline, since the examiners only set questions that the students can do, and the teachers only teach what the examiners will require the students to do.

Some progress has been made in recent years and assessment questions are now being seen that accord more with 'real' statistical practice. However, progress in this respect is slow and may depend on the characteristics and interests of the chief examiner for a particular examination board or syllabus.

A question such as:

'Compute the arithmetic mean of 6.3, 5.4, 4.9, 1.8 and 4.3'

does nothing to test the students' understanding of the *functional* characteristics of the mean as a representative statistic, or model of the given data, and so is a bad question. It can also be criticised because it is based on a small sample of meaningless figures.

The size of the data set in a written examination question is often constrained by examination conditions and the (un-) availability of relevant technical resources. Clearly there are 'reasonably-sized' data sets and there are those that are 'too small'. Debating appropriate sizes without reference to the assessment purpose, however, is much the same as discussing 'how long is a piece of string?'. In the case of numerical questions set merely to reinforce and test the students' understanding of definitions it may be advisable for the data and the results to be integers, and for the sample size to be relatively small. Some research has been done into generating such simple calculation examples (e.g. Posten, 1982; Read and Riley, 1983). A case may be made, however, for restricting the use of such questions to multiple-choice type examination papers.

Making data more meaningful by providing a context is not the

Exhibit 10.1 **Adding 'meaning' to numbers can equal nonsense**

The train to work should leave the station at 8.35 each morning. In one week, the train was late in departing on four days.

Monday	35 minutes (fire in the restaurant car)
Tuesday	6 minutes
Wednesday	On time
Thursday	2 minutes
Friday	3 minutes

What was the average number of minutes that the train was late leaving?

simple exercise it might appear to be. Exhibit 10.1 is an example of *bad* question design in this respect.

The official answer to this question was 9.2 minutes (the arithmetic mean). However, the figure for Monday clearly relates to an *exceptional* instance, and as such it is foolish to expect students to include it in computing the 'average' over all five days. Indeed, it is more than foolish because it implicitly 'teaches' students that to do so is correct practice. In fact, a candidate who excluded the Monday figure would have scored no marks on the question, and would presumably have learned as a result that to do *good* statistics is wrong.

If the above question is to be salvaged, it should at least ask students to comment on whether the 'average' is a good figure to use to represent the week's data, or indeed to stand for what passengers might expect in general. It would also have been possible to encourage students to propose better representative figures, with reasons, or to comment on the 'average' worked out with and without Monday's datum, with and without Wednesday's datum. None of these alternatives was included. It is clear that with a little care, the problem could have been turned into an interesting *statistical* exercise, highlighting the very real difficulties with which we may be faced when attempting to derive a representative summary statement about any real-life situation.

The deeper question of when an outlier is an outlier and when it is merely an extreme value is certainly an issue that teachers should be considering with their students. However, teachers are discouraged from *educating* students in 'real' statistics if examination boards set the above type of question, and if a simplistic 'right–wrong', 1-point marking scheme is used based merely on *computational* 'accuracy'.

The earlier example based on meaningless data would also be very hard for candidates who really do grasp the statistical concept of 'average'. They are placed in a considerable dilemma regarding whether or not the value 1.8 is or is not to be treated as an outlier, because there is no context to provide clues. As they stand, both questions examine only the *arithmetical* aspect of 'average' and are positively damaging to its more pertinent *statistical* aspects.

Of course, it is not just examiners who fall into the trap of designing bad *statistical* questions. It is often the case that writers of textbooks, and teachers themselves, dream up data sets that are not appropriate to the statistical processing then demanded of the students. As we saw in Chapter 6, research studies attempting to assess statistical understanding also have problems over ensuring that the intended task requirements are actually communicated to the respondent. Green's (1982) study attempted to design a paper-and-pencil test of probabilistic understanding, in which much thought and research went into the selection and design of the questions. One of the purposes of the study was to shed light on students' difficulties with statistical terminology. In fact, despite the extensive piloting of this assessment instrument, even this study had shortcomings with respect to the final choice of wording for some of the questions, showing how difficult it is to get it right.

In any event, it seems that the difficulties that students can have in *interpreting* the specific requirements of a problem, and the care taken in devising appropriate syntax for the sort of research into statistical and probabilistic misconceptions described in Chapters 3, 4 and 5, receive scant attention when it comes to designing statistical assessment and teaching examples, even to the point of encouraging 'wrong' interpretations.

It is still not uncommon to find questions that reflect back to the days when students were rehearsed in both 'regular' and 'computational' formulae. Such questions can only be justified if they serve to explore the students' deeper understanding of the concept as opposed to merely assessing their flexibility with a wider range of arithmetic exercises. It cannot, for example, be assumed that

'Find the arithmetic mean of 61, 62, 64, 65 and 67'

tests anything more substantial than the students' arithmetical capability with bigger numbers than the question

'Find the arithmetic mean of 1, 2, 4, 5 and 7'.

The examiners are probably only testing the ability to perform the *computation* in a *slightly* different way, one that may be based on the use of an arbitrary mean as the starting point.

A proper understanding of statistical concepts depends on an infrastructure of knowledge, thinking and experience which is probably far more constraining than that required for mathematical concepts, where it may be more easy to test isolated concepts. In statistics, the concepts are part of an intricately interwoven *whole*. This makes the assessment of statistics a much more difficult exercise than it might at first appear to be.

For example, there is a sense in which asking students to compute the 'average contents of a box of matches' (see Goodchild, 1987) should conjure up a different set of considerations and decisions from those that arise when the student is asked to compute the 'average contents of a bag of crisps'. These should include considerations related to discrete and continuous variables, decimal and integer values, approximations, and the practical use to which the derived 'average' is to be put. They might also include considerations of how to ensure that the 'average' is derived from a representative sample of boxes or bags, and so on. The infrastructure of statistical processing requires that assessment tasks should be designed with all these aspects in mind. Failure to do so, as has been seen, can lead to questions being set in which the required solution will flaunt other statistical considerations, and to data sets being chosen which are inappropriate for the processing task demanded.

Examination boards sometimes set questions where contextual considerations conflict with the conventions that the board expects the student to apply. As we saw in Chapter 7, the definition of class limits is a common example where, sometimes, even professional statisticians would disagree with one another in the face of the ambiguous examples used in examination questions. It is not fair to assess students assuming that they will apply one, rather than another, convention on any given occasion. However, it sometimes appears that the examiners are not themselves always aware of the issues involved.

Questions such as the following test only manipulative skills:

Show that $\dfrac{\Sigma(X_i - \bar{X})^2}{n - 1} = \dfrac{\Sigma X_i^2 - (\Sigma X_i)^2/n}{n - 1}$

The above example can be done without any reference to a sample variance. Indeed, if the algebraic manipulation is not new to the student, the question may merely be a test of memory and not of statistics, as would also be a question asking only for a definition of the variance. It might be argued that *mathematics* students could gain insight into the concept of variance through manipulating the mathematical language representing it. For example, a grasp of the mathematical schema for 'averaging' might yield generalisable insights into all kinds of index numbers, standard and mean deviations, and so on, while the general principle of squared deviations has analogies in a variety of contexts such as regression, variance and chi-square.

However, many students of statistics have not acquired the *vocabulary*, let alone the fluency and reasoning power, of what to them is the *foreign* language of *matheMAGICal* symbols. Unless the language is taught first, an alternative way is needed to educate these students statistically. In any case, to restrict the assessment of even those students who do have facility with mathematical language, to what is merely its manipulation, is to trivialise their skills.

Many questions fall into the 'test of memory' category. Questions asking for definitions and routine derivations obviously do this, but so too do many standard problems, especially those in the field of probability. It is not unreasonable to expect persons who are training to become expert in a discipline to be able to remember basic facts, and to some extent remembering and understanding do go together. However, when examination questions do not require the student to put what is recalled to good *statistical* use, they are not really assessing *statistics*. The provision of formulae sheets in examinations has been a step away from forms of assessment dominated by rote memory, but this cannot be a panacea for all the ills of statistics assessment.

Some questions, for example those of the 'Find a mean', or 'Fit the regression line' variety, which are designed to be done with the aid of a calculator or computer, may do little more than test the ability to use pre-packaged statistics functions. It has taken some time to convince examination boards that technical resources are here to stay, and so are here to be used. However, it is now generally accepted, and even required, that examination candidates will have such resources available, and moreover that these resources will have certain *minimum*, as distinct from *maximum*, functions. This should enable far more challenging questions to be set, for example those involving the exploration of a data set or those requiring the use of simulation, possibly to estimate probabilities where analytical solutions are too difficult, as was suggested in Chapter 8.

At present, however, examination boards still tend to be slow to introduce relevant types of questions. In this respect, the UK situation is not unique. Russell (1990) reported that

in some parts of the United States, there has been a push to have a certain percentage (up to 40% for example) of a student's examination permitting the use of calculators. The implication of this is that for that 40% the more traditional, computational, types of questions are not appropriate, and questions which emphasise skills of interpretation, etc., *are being* introduced'. [Current authors' emphasis. Note: Russell did not say 'have been'.]

MULTIPLE-CHOICE VS OPEN-ENDED QUESTIONS

Multiple-choice questions have become popular in many areas of the curriculum in recent years. They test similar aspects to other questions, but tend to preclude those that would require 'wordy' answers. They can assist students, since the correct answers are available for recognition as opposed to having to be recalled. There is a danger in this, however, because commonly held incorrect ideas may unintentionally be reinforced if they are supplied as distractors.

In designing a multiple-choice test, care has to be taken to ensure that the probability of gaining a pass by guesswork has an acceptably small probability of occurring. Because this topic is close to students' hearts, the use of multiple-choice tests can provide an important bonus for their statistical education. It can stimulate much interesting debate and encourage project work in probability, requiring as it does the operational definition of the problem and the choice of criteria of 'acceptably low'. It can also encourage theoretical, empirical and simulation studies with a number of variable factors such as length of test, number of distractors, random or systematic place ordering of the 'correct' response, and the comparison of a range of 'intuitively' optimal strategies of guessing.

In contrast to multiple-choice items, open-ended questions are often set. In general, these are a more promising way of assessing *real* statistics, especially in a classroom situation, but care is still needed in their design because they are not without problems of their own. Firstly, the concept of 'full marks' needs to reflect what the examiner believes the best candidates would be able to achieve in the time available. This may not be easy to define if the question is really open-ended because it may not be possible to predict exactly what the candidates will try to do or what they will actually do. Secondly, the examiner needs to consider whether any analysis done was appropriate and correctly performed, and to evaluate the standard of any accompanying comments.

A typical open-ended question might instruct the student to 'Analyse the following data: . . .'. The obvious danger of such a vague brief for an examination candidate is that there are no clues as to what the examiner expects (although if it is an internally set examination the examiner might feel that the students have been briefed as to what they should do). Consequently, students may spend inappropriate amounts of time on the different aspects of the question.

The following is a particularly bad example of an open-ended question:

'You will probably have encountered data of the sort given [which comprised students' marks on a range of school subjects]. Now analyse it *in as many different ways as you can think of.*'

This is very dangerous because it fails to encourage any critical approach to what is and what is not an appropriate or meaningful way of treating such data. It does not even ask for comments on such matters.

ESSAYS

Essay questions, although not traditionally used in assessing school mathematics, can be very useful for statistics, for example 'practical' essays requiring students to evaluate a proposed research design or to write a critical commentary on a given data analysis.

It is possible to ask for accounts of what are essentially concepts. For example:

'Discuss, if possible with reference to one of the projects you have completed, the relevance of the Normal Distribution.'

although it is difficult to know how the student is to respond to this in the absence of any indication of to what, or to whom, the distribution is to be 'relevant'.

In the past, this indirect form of project assessment has been seen as an important way of testing understanding of the particular concept specified in the question. It is clearly one that can save the assessor a great deal of time. The argument could be made that if the student can answer the question well, even in the absence of having done appropriate (or any) practical course-work, then he or she deserves the available marks. However, such an approach can never be a real substitute for assessing students' practical and project work directly in accordance with the recognition of statistics as an *applied* subject. Furthermore, experience has shown that this approach tends at best to encourage students to do only those simple simulation studies which derive data conforming to the popular distributions. Few 'real-life' practicals, where the concepts are seen in action and used, are tackled.

The allocation by examination boards in the past of only a few marks for answers given to this part of an examination question has also meant that teachers have not been encouraged to treat practical projects as a major part of the syllabus. Most of the marks have tended to be allocated to what was perceived to be the 'meat' of the question, that is, to the part requiring the students to carry out algebraic manipulations, statistical computations (or to substitute numbers in formulae). In cost-effective terms, of course, these other parts are easier to mark in large-scale programmes of assessment, and they ensure that most students can rely on at least some 'safe' marks.

Essays on the nature of statistics, its history and modern developments, and its philosophical underpinnings may also be used to explore students' awareness of the importance of statistics and its relationship to the other subjects they study. In fact, such areas are rarely debated at school level, but perhaps they should be if the student is to be statistically *educated* rather than merely being statistically *taught*.

Essays are less dependent on the remembering of fine details than are 'technique' questions. They test the ability to organise material from a broad spectrum, they may test creativity, and almost certainly they test understanding. They also allow the student some freedom to demonstrate his or her own particular statistical skills, and they assess skills that are much closer to those exercised in a vocational statistics context. Often, they may allow the student to show what he or she knows, or can do, as distinct from what he or she does not know, or cannot do. In point of fact, this aspect is somewhat in the hands of the students, being a matter of examination-taking technique which few are lucky enough to be taught.

ASSESSING PRACTICAL WORK AND PROJECTS

A problem arises in considering whether assessment procedures are likely to be valid and reliable indicators of whether students have a *vocational* aptitude for statistics. As yet the discussion has focused on individual assessment, but of course in a work context most statisticians, or people with statistical responsibilities, are required to work as individuals within a team of people who do not necessarily share the same statistical facility or responsibility as themselves. Adopting Gilchrist's (1980) distinction between 'practicals' and 'projects' (see Chapter 7) as a guideline, it can be seen that project work, in particular, should give students important preparation for such work. However, assessment of projects is a relatively new task for most teachers.

Timed written examination papers tend to be technique oriented, testing factual knowledge and computational skills. They give candidates little opportunity to demonstrate what they know or what they understand and they cannot assess practical skills and all that go with them, i.e. intuition, judgement, organisation of an extended piece of work, investigation of an open-ended problem, and so on. The National Curriculum for Mathematics suggests that a weighting of 15 per cent should be given to the assessment of practical applications of mathematics

(Department of Education and Science, 1987). Since statistics is generally seen as part of mathematics, and since it is essentially a practical subject, practical work should be an integral part not only of its teaching but also of its assessment.

In assessing practical work, marks will be given for its organisation, for the quality of the practical work itself, for the recording of the results, for any analysis done, for the logic of its progression from the planning to the conclusion stages, and for the write-up. Practical work is, of course, difficult to mark because, just as with essays on topics which try to be 'practical', there can be more than one correct answer, or indeed there may be no correct answer.

The kinds of questions that must be asked when marking practical work (and to some extent 'practical' essays) would include the following:

- Are the aims and objectives clearly spelt out?
- Was a clear, operational plan arrived at (and executed) and were the decisions based on that plan logical?
- Do the proposals (and methods) accord with the stated intentions?
- Is the design efficient, however this is defined? For example, is there evidence that it would lead to the obtaining of better, more reliable, more detailed, quicker, cheaper, data, for the same amount of cost or effort expended on an alternative design? A good sampling design might well score higher in some cases than a proposal for a census.
- Are the proposals and any research descriptions and interpretations clearly communicated? For example, could a research assistant put the proposal into operation?
- Have personnel considerations and other research management aspects been taken into account?
- Has the significance of the work taken account of its place in the on-going development of knowledge in the particular subject area, or has it been seen as too isolated a study?
- Has proper consideration been given to a range of possible sources of information, and has an appropriate balance been struck between the use of primary and secondary data?
- Are there any technical flaws in the use of the statistical techniques themselves, e.g. incorrect formulae, computation errors, wrong (probability) structures in any underlying models?
- Are the significance and implications of the study subjected to appropriate critical evaluation?
- Has the use of technical resources been sensibly and efficiently incorporated (allowing for their availability not being universally consistent)?

- Do the students show an awareness of the need for, and use of, relevant pilot work?

It is open to the assessor either to evaluate the performance of some of the tasks involved in a project directly (according to behavioural criteria) or to assess them less directly (on the basis of 'hear-say') by evaluating the student's report of the work undertaken. It is reasonable to assume that the production (and delivery, if oral) of a *good report* will be dependent on the student having a good *understanding* of the relevant issues. The development of both written and oral communication skills may be considered to be an important aspect of students' statistical education. Employers of statisticians place great stress on communication skills when deciding whom to appoint. Whatever the medium, in addition to evaluating the actual practical work undertaken, it will be necessary to determine whether the quality of the report is satisfactory, namely whether it communicates the nature and results of the study clearly, unequivocally and efficiently.

Many schemes for assessing projects have been suggested. At one end of the spectrum there are extremely detailed schemes with marks allocated to specific, predetermined aspects of the different stages in the work. The assessment for the public examinations taken at age 16+ usually takes this form. In contrast, sometimes there may be almost no such pre-ordained marking scheme. Free-format marking of this kind is more often found in institutions of higher education. The very detailed schemes give no flexibility for assessing those projects which do not follow what is thought to be the standard pattern, but it is useful to have some broad breakdown and guidance as to the weighting to give each component.

The three main components in the assessment of a project are:

1. the general approach and attitude towards the project;
2. the actual execution of the work; and
3. the report.

We suggest that the first and third of these might each account for about 25 per cent of the marks available and that the execution would then account for about 50 per cent. Within 'approach and attitude' are included planning of the project, initiative, background reading, the ability to work without supervision, and, in the case of group projects, interaction with others. 'Execution' would include collection and analysis of the data, including computing work, whether appropriate techniques were used, and whether the conclusions were drawn correctly.

Both the quality and the quantity of the work contribute to the assessment. As regards quantity, the assessor has to consider how the amount done compares with what he or she feels would be reasonable in the time available to someone at the student's stage of knowledge. It is important to remember that in statistics it is just as possible to do too much analysis, collect too much data, etc., as too little, especially if the processes are inappropriate or extraneous to the purpose of the study. By first making checklists and putting projects in rank order, a good feel for the overall standard can be obtained, thereby constructing a framework within which to discriminate between individual students' work.

In assessing a report of a project, matters to be considered include saliency, the description of the study, the organisation into sections, and the presentation of data, tables, results, and diagrams. The assessment of a project, however, clearly involves far more than marking its final report. Project assessment will probably take the form of continuous assessment, since to some extent the teacher has to assess work on a project by observing the students. Asking students to keep a log-book which shows the time spent on different activities can be helpful at the assessment stage. If at all possible at least two assessors should evaluate each project, because there are so many different facets to any given project. Some of these will be specific to the context of study, in which case an assessor from the appropriate 'user'-area may be helpful.

As we saw in Chapter 7, the trend towards *group* project work is an important development and one that has great relevance for statistical education. Skills of 'assessing the individual *within* the group context' are no doubt going to be a further problem area for the teacher, being innovatory for most school subjects, and especially for mathematics. Indirectly this has been attempted within the context of the Annual Applied Statistics Prize where team projects are the requirement. Here, however, the assessment is of the *team's effort as a whole*, and criteria such as appropriate management and synthesis of individual skills and effort are relevant. (See Hawkins, 1989b, for a fuller discussion about the difficulties of making such evaluations.) The balance between assessing teamwork and individual work is a current debate about which our education policy makers still have many decisions to make. Communication skills, motivation, attitude, contribution to group decision processes and other somewhat elusive concepts related to teamwork could all too soon become criteria against which the teacher must assess the student. We are not convinced that the teaching profession is fully prepared for this yet.

It is probably the case that only someone in the classroom can successfully evaluate the *individual as a team member*. One technique that might help sort out how much each student has contributed is to ask each student individually about the division of responsibility for the project tasks and about the relative contribution made by each member of the group. It is recommended that the students give this information on a self-completion questionnaire, not verbally. Another technique is to give each student a test on the project (possibly in a written format, but preferably by means of a *viva voce* or oral presentation format to reflect subsequent vocational needs) so that the individual's *understanding* of those aspects of the project of which he or she has had only *indirect experience* may be probed.

ORAL ASSESSMENT

As we have seen, oral tests are sometimes used to supplement other methods of assessment, for example, for clarification of points in written scripts, and for trying to ascertain the contribution of individuals to group work. Although it is a relatively new development in statistics, oral assessment is increasing in importance, partly as a result of a move away from timed examinations to practical and project work, partly in response to an increasing concern that those with poor written language skills are disadvantaged by traditional methods of examining, and partly as a result of stated National Curriculum requirements (Department of Education and Science, 1987, 1989a,b). As is often the case when new methods of assessment are introduced, there is little experience on which to build, and little is known about the reliability and validity of this method of assessment. Zimmer (1983) asserts, however, that the verbal mode imposes a smaller mental workload in representing and in processing knowledge about uncertainty than does the numerical mode.

Diagnostic-type interviews have been used in *research* studies for a long time. The work of Piaget and Inhelder (1951, trans. 1975) with young children is a noteworthy example. Interviews may also be used for assessment purposes, or to identify the problems of low attainers and those with special educational needs. Such interviews must be carefully structured, and to some extent standardised, particularly if comparisons are to be made between students. When the alternative is making detailed notes of the children's responses during the session, the use of a tape recorder may be less disruptive, although some children may find this inhibiting. Research studies have also made use of tape-recordings of older subjects who were required to 'think aloud' as they solved statistical problems, e.g. Goodchild (1987).

Young children are sometimes tested by a teacher reading pre-prepared questions and showing them a prompt-sheet on which responses can be indicated. For example, a child might be asked to point to a modal group in a bar chart, or to draw a division in a circle to show what a pie chart representing two equal-sized groups would look like.

There are some negative aspects to oral assessment that should not be underestimated. While advocating the use of oral assessment for those who have difficulty in writing English, we should not ignore the fact that some of those who have difficulty in writing English often also have difficulty in speaking English (typically those students from minority language groups). Shy students and those with speech difficulties are likely to under-perform in an oral assessment. Furthermore, oral assessment is time-consuming and its standardisation may be difficult to attain, especially if teachers are unfamiliar with the method.

MONITORING ON-GOING PROGRESS

An important part of every teacher's job is to monitor the progress of individual students, that is to say, to make regular assessments and keep records of the student's knowledge and skills. The main purpose of this is to provide feedback:

- to the teacher concerning whether instruction has been effective;
- to the student concerning whether learning has been effective; and
- to parents, other teachers and so on, concerning progress and standard attained.

This is nothing new, but what are perhaps new are attempts to formalise and standardise the monitoring of progress, making this an integral part of teaching schemes. These include the externally determined standardised assessment tasks (SATs) of the National Curriculum and the required assessments made by teachers themselves. In mathematics (which here includes statistics) a number of research projects have been established in recent years to develop teaching materials and assessment schemes, which have been field-tested in schools. Common to many of these schemes is the involvement of the students in the assessment process. They are aware of the 'rules' and receive information regarding their performance.

One such scheme is GAIM (Graded Assessment In Mathematics)[1] which is designed for 11–16 year olds. GAIM consists of student activities, a teacher's handbook and topic criteria, together with record sheets for use in assessment. Topic criteria are classified under logic, measurement, number, space, algebra and functions, and statistics. These are divided into fifteen levels for assessment purposes, the highest level corresponding to an 'A' grade at GCSE. There are plans for a GAIM GCSE. All student activities are open-ended in nature, encouraging the student to make decisions and to integrate different skills.

The topic criteria are profile statements which describe the mathematics that students should know, understand and can apply. For example, under Statistics level 6, Probability, the requirement is: 'Understands and can use the idea of "evens", "1 in 2" or "50–50" chances, and can say whether events are more or less likely than this.' One or two examples are given with each criterion. The record sheets provide a convenient method of storing information about who has done what and levels that have been reached.

The student activities are of two types: practical realistic problem solving, and investigations. A student's solution to a practical problem would be at a level of sophistication appropriate to his or her mathematical achievement, rather than an answer that has been pre-ordained to be 'right' by the assessors. Some problems are very obviously mainly statistical, such as finding the breakfast cereal which is most popular with students in the class. Others involve statistics being one of several approaches that could be used, such as in the study of possible car park layouts for a given location.

The investigations are exploratory, giving students an opportunity to develop their own systems for obtaining results and to identify and describe any patterns found. The teacher's handbook gives guidance on how to use the student activities, and describes the likely outcomes and how to assess them according to the topic criteria. All student activities are open-ended in nature, encouraging the student to make decisions and to integrate different skills. They are a useful teaching resource whether or not the assessment side of GAIM is used. Unfortunately, just as with the National Curriculum in mathematics, the possibility of investigating the characteristics of *statistical* concepts in their own right is apparently over-looked.

The SMILE (Secondary Mathematics Independent Learning Experience) scheme has grown out of the sharing, by teachers in the Inner London Education Authority area, of ideas that work well in a mathematics classroom. It continues to be a project where the major input as regards development of materials comes from teachers, but the central organisation is now overseen by the SMILE Centre[2] which also runs in-service training courses for teachers.

SMILE classrooms are now found in many different parts of the country. SMILE consists of learning materials for use by secondary school students of all abilities. It is particularly suitable for use in mixed ability classes, because it is a flexible scheme in which students work at their own pace and programmes of work are tailored to each individual student. The materials include work cards, references to suitable tasks in textbooks, games, and microcomputer activities, grouped by topic and level. Materials are revised and extended in accordance with teachers' requirements and changes in the educational system. Many tasks involve students working on their own, although there are also some group activities. Tasks for a student are chosen in sets of approximately ten and tests are given on the completion of a set. All the tasks attempted by a student and the test results are entered on a record sheet which shows attainment to date and is used as a basis for choosing the next set of tasks. An investigative approach is encouraged and students are partially responsible for organising their own work. Using SMILE is quite hard work for the teacher, but those who like the scheme tend to be very enthusiastic about it.

There is currently not much statistical material in SMILE, although there are plans to extend this. The network of tasks includes a section on Handling Data subdivided into Logic, Sets, Graphical representation, and Probability. Within this there are a few statistical tasks including some on arrangements and combinations, experiments with dice and coins, and surveys. There is an experiment on growing mustard seed, and a survey involving visits to retail outlets to find the best buy of, for example, instant coffee. There is really nothing on probability distributions or inference, and the descriptive statistics consist mainly of bar charts, pie charts and scatter diagrams.

ARE SOME GROUPS DISADVANTAGED BY THE ASSESSMENT METHODS IN USE?

When statistics is seen as an applied subject where the data have meaning and derive from a context, it becomes clear that it is easy to disadvantage particular groups of students for reasons of their gender, culture or socio-economic background. Either the assessment of applied skills and understanding needs to allow for possible differences in perspectives associated with such group membership, or the assessment instruments need to be proof against them. Much can be achieved in this respect by the careful choice of context and the nature of the data. On-going coursework, chosen and developed by the student, may also be a safer form of assessment medium. It allows the student to adopt contexts and areas of study that are relevant to his or her own interests and perspective. It also allows time for the teacher to develop the students' objectivity and to educate out their biases, both of which are important stages in the statistical learning process.

Several research projects in various countries have looked at the differences between girls and boys in learning and attainment in mathematical subjects. The newsletter of the International Organisation of Women and Mathematics Education (IOWME)[3] is a useful source of references to work in this area, as is the newsletter of the Gender and Mathematics Association (GAMMA).[4] In general, boys tend to perform better than girls in timed examinations, but girls perform better than boys in assessments done over a longer time period. Other findings relevant to the assessment of statistics are that girls are disadvantaged when applications relate to male interests, multiple-choice tests discriminate against girls but girls tend to do better on essay-type questions, girls use the computer less than boys, and girls have more collaborative and less competitive styles of working than boys, preferring creative work. Girls tend to be better than boys on the kinds of operations that are most susceptible to drilling, for example, vectors and matrices, and there is some thought that girls would find modern mathematics less demanding and more stimulating than traditional mathematics. Girls tend to prefer work that is ordered to problems that are open-ended. This list would suggest that girls' superiority, or otherwise, in statistics compared to boys would not be clear-cut. Statistics involves a range of skills and their associated assessment methods would not be expected universally to favour girls rather than boys, or vice versa.

In the past, the content of public examinations in the UK has tended to favour boys rather than girls. A position where the reverse is true should be avoided, but an awareness of the problem will hopefully mean that teachers and examiners can aim to set questions which reflect gender equity by covering a wide range of human activities and interests. This is relatively easy in statistics which has applications in every subject area, but more research is needed on the effects of question context. More extensive use of project and course work may help to redress the balance between the genders as regards measured attainment in the sense that gender biases related to subject matter can be eliminated when students are given a free choice of study contexts.

Some studies by Wood (1976) and Wood and Brown (1976) are particularly relevant to probability and statistics. An analysis of GCE 'O'-level (age 16+ examination) results showed that girls were particularly bad at questions on scale or measurement, probability, space/time relationships, and spatial visualisation. Probability questions were not done well by either boys or girls, but girls were more likely to confuse the addition and multiplication laws, and were more likely to be muddled about complementary events. Green (1982, and see Chapter 6) also found that boys did better than girls on the probability items in a multiple-choice GCE 'O'-level Mathematics paper, and also in a CSE Mathematics examination (both age 16+ examinations). These observed differences appeared to reflect the gender difference in mathematical ability, and to be less marked or even non-existent if only the more able mathematics students were considered.

In a recent Mathematics with Statistics scholarship examination in New Zealand, females were found to prefer to answer questions on statistics rather than those on mathematics, and the difference between the performance of boys and girls was found to be less marked in the statistics than in the mathematics section (Forbes, 1988). As with all studies on gender difference in attitude or attainment, however, it is very difficult to establish that the findings are not merely related to differential teaching approaches and content. More research is clearly necessary.

Rouncefield (1989) reported on a study of the performance of 2884 candidates on the June 1988 SMP (School Mathematics Project) 'A'-level examination (age 18+) and this serves to highlight some of the difficulties in attributing gender differences to particular types of subject matter as opposed merely to differences in examination-taking strategies. In this study, Rouncefield found that girls were more likely than boys to *attempt* examination questions, but might well obtain lower total marks than boys. This suggests that the girls may have had poor examination strategies, wasting time on questions they could not really do. The research also gave some support for the theory that in this type of examination girls tend to use a serialist strategy and boys a holist strategy in answering questions, which may also underly their relative performance levels. With respect to how well the girls did compared to the boys on *statistics* questions, no clear picture emerged. Subgroupings within the sample of girls were such as to suggest that whether they performed better or worse than, or equivalently to, the boys on particular items was more likely to be explained by their background training than by inherent differences in statistical ability associated with gender.

Green's (1982) findings based on his Probability Concepts Test, where most of the questions comprised separate items, were that boys generally outscored girls on the overall test score, but that this was not the case on the questions classified as testing the understanding of combinatorics. He further reported that girls performed significantly better than boys on only one of his test items, which is shown in Exhibit 10.2. At the First International

Exhibit 10.2 **Item 20 from Green's (1982) test of probability concepts for 11–16-year-old pupils**

A teacher asked Clare and Susan each to toss a coin a large number of times and to record every time whether the coin landed Heads or Tails. For each 'Heads' a 1 is recorded and for each 'Tails' an 0 is recorded. [*sic*]

Here are the two sets of results:

CLARE: 010110011001010110110100011100011011010101100100 01
                      0101001110011010110010110010110010010111011001 1011
                      0101001011001010110001001101011001110111010110 0011

SUSAN: 100111011110100111001001110010001110111111010 10101
                      1110000000100010100100000100011000101000000000 011001
                      0000000111110000110101001001001111110100111000 11000

Now one girl did it properly, by tossing the coin. The other girl cheated and just made it up.

(a) Which girl cheated? ....
(b) How can you tell? ....

Conference on Teaching Statistics, Varga elegantly demonstrated, using a group of conference delegates as his subjects, that the females appeared to be better at generating hypothetical sequences of 'Heads' and 'Tails' which were random than were the males. In the light of this, one might be tempted to attribute Green's findings to the same principle, namely 'Girls can be more random than Boys!' However, there are two things that should be noted: (1) Green's test item is one concerned with recognition rather than generation of random sequences which may make it a totally different assessment instrument; and (2) this item was in fact the only test item out of the 26 (some of which had several parts to them) in Green's questionnaire that featured girls' rather than boys' names.

Of course, it may seem somewhat difficult to feel that there is a correct answer to such a question. Green (1982) took 'Clare' to be the correct answer to question (a), although if *random* implies that any sequence is possible, there would be those who would argue that *it is impossible to tell* might be more correct. Green's wording of the test item did not encourage this response and not surprisingly very few pupils gave it. Indeed, this example serves to illustrate the point already made that it is exceedingly difficult to design questions that are *guaranteed* to test the elusive concepts of probability and statistics in a totally unambiguous way. For further discussion about research into the understanding of randomness, see Chapter 6.

Konold (1989a) advocates caution in interpreting findings on probability items of the type found in National Assessment of Educational Performance (NAEP) tests where he found that inappropriate wording of the questions may in fact fail to distinguish adequately between those students who do, and those who do not, understand concepts such as independence.

Several studies have considered whether attitudes and anxiety account for some of the differences observed in mathematics performance between female and male students. A fear of mathematics can result in a fear of statistics. Boys expect to do well in mathematics, but girls are less certain about their performance. In fact boys tend to do worse than they expect, but girls do better (Joffe and Foxman, 1984). Questions arranged in order from easy to more difficult might have a different effect on boys' performance than on girls'. Boys tend to rise to the challenge of more difficult questions whereas girls give up, possibly due to anxiety. An analysis of distractor choices in multiple-choice questions (Marshall, 1983) has shown gender differences in the choice of wrong distractors, as opposed to omitted items. One reason for this might be that boys and girls have different approaches to problem solving. Girls tend to say that they 'do not know how to do it' more than boys do.

Recent studies by Spear on marking written science work have shown that teachers are influenced by the gender of the pupil. Science teachers expect boys to perform better than girls, and work on average received higher ratings when labelled as done by a boy than when labelled as done by a girl (Spear, 1984). Science teachers also tend to think that girls' work is neat and well presented, but that of boys is untidy. They tend to say that girls are conscientious, but too wordy, whereas boys hurry their work but cover the essential points (Spear, 1989). It is likely that teachers of mathematics and statistics would have similar feelings about work in their areas. Either substantial differences do exist between the genders, or teachers are accepting popular cultural stereotypes. Teachers and assessors need to be aware of these findings. In public examinations anonymity of scripts would seem to be desirable, and anonymity of centres when some are single gender institutions.

There is much folklore but little published evidence concerning the extent to which various other groups of students are disadvantaged by some methods of assessment. Most assessors and instructors are aware that there could be a cultural bias in applications and questions. This could mean that students from minority ethnic groups are disadvantaged. It is less easy to study or to counteract than a gender bias, but awareness of possible cultural bias is the first step towards an improvement of the situation. The second step is to ensure that statistics teaching acknowledges the different starting points of students from different subgroups. For example, Garfield and Ahlgren (1988) discuss the difficulties that are faced by the teacher when formal instruction runs counter to the existing intuitions and belief systems of the students. One of us once had in a probability class an African student who was unfamiliar with packs of cards, yet examples based on cards and card games are commonly used because they are thought to belong to students' prior experiences.

Wright and Phillips (1980) observed that

> Strong differences exist between people raised within Asian and British culture on our measures of probabilistic thinking; these differences outweigh any influence of sub-culture, religion, occupation, arts/science orientation or sex, at least within the contexts studied. Generally, Asians adopt a less finely differentiated view of uncertainty, both numerically and verbally, than do the British. In cases where a numerical probabilistic set is adopted by Asians the probabilities assessed are much more extreme and much less realistic than those assessed by the British. This finding has clear implications for communication of uncertainty across cultures and to the potential inapplicability of decision analysis as a means of decision making to Asian culture. [The present authors see the finding as also having implications for the respective 'starting points' for the education of students from different cultures, and for the appropriate choices of teaching methods and materials, especially in multi-cultural classrooms.]

In addition to such fundamentally different starting points for the students, however, the teacher must also have concern for differentials that are introduced because of the particular style or method of assessment chosen. The difficulty here is that understanding and assessment differentials are often irretrievably confounded.

Students whose mother tongue is not English often have language difficulties, possibly in addition to the difficulties of having a different cultural background, and some students, even though their mother tongue is English, still have poor *writing* skills. Those methods of assessment of statistics which rely heavily on written work will disadvantage all students whose ability in writing English is poor. There might therefore be a strong case for making some at least of the assessment procedure oral. However, research has shown that females and students from minority groups, especially those who cannot speak the dominant language, may be disadvantaged by this. Of course, all teachers need to find out how students can *best* express their ideas, but possibly teachers of statistics need *special* training in how to help students to formulate and to express their statistical thoughts both orally and in writing.

Since practical work is less dependent on language ability than written and oral work, a greater use of practicals for assessment purposes might be fairer to some students. Practical work, especially if done in groups, can in fact help to remove differences between students caused by culture, language, and even gender, provided that the teacher is aware of the potential disadvantage to some members of the group and takes steps to avoid it.

Equal opportunity clearly provides an area that should be researched in the context of statistical education where changes in assessment procedures are now taking place. Subgroup differences in applied project work, team-work, and written and oral communication skills must be high on the research agenda if we are to prevent them becoming major problem areas with respect to the reliable and valid assessment of statistical skills.

EXPERIENCES OF CHANGING METHODS OF ASSESSMENT

From what has been said earlier, it seems that the situation with regard to assessing statistical knowledge, understanding and skills is far from being universally satisfactory for either teachers or their students. However, introducing changes is not easy. It is undoubtedly the case that there is a strong interrelationship between changes in teaching methods or content and changes in assessment methods. Sharpe (1990) feels that the best way to stimulate changes in ways of assessing statistics is by pointing out the influence that the type of examination has in either promoting or negating the aims of curricular or syllabus changes to which the policy makers are already committed.

In Australia, two different types of assessment moderation schemes have been applied to internally assessed examination components: (i) Statistical Moderation, which involves a comparison of internal with external grades where the grades are awarded for different aspects of the course; and (ii) Consensus Moderation, where groups of teachers moderate each others' students' work. The former has been found to be counter-productive, by leading to the external grades being given more weight because adjustment is made to the internal grades if there is a discrepancy between the two. Consensus Moderation is a more promising way of stimulating progress in statistical education, but its cost, in terms of time and money, is generally prohibitive.

Pereira-Mendoza (1990) describes a case involving internal and external assessment on a 50 : 50 basis. He observed that Statistical Moderation actually undermined the creative work being done in schools. If the internal and external grades did not correlate, teachers gave up the creative work and taught material which paralleled what would be externally assessed in order to ensure that the grades from the different sources *did* agree.

Pereira-Mendoza is of the opinion that in fact there are many activities and discussions for teachers and their students based on EDA with real data which cannot legitimately be assessed by means of traditional examinations. He feels that Teacher Consensus Moderation, or something similar, is necessary. It is crucial that a satisfactory way should be found to assess such aspects of statistics, or the curriculum progress being made in statistics may regress.

If those more creative skills which are not amenable to traditional forms of assessment are not directly assessed, students (and their teachers) will tend to ignore them, assuming that they are not important. Byrt (1990) agrees that this is a really serious danger. In his experience, 'without changes in assessment in Victoria [Australia], teachers would not have been sufficiently interested for a teacher-training programme in statistics to have been initiated'.

ASSESSMENT OF TEACHERS

Although this chapter has been mainly concerned with the assessment of students, it would be incomplete without some consideration of how to assess teachers of statistics. Clearly their technical competence could be measured to some extent by their qualifications, but many of those who teach statistics have not taken examinations in the subject recently, if at all (see Cockcroft, 1982; Hawkins, 1990). It is very difficult to find out exactly what comprises a teacher's statistical background since statistics can be encountered in many different contexts, at many different levels, and can be taught from a variety of different perspectives. For example, merely to ask teachers whether they studied statistics at university or college level will not discriminate between those who took it as a third-year option within an honours mathematics degree and those who met it as a series of five or six general lectures introducing them to the more quantitative aspects of a 'user'-discipline degree. For a fuller discussion about efficient ways to establish the real nature and extent of teachers' statistical background, see Hawkins (1989a).

Akbar (1990) adopted a different approach to this problem. Her concern was that there were discrepancies between the intended, taught and learned curricula at secondary school level. She hypothesised that one reason for the discrepancies was that the teachers themselves did not have an adequate understanding of the statistical concepts that their students were to be taught. Akbar's work included testing teachers and their students on a wide range of statistical and probability concepts, as well as assessing the two groups' perceptions of where and how particular statistical ideas were being taught. Her findings indicate that there are indeed discrepancies between the understanding and perceptions of the two groups. She therefore concluded that it is likely to be very difficult implementing the National Curriculum effectively.

Even given personnel with a good knowledge and understanding of the subject area, this does not in itself guarantee that they will be good statistics teachers. As Cockcroft (1982) and Hawkins (1990) point out, there are very few teachers who have been trained in how to teach statistics, and therefore very few have been assessed in their teaching of the subject. At *pre-service* training levels, those who do, often almost by chance, find themselves teaching some statistics while on teaching practice, may then be assessed as they would be for any other teaching discipline. At *in-service* levels, assessment of teachers is generally limited to those who enrol for courses carrying awards of diploma or taught Masters degrees, although, as has been said, there are very few opportunities for teachers to study statistical education at these levels. For those who do, their assessment will then mainly be based on their ability to *write* about curriculum issues, the pedagogy and the research associated with statistical education, and *not* on their ability to *teach* statistics. In some cases, their competence in statistics may also be evaluated by written examinations or course work. The Sheffield City Polytechnic Postgraduate Diploma (by distance learning) in Statistics and Statistical Education is a good example of such a programme, incorporating both pedagogic and statistical skills, but no assessment of students' teaching practice. At Masters and Doctorate research degree levels, assessment is generally based on students' ability to conduct and report some kind of research in the area of statistical education, and again there would be no assessment of their practical teaching skills.

The statistical assessment of teachers who study other subject areas, i.e. those who will almost certainly teach some statistics by virtue of the subject pervading all parts of the curriculum, must be assumed to be essentially non-existent. A *few* may have had to satisfy first-degree examiners that they had some working knowledge of statistics, because the particular institution that they attended designed its 'user'-discipline degree courses in this way. After that, they are unlikely to have been evaluated in the statistical areas of their discipline during their professional training. As Rouncefield (1990) said, even in mathematics teacher-training courses, statistics or statistical education is only minimally taught, let alone assessed. Subsequently, few teachers publish papers in teaching journals, and those who do so rarely write articles based on empirical research, so even the indirect assessment of their statistics by the refereeing route is precluded.

If 'user'-discipline teachers later return to study at diploma or higher degree levels, they *might* then undertake some statistical training to support their chosen areas of research. If so, assuming that their research is of a quantitative kind, which not all would be, their use of statistical methods in their research might be included but would not be the main thrust of the assessment process. Indeed, a look at dissertations and theses held in academic libraries will show a great many, and sometimes gross, statistical flaws which seem to have been totally ignored when the reports were assessed, presumably by examiners looking at other aspects of the students' work. Indeed, such examiners themselves may not have had the necessary statistical expertise to look at that aspect of the work, which has therefore to be assumed by them to be of secondary or incidental importance to the substantive discipline content. Even if, and certainly not unless, the particular project is *highly* quantitative, and obviously wholly dependent on its statistical content, it is rare for 'user'-discipline supervisors to recommend the appointment of a second (statistical) examiner.

NOTES

1. GAIM, King's College London, 552 Kings Road, London, SW10 0UA. (GAIM is published by Thomas Nelson and Sons, Mayfield Road, Walton-on-Thames, Surrey KT12 5PL.)
2. SMILE Centre, Isaac Newton Centre for Professional Develoment, Lancaster Road, London, W11 1Q6.
3. Convener: Gila Hanna, Department of MECA, Ontario Institute for Studies in Education, 252 Bloor Street West, Toronto, Ontario, Canada M5S 1V6. e-mail: G_Hanna@utoroise.bitnet. UK contact: Veronica Ruth, 17 Dumont Road, London, N16 0NR.
4. Gender and Mathematics Association, c/o Lesley Jones, Faculty of Education, Goldsmith's College, University of London, Lewisham Way, New Cross, London, SE14 6NW.

CHAPTER 11

The future for statistics and statisticians

In 1978, Kish characterised the field of statistics in relation to other disciplines:

> ... statistics differs fundamentally from other sciences. The data of other scientists come chiefly from their own disciplines – though they also may take side trips into other fields. In stark contrast, statisticians have no fields of their own from which to harvest their data. Statisticians get all their data from other fields, and from *all* other fields, wherever data are gathered. Because we have no field of data of our own we cannot work without others, but they also cannot do without us – or not very well, or for very long.

In many respects, Kish may be accused of being complacent in expressing this view. Much of statistical education is, and will increasingly be, aimed at the non-specialist. What then will be left of the role and function of the specialist statistician? Our view is that there is a distinctive role for such a person, but that there is a great need for members of the profession to clarify for the outsider the skills and services a statistician has to offer, and when, how and why such a specialist should be consulted. Statistics teachers must also share some of the responsibility for giving students an awareness of such issues.

In fact, there is evidence that there are differences of opinion within the profession as to exactly what role a statistician should take. According to Moore (1990), Hamaker (1977) argued that '. . . the professional role of the statistician must stop short of offering direct advice to the decision maker', but many statisticians would not share this view. Moore (1990, 1978), for example, is of the opinion 'that statistics should be the glue that binds together the various functional areas of business. Statisticians see more of the total picture than is commonly the case, and hence should be encouraged to proffer policy advice when appropriate.'

Bost (1990) in a *2120 Hindsight* article states:

> I am happy to report that there are very few professional statisticians left nowadays. Instead almost everybody could be considered a statistician of one sort or another . . . Just as you do not need experts in the field of

multiplication and division, we no longer force a frustrated statistical minority to perpetually attempt salvaging tons of carelessly accumulated data. The few professional statisticians we do have work with the BIG BRAINS (we do not call their intelligence 'artificial' any more). Together they are into founding or strengthening new sciences and arts and enhancing socioeconomic theories.

Brailsford (1990) also predicted the demise of the statistical profession although he is less sanguine about the outcome. He feels that the practising statistician will be extinguished if:

1. statisticians focus on refining minute details of certain applied tools while neglecting the needs of the problems to which these, or different tools, should be applied, or worse if they over-concentrate on theoretical developments, ignoring the applications altogether;
2. statistics continues to be fragmented into other specialist areas like OR, management science, psychology, etc. (as described by Zidek, 1988) because this could mean that although statistical procedures will still be practised, there will be no discipline to 'champion the statistical thought process';
3. existing statistical units are dispersed into other management structures; in such circumstances Brailsford fears that 'the ability to hire workers from other disciplines, whose course work has included some statistics, makes it difficult for the existing statistical staff members to object too vehemently' resulting in an erosion of *statistical identity*;
4. expert statistical systems come to be seen as adequate replacements for real-life professionals; such systems will, says Brailsford, 'give statistical analysis a bad name because the unknowing user will be feeding them data that are inconsistent, ill-conceived, poorly measured, and full of holes'.

If not responded to appropriately, Brailsford (1990) sees all these pressures as direct threats to the statistics profession, the only saving grace being if they led to 'the universal acceptance of the statistical method, or problem-solving paradigm, as a way of thinking'.

Hamming (1990) points to another problem that contrives to prevent the establishment of appropriate curricula and also places the future of the statistics profession in jeopardy. As he says, statistics used to be

consistent in the sense that various statisticians given essentially the same data would come to the same conclusions. . . . Now [however in statistics and statistical applications] there are not mutually agreed upon theories and methods; rather, there are various schools of statisticians that under some circumstances will give quite different answers to the same problem.

In Hamming's view, unless this is rationalised within statistics, the profession will become very vulnerable to the influence of the user areas which will force their own standards on the practice of statistics from outside.

In the discipline of computer science as it looks forward in the 1990s, the emphasis is being placed on *data objects* (the object-oriented approach to software systems). The dominant position of algorithmic procedures is losing ground. Statisticians too must loosen their grip on the 'methods and techniques' approach and concentrate on *data* – data collection, data validation, preparation of data for eventual analysis, presentation of data and results, data management – all of these to be implemented in a computing environment. The statistician will have to ensure that these aspects conform to the demands of *total quality* – a 'buzz word' expression in software engineering that is penetrating the statistical profession as well, appearing in several issues of the Royal Statistical Society's *News and Notes* in 1990 and 1991. The 'methods and techniques' statistician will probably have disappeared by the twenty-first century to be replaced by the 'data consultant'. Teachers of statistics and trainers of such teachers must ensure that the curriculum reflects these changes of emphasis.

It is certainly not clear that teachers themselves have a very highly developed understanding or insight into such vocational issues. There is much to recommend the various work experience schemes allowing teachers and students to gain insight into the professional lives of practising statisticians, preferably in a range of different application contexts throughout commerce, industry, government and research. Schemes which bring the professional into the classroom are also valuable opportunities for capitalising on an important teaching resource.

Whatever one's position on the exact role of statisticians, it is abundantly clear that communication with non-specialists is the one essential skill that all statisticians must acquire. In a sense, however, the training given to the non-specialists should also make them more receptive to the specialists' communications. Moore (1990) addressed both these issues:

For those whose vocation is statistics and statistical methods, it is not enough to concentrate on communicating with others in terms of coded messages. . . . It is essential that statisticians . . . [champion] basic numeracy . . . arguing that it provides a powerful means of reinforcing communication and understanding.

Whilst the statistical community needs to increase its numbers, it should be pleased, rather than dismayed, if we can mould other professionals to develop into parastatisticians. Our crusade must be to seek to make numeracy an equal partner with literacy.

As teachers of statistics, we need to consider how to prepare both the specialist *and* the non-specialist, developing common ground between the two and preventing the gap that otherwise forms between them. Many of the fundamental skills are equally accessible, and equally elusive, to both types of student. There is no research to suggest that statisticians are born rather than made.

By 1978, Kish was mindful that during the preceding thirty years there had been an explosion in the number of university statistics departments, and that this could not continue indefinitely. He argued that statistics departments must change their teaching strategies to put right the unsatisfactory situation described by Box (1976):

. . . one had the curious situation where the highest objective of the teacher of statistics was to produce a student who would be another teacher of statistics. It was thus possible for successive generations of teachers to be produced with no practical knowledge of the subject whatever.

While acknowledging the need for practical experience of applying statistics for those who become teachers (which is still rarely satisfied), we also feel it necessary to say that the supply of teachers of statistics is still not yet adequately served. At the 3rd International Conference on Teaching Statistics (1990) a common concern that was expressed was that fewer first-degree statisticians were progressing to postgraduate studies and hence the pool of potential researchers and university teachers was being depleted. A further problem is that there is very little appropriate teacher-training available for those few statisticians who do become teachers, irrespective of the level at which they teach, and no expectation of tertiary level teachers to take advantage of what there is. Lastly, there is a widespread shortage of teachers of statistics at the school level who have been trained more than superficially in statistics.

The relatively recent developments in the professional practice of statistics are providing major opportunities for narrowing the gap between specialist and non-specialist. It would be misleading, however, to suggest that this is an altogether new movement. Ehrenberg's (1975) pioneering work in the area of data presentation, for example, has been available for many years now, but rarely does one hear of courses teaching the skills of data presentation that he advocates. Far more often, one might see Ehrenberg's book on an introductory student's reading list, with no consolidatory lectures to explore or develop the skills described in that book. If this is because the teachers believe that such skills are in some sense instinctive, and that they therefore do not need to teach them, then the teachers are blind to the misuse and abuse of statistics which surrounds them. We feel that it is more likely that the teachers do recognise the need to teach them, but do not feel confident that they possess the relevant statistical skills; nor do they know how to teach them, having not themselves been trained in their pedagogy.

Good (1990) reported that a number of professional statisticians believed that the emphasis in high school teaching should be on the training of intuition. Baxter (1990) tried to be more specific, considering that the most useful content for introductory statistics courses would now be:

- exploratory data analysis (emphasising the processes of *looking at data* as much as the specific Tukey-type techniques);
- parametric modelling of data by computer as opposed to merely *number crunching*;
- simple forecasting techniques.

Assuming that Baxter's view of the future direction statistics will take is correct, the question that remains is: 'to what extent can school curricula provide foundations for these emphases?' It is clear that, as they stand, existing school syllabuses continue to emphasise those areas which Baxter considers to be of less long-term use.

A prototypical course will contain a brief introduction to the presentation of data, enough probability to confuse the novice, point and interval estimation, a great deal of hypothesis testing, and some linear regression. It is not at all clear that such a syllabus, dictated partly by demands from user departments, partly by available textbooks, and partly by inertia, provides a sufficiently cogent justification of statistics to the uninitiated. Certainly, there is very little reason for most instructors to explain the classical notions of confidence intervals and hypothesis tests when their theoretical foundation (hypothetical replications of an experiment) is so patently unconvincing. (Baxter, 1990)

As Norman (1980) says:

It is strange that we expect students to learn, yet seldom teach them anything about learning. We expect students to solve problems, yet seldom teach them the art of problem solving.

Here we would add that 'we expect students to apply statistics, yet seldom teach them the skills with which to do it'.

Statistical education is beset by a number of such 'chicken and egg' problems. As Shaughnessy (1992) says, research into stochastics (education) is crucial, but until statistics is in the mathematics curriculum in a significant way, such research will not be perceived as being important. Putting statistics into the curriculum in a significant way, however, demands the prior belief that it should be in the curriculum, as well as the existence of teachers already trained to teach the subject. This requires policy decisions which are dependent on the policy makers' own knowledge and understanding of statistics, which in turn will be crucially dependent on their own experience of statistics during their education.

Considering the problems faced by this emerging educational discipline, great strides have been and are being made. Anything that can be done to facilitate cooperation and communication between educationalists, teachers, practitioners and users, researchers and policy makers can only be for the betterment of the subject. There is great scope for establishing good practice in terms of teaching methods and content. However, as well as the need for statisticians to practise their profession, there is still a great need for them to proselytise it. Much of the responsibility for doing this in a way which safeguards its fundamental characteristics must still fall on those who have trained as specialist statisticians, for it is they who should have insight into these fundamental characteristics. Many professional statisticians have not yet realised the importance of their role in this respect, and indeed there are those for whom the difference between 'selling' statistics as a subject for all, and preserving the distinctive nature of statistics as a profession, is a problem area that they have not yet been able to resolve.

The problem is echoed by Morrison (1991) who says that in the academic world he 'never understood why mathematical statisticians appeared to stand apart from other mathematicians. This leads me to think that the barrier that is thought to exist *between* statisticians and the rest of society is a barrier that *surrounds* statistics, and that statisticians themselves should be doing something about breaking it down.' We fully agree with Morrison, but would add that teachers of statistics (who do not necessarily consider themselves to be statisticians) have an important contribution to make in breaking down the barrier.

BIBLIOGRAPHY

Abele A 1983 Probabilities: Learning by doing or learning by imitating. In Grey D R *et al.* (eds) *Proceedings of the First International Conference on Teaching Statistics*. Teaching Statistics Trust, Centre for Statistical Education, University of Sheffield. Vol 2, pp 813–28

Addelman Sydney 1976 Teaching statistics sensibly. In Barnes Ronald, Nouri Esmat, Fraley J, Brown Foster Lloyd, (eds) *Proceedings of the workshop on the teaching of statistics*. State University of New York, pp 111–18

Advisory Unit for Microtechnology in Education 1988 *British Educational Software Statistics Catalogue*. The Advisory Unit, Hatfield Polytechnic, Endymion Road, Hatfield, Herts., AL10 8AU

Ahlgren Andrew 1989 (in print) Probability and Curriculum. In Mayer Carolyn A, Goldin Gerald A and Davis Robert B (eds) *Proceedings of the 11th Annual Meeting of the National Chapter of the International Group for the Psychology of Mathematics Education*

Ahlgren Andrew, Garfield Joan 1991 Analysis of the probability curriculum. In Kapadia R and Borovcnik M (eds) Chance encounters: probability in education. Reidel, Dordrecht

Akbar, Aysha 1990 The place of stochastics in the secondary school curriculum. Unpublished MSc dissertation, University of London

Allwood C M, Montgomery H 1982 Detection of errors in statistical problem solving. *Scandinavian Journal of Psychology* 23: 131–9

Anderson A J B 1989 *Interpreting Data. A first course in statistics*. Chapman & Hall

Anderson N H 1964 Test of a model for number-averaging behaviour. *Psychonomic Science* 1: 191–2

Anderson O D 1989 Statistics instruction in the U.S.A. *The UMAP Journal* 10: 1–9

Andrews D F 1972 Plots of high dimensional data. *Biometrics* 28: 125–36

Arbel T 1986 Minimising the sum of absolute deviations. *Teaching Statistics* 7: 88–9

Bar-Hillel M, Falk R 1982 Some teasers concerning conditional probabilities. *Cognition* 11: 109–22

Barford N C 1985 *Experimental Measurements: Precision, Error and Truth* 2nd edition. Wiley

Barnett Vic (ed.) 1987 *The Statistician at Work*. 2 audio-tapes available from the Centre for Statistical Education, University of Sheffield

Barr G V 1980 Some student ideas on the median and the mode. *Teaching Statistics* 2(2): 38–41. Reprinted in Holmes P (ed) 1986 *The Best of 'Teaching Statistics'*, Teaching Statistics Trust, pp 79–82

Bassett E E, Bremner J M, Jolliffe I T, Jones B, Morgan B J T, North P M 1986 *Statistics Problems and Solutions*. Edward Arnold

Baxter Laurence A 1990 Futures of statistics. *The American Statistician* **44**(2): 128–9

Becker Richard A, Cleveland William S 1987 Brushing scatterplots. *Technometrics* **29**(2): 127–42

Beniger J R, Robyn D L 1978 Quantitative graphics in statistics: a brief history. *American Statistician* **32**(1): 1–11

Beyth-Marom R, Dekel S 1983 A curriculum to improve thinking under uncertainty. *Instructional Science* **12**: 67–82

Bibby John 1986 *History of Teaching Statistics*. John Bibby (Books)

Biehler Rolf 1984 Exploratory data analysis – a new field of applied mathematics. In Berry J S *et al.* (eds) *Teaching and Applying Mathematical Modelling*. Ellis Horwood Ltd, pp 117–30

Biehler Rolf 1985 Interrelations between computers, statistics, and teaching mathematics. In *The Influence of Computers and Informatics on Mathematics and its Teaching*. ICMI, pp 209–14

Biehler Rolf, Rach W, Winkelman B 1988 Computers and mathematics teaching; the German situation and reviews of international software. Occasional Paper No.103. Institut für Didaktik der Mathematik, Bielefeld, FRG

Bost R H 'Butch' 1990 2120 Hindsight. *The American Statistician* **44**(2): 130–1

Bowman A W, Robinson D R 1987 *Introduction to Statistics*. Institute of Physics Publishing

Bowman A W, Robinson D R 1990 *Introduction to Regression and Analysis of Variance*. Institute of Physics Publishing

Box G E P 1976 Science and Statistics. *Journal of the American Statistical Association* **71**: 791–9

Brailsford Thomas W 1990 The future of statistics in the next *n* years ($25<n<150$). *The American Statistician* **44**(2): 131

Braithwaite G R 1976 Coursework, a discussion of its role and assessment. *The Statistician* **25**(2): 129–35

Brewer J K 1985 Behavioural statistics textbooks: source of myths and misconceptions? *Journal of Educational Statistics* **10**: 252–68

British Broadcasting Corporation 1982 *Mathematics Topics*. A series of five 20-minute films on statistics for GCSE (originally GCE 'O'-) level students. Adviser to series Peter Holmes

British Broadcasting Corporation 1984 *Advanced Level Studies – Statistics*. A series of five 20-minute films. Adviser to series Peter Holmes

British Computer Society 1990 *Software for Statistical and Survey Analysis 1989–90*. The Study Group on Computers in Survey Analysis (SGCSA), 4 Mansel Drive, Rochester, Kent, ME1 3HX

Burrill Gail 1990 Quantitative literacy: leadership training for Masters teachers. In Hawkins Anne (ed) *Training Teachers to Teach Statistics*. International Statistical Institute, Voorburg, pp 219–27

Butt Peter J 1986 Of the micro-worlds of random squares and snakes. *Teaching Statistics* **8**(3): 72–7

Buxton R 1970 Probability and its measurement. *Mathematics Teaching* **49**: 4–12

Byrt Ted 1990 Contribution to Closing Discussion. In Hawkins Anne (ed) *Training Teachers to Teach Statistics*. International Statistical Institute, Voorburg, p 284

Central Statistical Office (annual) *Annual Abstract of Statistics*. HMSO

Central Statistical Office (annual) *Key Data*. HMSO

Central Statistical Office (annual) *Regional Trends*. HMSO

Central Statistical Office (annual) *Social Trends*. HMSO

Centre for Statistical Education 1985 *Statistical Needs of Non-specialist Young Workers*. University of Sheffield

Centre for Statistical Education 1986 *A Review of Micro-computer Programs for Teaching Statistics*. University of Sheffield

Centre for Statistical Education 1988 *Design for Education*. Teachers' notes accompanying statistical template. University of Sheffield

Chambers J M, Cleveland W S, Kleiner B, Tukey P A 1983 *Graphical Methods for Data Analysis*. Wadsworth International Group, Duxbury Press

Chapman Myra (in collaboration with Basil Mahon) 1986 *Plain Figures*. Cabinet Office (Management and Personnel Office), Civil Service College, London, HMSO

Chaterjee S, Price B 1977 *Regression Analysis by Example*. Wiley

Chatfield C 1985 The initial examination of data. *Journal of the Royal Statistical Society, Series A* **148**(3): 214–53

Chernoff H 1973 Using faces to represent points in k-dimensional space graphically. *Journal of the American Statistical Association* **68**: 361–8

Chervany Norman L, Benson P.George, Iyer Raja K 1980 The planning stage in statistical reasoning. *American Statistician* **34**(4): 222–6

Chervany Norman L, Collier Raymond O, Jr, Fienberg Stephen E, Johnson Paul E, Neter John 1977 A framework for the development of measurement instruments for evaluating the introductory statistics course. *American Statistician* **31**: 17–23

Chung K L 1979 *Elementary Probability Theory with Stochastic Processes*, 3rd edition. Springer-Verlag

Cleveland William S 1987 Research in statistical graphics. *Journal of the American Statistical Association* **82**: 419–23

Cleveland William S, Diaconis P, McGill Robert 1982 Variables on scatterplots look more highly correlated when the scales are increased. *Science* **216**: 1138–41

Cleveland William S, McGill Robert 1986 An experiment in graphical perception. *International Journal of Man-Machine Studies* **25**: 491–500

Cobb G W 1987 Introductory textbooks: a framework for evaluation. *Journal of the American Statistical Association* **82**: 321–39

Cochran W G, Cox G M 1957 *Experimental Designs*, 2nd edition. Wiley

Cockcroft W H 1982 *Mathematics Counts*. HMSO

Cox D R 1958 *Planning of Experiments*, 2nd edition. Wiley

Daniel W W 1977a Statistical significance versus practical significance. *Science Education* **61**: 423–7

Daniel W W 1977b What are p-values? . . . *Nursing Research* **26**: 304–6

Davies Hilda 1970 The role of practical experimentation in the teaching of probability and statistics. In Råde L (ed) *The Teaching of Probability and Statistics*. Wiley pp 69–77

Davies Owen L 1954 *Statistical Methods in Research and Production*. Oliver and Boyd

Davis R B 1984 *Learning Mathematics: a cognitive science approach to mathematics education*. Croom Helm

Department of Education and Science 1987 *National Curriculum – Consultation Document*. HMSO

Department of Education and Science 1989a *Mathematics from 5 to 16*. HMSO

Department of Education and Science 1989b *Mathematics in the National Curriculum*. HMSO

Department of Education and Science 1991 Survey of Information Technology in Schools. *Statistical Bulletin*, 11/94

Department of Employment 1987 *New Earnings Survey*. HMSO

Donaldson M 1978 *Children's minds*. Fontana Original

Draper N R, Smith H 1981 *Applied Regression Analysis*, 2nd edition. Wiley

Dunkels Andrejs 1990 Examples from the in-service classroom (age group 7–12). In Hawkins Anne (ed) *Training Teachers to Teach Statistics*. International Statistical Institute, Voorburg, pp 102–9

Eddy David M 1982 Probabilistic reasoning in clinical medicine: problems and opportunities. In Kahneman D, Slovic P, Tversky A (eds) *Judgment under Uncertainty; Heuristics and Biases*. Cambridge University Press. Chapter 18, pp 249–67

Ehrenberg A S C 1975 *Data Reduction; analysing and interpreting statistical data*. Wiley

Ehrenberg A S C 1982 *A Primer in Data Reduction – an introductory statistics textbook*. Wiley, New York

Ehrenberg A S C 1983 We must preach what is practised. *The American Statistician* **37**: 248–50

Engel A 1965 *Les répercussions de la récherche mathématique sur l'enseignement*. Conférences CIEM, Echternach. Cited in Freudenthal H 1973 *Mathematics as an Educational Task*. Reidel Dordrecht, p 613

Engel A 1970 Teaching probability in intermediate grades. In Råde L (ed) *The Teaching of Probability and Statistics*. Proceedings of the CSMP International Conference. Almqvist and Wiksell, Stockholm/ Wiley Interscience Division. Cited in Freudenthal H 1973 *Mathematics as an Educational Task*. Reidel Dordrecht, p 613

Engel A, Varga T, Walser W 1976 *Hasard ou Stratégie*. O.C.D.L. (Also published as *Zufall oder Strategie*, 1972)

Ernest P 1984 Introducing the concept of probability. *Mathematical Teacher*, **77**: 524–5

Evans J St B T 1986 Estimating sample size requirements in research design: a study of intuitive statistical judgment. *Current Psychological Research and Reviews* **5**: 10–19

Evans J St B T 1989 *Bias in Human Reasoning, Causes and Consequences*. Essays in Cognitive Psychology, Lawrence Erlbaum Associates Inc.

Falk R 1986 Misconceptions of statistical significance. *Journal of Structural Learning* **9**: 93–6

Falk R 1988 Conditional probabilities: insights and difficulties. In Davidson R, Swift J (eds) *Proceedings, 2nd International Conference on Teaching Statistics*. University of Victoria, British Columbia, Canada, pp 292–7

Falk R, Falk R, Levin I 1980 A potential for learning probability in young children. *Educational Studies in Mathematics* **11**: 181–204

Falk Ruma 1983 Children's choice behaviour in probabilistic situations. In Grey D R *et al* (eds) *Proceedings of the First International Conference on Teaching Statistics*. Teaching Statistics Trust, Centre for Statistical Education, University of Sheffield. Vol. 2, pp 714–26

Farnum N R 1988 A short-cut formula for the mean absolute deviation. *Teaching Statistics* **10**: 87–9

Fechner G T 1860 *Elemente der Psychophysik*. Leip., Breitkopf & Härtel

Fiedler Klaus 1983 On the testability of the availability heuristic. In Scholz A (ed) *Decision Making under Uncertainty*. North-Holland, pp 109–19

Fienberg S E 1979 Graphical methods in statistics. *American Statistician* **33**(4): 165–78

Fischbein E 1975 *The Intuitive Sources of Probabilistic Thinking in Children*. Reidel, Dordrecht, tr. Sheppard C A

Fischbein E, Pampu Ileana, Minzat I 1967 The child's intuition of probability. *Enfance* **2**: 193–206

Fisher R A 1925 *Statistical Methods for Research Workers*, 14th edition 1970. Edinburgh

Fong Geoffrey T, Krantz David H, Nisbett Richard E 1986 The effects of statistical training on thinking about everyday problems. *Cognitive Psychology* **18**: 253–92

Forbes Sharleen D 1988 Gender differences in performance in the 1986 Mathematics with Statistics scholarship examination. *New Zealand Statistician* **23**(1): 17–25

Ford M M 1912 The position of mathematics in the education of girls. *Journal of the Association of Teachers of Mathematics* **3**: 32–40

Freedman D, Pisani R, Purves R 1978a *Instructor's Manual for Statistics*. Norton

Freedman D, Pisani R, Purves R 1978b *Statistics*. Norton

Freudenthal H 1973 *Mathematics as an educational task*. Reidel, Dordrecht

Freund J 1980 *Mathematical Statistics*, 3rd edition. Prentice-Hall

Freund J 1988 *Modern Elementary Statistics*, 7th edition. Prentice-Hall

Fuller, Michael 1980 Problems of learning statistics. Unpublished paper given at conference on *Teaching Statistics using Practicals*, Sheffield City Polytechnic

Gardner Martin J, Altman Douglas G (eds) 1989 *Statistics with Confidence*. British Medical Journal

Garfield Joan, Ahlgren Andrew 1988 Difficulties in learning basic concepts in probability and statistics: implications for research. *Journal for Research in Mathematics Education* **19**(1): 44–63

Garfield Joan 1988 Obstacles to effective teaching of probability and statistics. Paper for the Research Presession of the NCTM 66th Annual Meeting, Chicago

Gibbons J D, Pratt J W 1975 P-values: interpretation and methodology. *American Statistician* **29**: 20–5

Gilchrist Warren 1980 Unpublished introductory paper given at conference on *Teaching Statistics using Practicals*, Sheffield City Polytechnic

Gilchrist Warren 1982 The role of practicals in statistics. *Teaching Statistics* **4**(1): 2–5. Reprinted in Holmes P (ed) 1986 *The Best of 'Teaching Statistics'*, Teaching Statistics Trust, pp 52–54

Giles G 1979 The Stirling Recording Sheet for experiments in probability. *Teaching Statistics* **1**(3): 84–91. Reprinted in Holmes P (ed) 1986 *The Best of 'Teaching Statistics'*, Teaching Statistics Trust, pp 8–14.

Glickman L V 1982 Families, children and probabilities. *Teaching Statistics* **4**: 66–9

Glickman L V 1990 Lessons in counting from the history of probability. *Teaching Statistics* **12**: 15–17

Glickman L V (1992, in preparation) *Displaying the Discrete and the Continuous in EDA*

Gnanadesikan M, Scheaffer R L, Swift J 1987 *The Art and Techniques of Simulation*. Dale Seymour, Palo Alto

Gnanadesikan R 1977 *Methods for Statistical Data Analysis of Multivariate Observations*. Wiley, New York

Good I J 1990 Abstract of 'Speculations concerning the future of statistics'. *The American Statistian* **44**(2): 132–3

Goodall G W, Jolliffe F R 1988 The training of Brunel University undergraduates who intend to become statistics teachers. In Davidson R *et al.* (eds) *Proceedings of the Second International Conference on Teaching Statistics*, University of Victoria, Canada, pp 137–40

Goodchild Simon 1987 An investigation of 3rd Form secondary school pupils' understanding of 'average' and their ability to solve 'weighted mean' problems, Unpublished MSc report, University of London

Goodchild Simon 1988 School pupils' understanding of average. *Teaching Statistics* **10**(3): 77–81

Graham A T 1976 Choosing a statistics textbook. *Mathematics Teaching* **75**: 34–6

Green D R 1979 The chance and probability concepts project. *Teaching Statistics* **1**(3): 66–71

Green D R 1982 *Probability Concepts in 11–16 year old Pupils*, 2nd edition. Centre for Advancement of Mathematical Education in Technology, University of Technology, Loughborough

Green David 1989 Review of audiotapes. *Teaching Statistics* **11**(3): 93

Green David 1990 Using computer simulation to develop statistical concepts. *Teaching Mathematics and its Applications* **9**(2): 58–62

Green David, Knott R P, Lewis P E, Roberts J 1986 *Probability and Statistics Programs for the BBC Micro*. Microelectronics Education Programme

Hamaker H C 1977 Bayesianism; a threat to the statistical profession. *International Statistical Review* **45**: 111–15

Hamdan M A 1978 A systematic approach to teaching counting formulae. *International Statistical Review* **46**: 219–20

Hamming Richard W 1990 The future of statistics. *The American Statistician* **44**(2): 133–5

Hansen R S, McCann J, Myers J L 1985 Rote vs. conceptual emphases in teaching elementary probability. *Journal of Research in Mathematics Education* **16**(5): 364–74

Hardiman Pamela Thibeau, Well A D, Pollatsek A 1984 Usefulness of a balance model in understanding the mean. *Journal of Educational Psychology* **76**(5): 792–801

Harding C M, Riley I S, Bligh D A 1981 A comparison of two teaching methods in mathematical statistics. *Studies in Higher Education* **6**(2): 139–46

Harterink Joy 1987a The concept of average and some comments on methodologies for research. MSc dissertation, University of London

Harterink, Joy 1987b Classroom practicals in A-level statistics. Unpublished MSc report, University of London

Hawkins Anne 1984 Teaching pupils to 'do statistics' using a PET. In Ramsden E (ed.) *Microcomputers in Education 2.* Ellis Horwood, chapter 15, pp 151–60

Hawkins Anne 1985 Stretching the imagination. *Teaching Statistics* **7**(1): 6–11

Hawkins Anne 1989a unpublished report, University of London Central Research Fund

Hawkins Anne 1989b The Annual United Kingdom Statistics Prize. In Morris R (ed.) *Studies in Mathematics Education*, Vol 7, Teaching Statistics in Schools. UNESCO, chapter 17, pp 217–27

Hawkins Anne (ed) 1990 Training teachers to teach statistics. *Proceedings of the International Statistical Institute's Round-table Conference*, Budapest, 1988. International Statistical Institute, Voorburg

Hawkins Anne 1991a Students' Project Work and the UK Applied Statistics Competition. In Vere-Jones David *et al.* (eds) *Proceedings of the Third International Conference on Teaching Statistics*. International Statistical Institute, Voorburg, Vol 1, pp 209–13

Hawkins Anne 1991b Success and Failure in Statistical Education. In Vere-Jones David *et al.* (eds) *Proceedings of the Third International Conference on Teaching Statistics*. International Statistical Institute, Voorburg, Vol 1, pp 24–32

Hendrick C, Constanini A F 1970 Number averaging behaviour: a primacy effect. *Psychonomic Science* **19**: 121–2

Hill I D 1979 On calculating a standard deviation. *Teaching Statistics* **1**(3): 81–4

Hille J W 1978/79 A Bayesian look at the jury system. *Mathematical Spectrum* **11**: 45–7

Hinderer K 1990 Non-traditional approaches to some classical topics in probability and estimation. *European Journal of Engineering Education* **15**: 213–22

Hinders D C 1981 Monte Carlo, probability, algebra, and pi. *Mathematics Teacher* **74**(5): 335–9

Hirst H 1977 Working with WISKOBAS: Probability. *Mathematics Teaching* **80**: 6–8

Hodges J L, Krech D, Crutchfield R S 1975 *Statlab: an Empirical Introduction to Statistics.* McGraw-Hill

Holmes Peter 1991 *Statistics in your World – Laying the Foundation* and *Statistics in your World – Solving Real Problems*. New edition and format of 1982 materials. Foulsham Press

Holmes Peter, Kapadia R, Rubra G N 1981 *Statistics in Schools 11–16; a review*. Schools Council Working Paper 69, Turner D (ed). Methuen International

Holmes Peter, Rouncefield Mary 1990 *From Cooperation to Coordination* (*A file for coordinating school statistics*). Centre for Statistical Education, University of Sheffield

Hooke R 1983 *How to Tell the Liars from the Statisticians*. Popular Statistics Series, 1. Marcel Dekker, New York

Huck S W, Cross T L, Clark S B 1986 Overcoming misconceptions about z-scores. *Teaching Statistics* **8**: 38–40

Huff B W 1971 Another definition of independence. *Mathematics Magazine* 196–7

Huff D 1954 *How to Lie with Statistics*. Norton, London

Iman R L, Conover W J 1989 *Modern Business Statistics*, 2nd edition. Wiley

Jaffe A J, Spirer H F 1987 *Misused Statistics: Straight Talk for Twisted Numbers*. Popular Statistics Series, 5. Marcel Dekker, New York

Jennings Dennis L, Amabile Teresa M, Ross Lee 1982 Informal covariation assessment: data-based versus theory-based judgments. In Kahneman D, Slovic P, Tversky A (ed) 1982 *Judgment under Uncertainty; Heuristics and Biases*. Cambridge University Press. Chapter 15, pp 211–30.

Joffe L, Foxman D 1984 Assessing mathematics 5. Attitudes and sex differences. Some APU findings. *Mathematics in School* **13**(4): 22–6

John J A and Quenouille M H 1977 *Experiments: Design and Analysis*, 2nd edition. Griffin

Johnson L W 1981 Teaching hypothesis testing as a six step process. *Teaching Statistics* **3**: 47–9

Jolliffe Flavia R 1991 Assessment of the understanding of statistical concepts. In Vere-Jones David *et al.* (eds) *Proceedings of the Third International Conference on Teaching Statistics*. International Statistical Institute, Voorburg, Vol 1, pp 461–6

Jolliffe Flavia R, Sharples Fay 1991 An investigation of the knowledge of proportion and probability that students bring to University with them. In Vere-Jones David *et al.* (eds) *Proceedings of the Third International Conference on Teaching Statistics*. International Statistical Institute, Voorburg. Vol 1, p 370.

Jowett G H, Davies Hilda M 1960 Practical experiments as a teaching method in statistics. *Journal of the Royal Statistical Society, Series A* **123**: 10–35

Kahneman D, Slovic P, Tversky A (eds) 1982 *Judgment under Uncertainty; Heuristics and Biases*. Cambridge University Press, New York

Kepner Henry 1989 The NCTM Standards for curriculum and evaluation in school mathematics (first of two-part presentation). *Statistics Teacher Network* **22**: 5–8

Kepner Henry 1990 The NCTM Standards for curriculum and evaluation in school mathematics (second of two-part presentation). *Statistics Teacher Network* **23**: 5–8

Kerridge D 1973 Discussion on computers in the teaching of statistics, by R Mead and R D Stern. *Journal of the Royal Statistical Society, Series A* **136**(2): 205 in 191–225

Kish Leslie 1978 Chance, statistics, and statisticians. *Journal of the American Statistical Association* **73**: 1–6

Knuth D E 1969 *The Art of Computer Programming*. Vol 2 *Seminumerical Algorithms*. Addison-Wesley

Konold Clifford 1989a *An outbreak of belief in independence?* Paper for the 11th annual meeting of the North American chapter, International Group for the Psychology of Mathematics Education

Konold Clifford 1989b Informal conceptions of probability. *Cognition and Instruction* **6**: 59–98

Koopmans L H 1981 *Introduction to Contemporary Statistics*. Duxbury Press

Koopmans L H 1982 A new introductory course in statistics. In Rustagi J S, Wolfe D A (eds) *Teaching of Statistics and Statistical Consulting*. Academic Press pp 135–63

Kunda Z, Nisbett R E 1986 The psychometrics of everyday life. *Cognitive Psychology* **18**: 195–224

Landwehr J 1989 (unpublished discussion paper) A reaction to alternative approaches to probability concepts. *The 11th Annual Meeting of the North American Chapter of the International Group for the Psychology of Mathematics Education*

Landwehr J, Swift J, Watkins A E 1986 *Exploring surveys*; *Information from Samples*. Dale Seymour, Palo Alto

Landwehr J, Watkins A E 1986 *Exploring Data*. Dale Seymour, Palo Alto

Laplace Pierre Simons de 1812 *Théorie Analytique des Probabilités*. (See also Simons P, 1812)

Lee A S 1989 The pattern-forming mode of teaching and learning statistics. *International Journal of Mathematical Education in Science and Technology* **20**: 321–8

Lee M P, Soper J B 1987 Using spreadsheets to teach statistics in geography. *Journal of Higher Education in Geography* **11**: 27–33

Leon Marjorie Roth, Zawojewski Judith S 1991 Use of the arithmetic mean: an investigation of four properties. Issues and preliminary results. In Vere-Jones David *et al.* (eds) *Proceedings of the Third International Conference on Teaching Statistics*. International Statistical Institute, Voorburg, Vol 1, pp 302–6

Lindley D V, Tversky A, Brown R V 1979 On the reconciliation of probability assessments. *Journal of the Royal Statistical Society, Series A* **142**(2): 146–80

Lindsay P H, Norman D A 1972 *Human Information Processing*. Academic Press

Litwiller B H, Duncan D R 1982 Probabilities in Yahtzee. *Mathematics Teacher* **75**: 751–4

Lopes Lola L 1982 Doing the impossible; a note on induction and the experience of randomness. *Journal of Experimental Psychology* **8**(6): 626–36 (Also in Arkes H R, Hammond K R (eds) 1986 *Judgment and Decision Making*, Chap. 43 pp 720–38)

Loyer M W 1987 Using classroom data to illustrate statistical concepts. In Nouri E (ed) *Proceedings of the 2nd Conference on the Teaching of Statistics*. New York College, Oneonta, pp 43–73

Lundberg B 1955 Fatigue failure of airplane structures. *Journal of Aeronautical Sciences* **22**: 394

Macdonald-Ross M 1977a How numbers are shown, A review of research on the presentation of quantitative data in texts. *AV Communication Review* **25**: 359–409

Macdonald-Ross M 1977b Graphics in texts. In Shulman L S (ed) *Review of Research in Education 5*. F E Peacock Publishers, Illinois, pp 49–85

Mainland D 1983 Medical Statistics – suggestions for the evaluation of introductory textbooks. *Journal of Chronic Diseases* **36**: 345–51

Mangles T H 1984 Application of micros and the use of computer graphics in the teaching of statistical principles. *The Professional Statistician* **3**(7): 24–7, 49

Margenau H 1950 The nature of physical reality, cited in Van Brakel J 1976 Some remarks on the prehistory of the concept of statistical probability. *Archive for History of Exact Sciences* **16**: 119–36

Marsaglia G 1968 Random numbers fall mainly in the planes. *Proceedings of the National Academy of Sciences* **61**: 25–8

Marsh C 1988 *Exploring Data: An Introduction to Data Analysis for Social Scientists*. Polity Press in association with Basil Blackwell

Marshall S P 1983 Sex differences in mathematical errors: an analysis of distractor choices. *Journal for Research in Mathematics Education* **14**(4): 325–36

Mathematical Association of America: Committee on the Teaching of Undergraduate Mathematics, 1979. *College Mathematics: Suggestions on How to Teach It.*

Mayer R E, Greeno J G 1972 Structural differences between learning outcomes produced by different instructional methods. *Journal of Educational Psychology* **63**(2): 165–73

Mevarech Z R 1983 A deep structure model of students' statistical misconceptions. *Educational Studies in Mathematics* **14**: 415–29

Milsom Mark M 1987 Perceptions of probability in school children. Unpublished MSc dissertation, University of London

Milton J S, Corbet J J 1982 Conditional probability and medical tests: an exercise in conditional probability. *The UMAP Journal* III: 157–62

Mitchem J 1989 Paradoxes in averages. *Mathematics Teacher* **82**: 250–3

Moore D S 1985 *Statistics: Concepts and Controversies*, 2nd edition. Freeman

Moore P G 1978 The mythical threat to Bayesianism. *International Statistical Review* **46**: 67–73

Moore Peter G 1990 The skills challenge of the nineties. *Journal of the Royal Statistical Society, Series A* **153**(3): 265–85

Morrison D E, Henkel R E (eds) 1970 *The Significance Test Controversy – a Reader*. Aldine

Morrison Jim 1991 Who should teach statistics? *News and Notes* **17**(8): 3

Mosteller F 1962 Understanding the birthday problem. *Mathematics Teacher* **55**: 322–5

Mosteller Frederick 1965 *Fifty Challenging Problems in Probability with Solutions*. Addison-Wesley, Reading, MA

Myers J L 1983 The role of explanation in teaching elementary probability. In Grey D R *et al.* (eds) *Proceedings of the First*

International Conference on Teaching Statistics. Teaching Statistics Trust, Centre for Statistical Education, University of Sheffield. Vol 2, pp 802–13

Myers J L, Hansen R S, Robson R C, McCann J 1983 The role of explanation in learning elementary probability. *Journal of Educational Psychology* **75**: 374–81

National Council of Teachers of Mathematics 1989 *Curriculum and Evaluation Standards for School Mathematics*. NCTM, Reston, VA

Navon D 1978 The importance of being conservative. Some reflections on human Bayesian behaviour. *British Journal of Mathematical and Statistical Psychology* **31**: 33–48

Neuwirth Erich 1990 Visualising correlation with spreadsheets. *Teaching Statistics* **12**(3): 86–9

Newman C M, Obremski T E, Scheaffer R L 1987 *Exploring Probability*. Dale Seymour, Palo Alto

Nisbett Richard E, Krantz David H, Jepson Christopher, Kunda Ziva 1983 The use of statistical heuristics in everyday inductive reasoning. *Psychological Review* **90**: 339–63

Norman Donald A 1980 Cognitive engineering and education. In Tuma D T, Reif F (eds) *Problem Solving and Education; Issues in teaching and research*. Chapter 7, pp 97–107

Office of Population Censuses and Surveys (annual) *The General Household Survey*. HMSO

Onions C R 1987 The longest run. *Mathematics in School* **16**(3): 12–13

Oskamp S 1965 Overconfidence in case-study judgments. *Journal of Consulting Psychology* **29**: 261–5

Papy G 1978 *Shunda's News Stand*. Comprehensive School Mathematics Program, CEMREL

Pearson Karl 1911 Cited in Bibby John 1986 *History of Teaching Statistics*. John Bibby (Books)

Pereira-Mendoza Lionel 1990 Contribution to Discussion. In Hawkins Anne (ed) *Training Teachers to Teach Statistics*. International Statistical Institute, Voorburg, p 283

Pereira-Mendoza Lionel, Mellor Judith 1991 Students' concepts of bar graphs – Some preliminary findings. In Vere-Jones David *et al.* (eds) Proceedings of the Third International Conference on Teaching Statistics. International Statistics Institute, Voorburg, Vol 1, pp 150–7

Perry Mike, Kader Gary, Harris Mark 1989 *SIMPAC – Simulation in Mathematics, Probability and Computing*. Appalachian State University, USA

Peterson C R, Beach L R 1967 Man as an intuitive statistician. *Psychological Bulletin* **68**: 29–46

Phillips E, Lappan G, Winter M J, Fitzgerald W 1986 *Probability*. Addison-Wesley, Menlo Park, California

Piaget Jean, Inhelder Bärbel 1951 (trans 1975 Lowell Leake Jr, Paul Burrell, Harold D Fischbein) *La genèse de l'idée de hasard chez l'enfant* (The origin of the idea of chance in children). Routledge & Kegan Paul

Plummer H C 1940 *Probability and Frequency*. Macmillan

Pollard P 1984 Intuitive judgments of proportions, means, and variances: a review. *Current Psychological Research and Reviews* **3**: 5–18

Pollatsek A, Konold C E, Well A D, Lima S D 1984 Beliefs underlying random sampling. *Memory and cognition* **12**: 394–401

Pollatsek A, Lima S, Well A D 1981 Concept or computation – Students' understanding of the mean. *Educational Studies in Mathematics* **12**: 191–204

Pollatsek Alexander, Well Arnold D, Konold Clifford, Hardiman Pamela, Cobb George 1987 Understanding conditional probabilities. *Organisational Behavior and Human Decision Processes* **40**: 255–69

Posten H O 1982 Neat data for teaching statistics. *Teaching Statistics* **4**: 42–5

Preece D A 1986 Illustrative examples: illustrative of what? *The Statistician* **35**: 33–44

Quandt R E 1974 Some statistical characterizations of aircraft hijacking. *Accident Analysis & Prevention* **6**: 115–23

Råde L 1983 Stochastics at the school level in the age of the computer. In Grey D R *et al.* (eds) *Proceedings of the First International Conference on Teaching Statistics*. Teaching Statistics Trust, Centre for Statistical Education, University of Sheffield. Vol 1, pp 19–33

Råde L, Kaufman B A 1980 *Adventures with your pocket calculator*. Penguin Books

Råde Lennart 1977 *Take a Chance with your Calculator*. Dilithium Press

Råde Lennart 1985 *Calculators and Statistical Calculations. An International Inquiry*. International Statistical Institute, Voorburg, Netherlands

Read K Q L, Riley I S 1983 Statistics problems with simple numbers. *The American Statistician* **37**: 229–31

Reinhardt H E, Loftsgaarden D O 1979 Using simulation to resolve probability paradoxes. *International Journal of Mathematical Education in Science and Technology* **10**(2): 241–50

Reynolds Christopher, Walkey Nigel 1990 Towards practical examinations in advanced level statistics. *Teaching Statistics* **12**(3): 82–3

Robinson D R, Bowman A W 1986 *Introduction to Probability*. Institute of Physics Publishing

Rouncefield Mary 1990 Preparing the statistics coordinator. In Hawkins Anne (ed) *Training Teachers to Teach Statistics*. International Statistical Institute, Voorburg, pp 250–8

Rouncefield, Mary 1989 Gender differences in performance on an A-level mathematics paper. Unpublished MSc thesis, Sheffield City Polytechnic

Rubin A, Rosebery A S, Bruce B 1988 *ELASTIC and Reasoning under Uncertainty*. BBN Systems Technologies Corporation, Boston, Research Report No. 6851

Rubin Andee *et al.* 1990 *ELASTIC: Environments for Learning Abstract Statistical Thinking*. BBN Annual Report No.7282. BBN Laboratories, Cambridge, Massachusetts

Russell Bertrand 1927 *Philosophy*. Norton, New York

Russell Susan Jo, Friel Susan, Corwin Rebecca 1990 *Used Numbers*. Series of six books. Dale Seymour, Palo Alto

Russell Susan-Jo 1990 Contribution to closing discussion. In Hawkins Anne (ed) *Training Teachers to Teach Statistics*. International Statistical Institute, Voorburg, p 284

Schell E D 1960 Samuel Pepys, Isaac Newton, and probability. *The American Statistician* **14**: 27–30

Schupp Hans 1990 Teacher training by teacher collaboration in a curriculum project. In Hawkins Anne (ed) *Training Teachers to Teach Statistics*. International Statistical Institute, Voorburg, pp 270–6

Searle Shayle R 1989 Statistical computing packages: some words of caution. *American Statistician* **43**(4): 189–90

Selkirk K 1973, 1974 Random models in the classroom: 1. An example, 2. Random Numbers, 3. Some ideas to try. *Mathematics in School* 2(**6**): 5–6, **3**(1): 5–7, **3**(2): 15–17

Selkirk K 1983 Simulation exercises for the classroom: 1. The bus company game, 2. Leaving the motorway, 3. Arriving at a campsite, 4. The potato beetle. *Mathematics in School* **12**(1): 2–4, **12**(2): 2–4, **12**(3): 20–22, **12**(4):10–13

Sharpe Ken 1990 Contribution to discussion. In Hawkins Anne (ed) *Training Teachers to Teach Statistics*. International Statistical Institute, Voorburg, p 283

Shaughnessy J Michael 1988 Computer simulations of probability challenges; from data to theory. Paper presented at the 6th International Conference on Mathematical Education, Budapest.

Shaughnessy Michael 1992 (in preparation) Research in probability and statistics: reflections and directions, to appear in Grouws Doug (ed) *Handbook on Research in Mathematics Education*. Macmillan

Simon Julian L 1990 *Resampling: Probability and Statistics a Radically Different Way*. Resampling Stats, Arlington VA.

Simon Julian L, Atkinson David T, Shevokas Carolyn 1976 Probability and statistics; experimental results of a radically different teaching method. *The American Mathematical Monthly* **83**: 733–9

Simon Julian L, Holmes Alan 1969 A really new way to teach probability and statistics. *The Mathematics Teacher* **62**: 283–8

Simon Julian L, Oswald Terry 1989 *Instruction Manual for RESAMPLING STATS* (Contact Peter Bruce, 612 N. Jackson St, Arlington, VA 22201)

Simons Pierre (Marquis de Laplace) 1812 *Théorie Analytique des Probabilités*

Singer Judith D, Willett John B 1990 Improving the teaching of applied statistics; putting the data back into data analysis. *American Statistician* **44**(3): 223–30

Skemp R R 1971 *The Psychology of Learning Mathematics*. Penguin

Smeeton N C, Smeeton E A 1984 Statistical ideas in English Studies. *Teaching Statistics* **6**(3): 92–4

Soper J B, Lee M P 1985 Spreadsheets in teaching statistics. *The Statistician* **34**: 317–21

Spear M G 1984 The biasing influence of pupil sex in a science marking exercise. *Research in Science and Technological Education* **2**(1): 55–60

Spear M G 1989 Differences between the written work of boys and girls. *British Educational Research Journal* **15**(3): 271–7

Spencer Brown G 1957 *Probability and Scientific Inference*. Longman Green & Co

Statistics Sweden 1990 *Women and Men in Sweden – Facts and Figures*. Statistics Sweden, S-115 81 Stockholm, Sweden. Tel: +46 8 783 40 00

Stevens S S (ed) 1951 *Handbook of Experimental Psychology.* Wiley, New York

Stevens S S 1961 To honour Fechner and repeal his law. *Science* **133**: 80–6

Stirling W D 1987 *StatLab.* New Zealand Statistical Association and Massey University, New Zealand

Strahan R F, Hansen C J 1978 Underestimating correlation from scatterplots. *Applied Psychological Measurement* **2**: 543–50

Strauss S and Bichler E 1988 The development of children's concepts of the arithmetic average. *Journal for Research in Mathematics Education* **19**: 64–80

Szekely G J 1986 *Paradoxes in Probability Theory and Mathematical Statistics.* Reidel, Dordrecht

Szmidt T, Bissell A F (eds) 1977 *Statistical Teaching Aids.* Institute of Statisticians

Tanner J R (ed) 1926 *Private Correspondence and Miscellaneous Papers of Samuel Pepys.* Bell and Son.

Taylor Robert T (1980) *The Computer in the School: Tutor, tool, tutee.* Teachers College Press

Tolman E C, Brunswick E 1935 The organism and the causal texture of the environment. *Psychological Review* **42**: 43–77

Travers K J, Gray K G 1981 The Monte Carlo method: a fresh approach to teaching probabilistic concepts. *Mathematics Teacher* **74**(5): 327–34

Travers K J, Stout W F, Swift J H, Sextro J 1985 *Using Statistics.* Addison-Wesley, Reading, MA

Tukey J W 1982 Thoughts on the evolution of dynamic graphics for data modification display. In Cleveland W S (ed) 1987 *The Collected Works of John W Tukey: Graphics.* Wadsworth, Monterey CA

Tukey John W 1977 *Exploratory Data Analysis.* Addison-Wesley, Reading, MA

Tversky A, Kahneman D 1980 Causal schemas in judgment under uncertainty. In Fishbein M (ed) *Progress in Social Psychology.* Lawrence Erlbaum

Tversky A, Kahneman D 1982 Evidential impact of base rates. In Kahneman D, Slovic P, Tversky A (eds) *Judgment under Uncertainty; Heuristics and Biases.* Cambridge University Press, Chapter 10, pp 153–60

Van Brakel J 1976 Some remarks on the prehistory of the concept of statistical probability. *Archive for History of Exact Sciences* **16**: 119–36

Vännman Kerstin 1990 Some aspects of statistical graphics for secondary school teachers. In Hawkins Anne (ed) *Training Teachers to Teach Statistics.* International Statistical Institute, Voorburg, pp 110–26

Velleman P F, Hoaglin D C 1981 *Applications, Basics, and Computing of Exploratory Data Analysis.* Duxbury Press.

Vere-Jones David 1990 Foreword. In Hawkins Anne (ed) *Training Teachers to Teach Statistics.* International Statistical Institute, Voorburg, pp vi–vii

Von Neumann J 1952 *Probabilistic Logics and the Synthesis of Reliable Organisms from Unreliable Components.* Printed notes of lectures given at the California Institute of Technology.

Wagenaar W A 1972 Generation of random sequences by human

subjects: a critical survey of literature. *Psychological Bulletin* **77**(1): 65–72

Wagenaar W A 1988 *Paradoxes of Gambling Behaviour*, Essays in Cognitive Psychology, Lawrence Erlbaum Associates Inc.

Wainer H 1980 A test of graphicacy in children. *Applied Psychological Measurement* **4**: 331–40

Wainer H and Thissen D 1981 Graphical data analysis. *Annual Review of Psychology* **32**: 191–241

Weber E H 1834 *De pulsu, resoptione, auditu et tactu.* Leip., Koehler.

Weiss G 1962 On certain redundant systems which operate at discrete times. *Technometrics* **4**: 69

Weissglass J, Thies N, Finzer W 1986 *Hands-on Statistics.* Wadsworth, Belmont, California

Well Arnold D, Boyce Susan J, Morris Robin K, Shinjo Makiko, Chumbley James I 1988 Prediction and judgment as indicators of sensitivity to covariation of continuous variables. *Memory and Cognition* **16**(3): 271–80

Well Arnold D, Pollatsek Alexander, Boyce Susan J 1990 Understanding the effects of sample size on the variability of the mean. *Organisational Behavior and Human Performance* **47**: 289–312

Wonnacott T 1987 Confidence intervals or hypothesis tests? *Journal of Applied Statistics* **14**: 195–201

Wonnacott T H 1986 Bayesian and classical hypothesis testing. *Journal of Applied Statistics* **13**: 149–57

Wood R 1976 Sex differences in mathematics attainment at GCE Ordinary level. *Educational Studies* **2**(2): 141–60

Wood R, Brown M 1976 Mastery of simple probability ideas among GCE Ordinary level mathematics candidates. *International Journal of Mathematical Education in Science and Technology* **7**(3): 297–306

Woodworth R S, Schlosberg H 1966 *Experimental Psychology.* Methuen

Wright George N, Phillips Lawrence D 1980 Cultural variation in probabilistic thinking; Alternative ways of dealing with uncertainty. *International Journal of Psychology* **15**: 239–57. (Also in Arkes H R, Hammond K R (eds) 1986 *Judgment and Decision Making*, Chapter 25, pp 417–31)

Wright P 1977 Presenting technical information: a survey of research findings. *Instructional Science* **6**: 93–134

Zidek James V 1988 Statistication; the quest for a curriculum. In Davidson R, Swift J (eds) *Proceedings 2nd International Conference on Teaching Statistics.* University of Victoria, British Columbia, Canada, pp 1–17

Zimmer Alf C 1983 Verbal vs. numerical processing of subjective probabilities. In Scholz A (ed) *Decision Making under Uncertainty.* Elsevier, pp 159–82

Index